BECOMING DRUSILLA

Richard Beard is the author of four critically acclaimed novels, *X20*, *Damascus*, *The Cartoonist* and *Dry Bones*, and two works of non-fiction, *Muddied Oafs* and *How to Beat the Australians*.

RICHARD BEARD

Becoming Drusilla

One Life, Two Friends, Three Genders

VINTAGE BOOKS
London

Published by Vintage 2009

2 4 6 8 10 9 7 5 3 1

First published in Great Britain in 2008 by Harvill Secker

Vintage
Random House, 20 Vauxhall Bridge Road,
London SW1V 2SA

www.vintage-books.co.uk

Addresses for companies within The Random House Group Limited can
be found at: www.randomhouse.co.uk/offices.htm

The Random House Group Limited Reg. No. 954009

A CIP catalogue record for this book
is available from the British Library

ISBN 9780099507734

The Random House Group Limited supports The Forest Stewardship
Council (FSC), the leading international forest certification organisation.
All our titles that are printed on Greenpeace approved FSC certified
paper carry the FSC logo.
Our paper procurement policy can be found at:
www.rbooks.co.uk/environment

Printed and bound in Great Britain by
CPI Bookmarque, Croydon CR0 4TD

O wad some Pow'r the giftie gie us
To see oursels as others see us!
Robert Burns

To which Dru adds:

. . . the giftie would be greater far
If they saw us for what we are.

BECOMING DRUSILLA

I

All paths go somewhere;
Some, the place you're hoping for;
Some go somewhere else.

The first time I saw my friend Dru in pearl earrings I coughed and pretended nothing had changed, sat down at the kitchen table, cleared a space for the tea. Then I made a big effort not to say anything stupid, meaning saying what in fact I was thinking – *You are a 43-year-old man whose wife has just left you for another bloke, taking your daughter with her. You have a dismantled crankcase on the table in your front room. You drink lunchtime pints of Smiles Old Tosser and you work in the engine room of a 7,000 ton passenger ship. You are not a woman.*

We sat opposite each other and drank mugs of tea. Dru smiled happily.

'From now on I want you to think of me as she.'

She'd shaved her forearms.

I listened hard and looked too closely at the earrings, the pearl studs a delicate shade of Debenhams pink, set in lace-worked gold. It was 16 September 2001, and Dru had phoned me the day before.

'There's something you ought to know.'

'Tell me tomorrow. I'm coming round.'

'That's why I want to tell you now. Give you a chance to get over the giggles.'

'Try me.'

I wasn't expecting any surprises because once a year, for five or six years in a row, the two of us had made a habit of sleeping together somewhere outside. Dru was an excellent person to go camping with. She knew the names of flowers and birds, liked a drink and wasn't fussy about lunch. She was also immensely, impressively practical. In Bristol she'd taught me to clean carburettors with a toothbrush, and how to cut a gasket from a cornflakes box.

The idea of our annual camping trips, or at least my idea, was that it was worth remembering on a regular basis how it felt to live without a roof. They were a back-to-nature quest for what it meant to be alive, truly alive; and more than likely as the cold and the blisters cut in, what it meant to be a man.

Dru had a slightly different idea. She liked to pitch the tent close enough to civilisation for breakfast, usually a market town like Monmouth or Harlech. Most mornings, not long after daybreak, we'd push away the plates and sit side by side in front of an open OS Voyager map. I'd be searching for the steepest hills, Dru for a pub we could safely reach on foot by lunchtime.

We'd covered most of Wales, starting with a trip to the Lleyn mountains in the north. We'd climbed Cader Idris and Snowdon, cycled from Bristol to St David's and one year, after I sold a book, we hiked across the First World War battlefields in northern France. When we'd had enough, usually after four or five days, Dru would brew some tea, I'd finish the cigarettes, and we'd happily go back home.

We knew each other pretty well. How well? Well enough to share the one-and-a-half-man space in your average two-man tent. And want to do it again.

That well, and not at all.

Dru's flat, then as now, was on the top floor of a large Victorian semi near the Downs in Bristol. When she opened the door on the day after the phone call, she looked the same as ever. About five foot eight, shortish blonde hair, high cheekbones. She was in her early forties but passed for younger; also stockier than she was because her forearms and hands were out of proportion, thick and strong from work on the boats, a permanent tidemark of engine oil lined beneath her fingernails. She didn't often smile because her teeth were dreadful, but her round-framed specs brought out the intelligence in her face, in her restless copper-coloured eyes. She was familiar to me down to the sharpened Buck knife in its worn leather pouch, clipped as ever to her broad black belt.

That day, as well as black combat trousers and a fleece, she was also wearing the neat pearl studs. And she'd combed down her hair to make a wispy fringe. 'I know,' she said, 'don't tell me, it shows my bald spot.' She pirouetted on the heel of her paratroop boot. 'See if I care. Hello oestrogen, goodbye male pattern hair loss.'

This kind of awakening belonged on television, and I sat there with my tea imagining a panel of TV experts in a hidden control room. They were measuring the decency of my response, seeing if I reacted like a good friend should. Although, perhaps prompted by the sense of melodrama, I was already entertaining self-important thoughts of being Dru's *special* friend. I would be the only person on earth truly to understand.

A good beginning would be to contain the most obviously wrong and frankly absurd thoughts that blundered into my head – 'Is it catching?' – followed closely by the least of both our worries – 'I suppose camping's out of the question, then?'

*

I did not cover myself in glory.

Dru had been right to ring the day before, right to be cautious, because on the phone I did giggle. It was involuntary, not amusement but nerves. I had an awful, immediate sense that it was true. Followed just as quickly by an attack of paranoia: if this was funny (and it was second nature with male friends to look for the joke, the protection) it was a boyish prank being played at my expense.

Men pretending to be women are funny. They're having a laugh, an old favourite from the dressing-up chest at the back of the British music hall. But how funny is it to be a woman trapped in a man's body? Is it alright to have a sense of humour about this? What exactly is the *joke* when Bugs Bunny dresses as a lady?

Easy. He's a rabbit.

I'd fallen for it, yes that was it. Dru was having a laugh, mocking my chronic weakness for ludicrous ideas like looking for what it meant to be a man in a two-man tent. I was just the kind of bookish patsy to fall for something as absurdly far-fetched as Dru the engine-room mechanic in twinset and pearls.

My attempt to defuse what Dru was saying, make it centre on me (the joke's on me, me, me) was an act of denial. More would follow. Sitting in her kitchen that first day, when some unknown and idle-handed force had doodled pearl-stud earrings on to the person I thought I knew, I found everything she was telling me questionable.

When did this start? How did you tell your wife? Is that why she left you? The predictable, loaded enquiry about sex – are you now or have you ever been attracted to men? (To me. That's what I was wondering. To me, me, me.) It was hard to avoid a nasty tone of inquisition, because the information she was offering seemed unreliable. We'd known each other for more than ten years. If she could hide the truth that she was secretly a woman, then why believe anything else she had to say?

The TV experts conferred, frowned, but let me stay for another episode.

I went home and did what I usually do when life surprises me – I read some books. They didn't always help. The medical information had me squeezing my legs together while the personal accounts were mostly witness autobiographies by Americans. America loves the transgender story ('As Seen On Oprah!') because it has obvious themes of transformation and reinvention, liberating a you-go-girl inner being just bursting to get out there and shake it.

The transgender story has a recognisable shape, plotted most commonly as a Hollywood heart-warmer. It embodies the pursuit and capture of happiness with the bonus excitement of dispatches from the exotic margins, often involving vaginal dilators. This standard version of the story is dramatic and extreme – the protagonist starts out as redneck

Bubba and ends up a torch singer in a velvet lounge bar. If she's lucky. If not, she's the strapline on an afternoon victim show – 'My Wife Is A Man!'

I wasn't convinced that this model offered a true reflection of how it was for Dru, how it started, how it was going to end up. As I exhausted the gender shelves at the library, it seemed that only those British women who conformed to the familiar narrative were permitted to tell their story. Caroline Cossey (*My Story*) is a Norwich butcher's apprentice called Barry who reinvents herself as Tula, Page Three girl, model, and slinky half-naked background in a James Bond film. Even Jan Morris, the highly esteemed travel writer who became a transsexual pioneer, shapes her book *Conundrum* as a glorious transformation, a fresh start 'like a princess emancipated from her degrading disguise, or something new out of Africa.'

Dru, on the other hand, switched her combat trousers for a denim skirt, with a multi-purpose tool on a red lanyard clipped to the belt loop. I went round again a day or two later to make a second attempt at an acceptable first reaction. I sat down. I drank tea.

Some of Dru's explanations sounded learnt, memorised from numbered FAQs on specialist transgender websites. She admitted that to get female hormones on prescription she'd have to jump through the right hoops for a psychiatrist, probably at the Gender Identity Clinic at Charing Cross Hospital in London. The interview was rumoured to follow a set pattern – correct answers could be found on the Internet. That was just the way it was; everyone cheated, because the first step of the journey was too important to leave to chance. Dru even talked about 'putting a name to my gender issues', a sure sign she'd been exposed to language a psychiatrist might like to hear. It didn't sound like something she'd normally say. But then the denim skirt didn't look like something she'd normally wear.

For Dru it had started, so she said, at the end of 1993. That was the year we camped behind the car park at Cader Idris, and spent too much time on the computer playing *Aces over Europe*. On New Year's Eve, however, which we did not spend together, Dru was given shore leave from the MV *Havelet*, berthed in Weymouth for the holidays. Her girlfriend travelled down from Bristol, and before hitting the town's party pubs the two of them swapped clothes.

'Low-necked three-quarter length black velvet dress, mid-length sleeves,' Dru tells me, with instantly perfect recall.

'Make-up?'

'Oh yes.'

'Shoes?'

'Alas, no. My Doc Martens. Size ten women's pumps are hard to find in Weymouth on New Year's Eve.'

'I bet they are.'

'And in fact at any other time.'

Footwear apart it was a more than fair swap against an engine room boiler suit, but had the change really started so late? In 1993 Dru was thirty-five years old. Was it believable to have waited so long? What the hell did *I* know?

Only what I'd read in books, so in Dru's flat, the second time round, I resolved that the best course of action was to keep my mouth shut and avoid the more bone-headed questions.

'Why dresses?' I couldn't help it. 'Why can't transsexuals wear trousers? Women do.'

That'll be the doctors again. The Internet gospel claimed that anyone turning up at Charing Cross in trousers could be marked down for not showing enough commitment.

'To what? *Marie Claire* and side salads?'

'To the operation.'

Christ, I thought, you only put the earrings in a week ago.

'And by the way,' Dru corrected me, 'transsexual is an adjective.'

Because she was my friend, I'd assumed our uncomplicated friendship helped her to be happy, and I was suddenly hopeless at the effort needed to imagine her unhappiness. If, that is, she had actually been unhappy. If Dru as a woman was true, then the conventional story of renewal cast her life before now under a desperate shadow. The subterfuge of pretending to be a man, if that's what it was, devalued our earlier supposed friendship. Friends? We knew nothing about each other.

At the same time, she seemed strangely unchanged. There were the clothes and the jewellery and the make-up, but these were on the surface. Underneath, the old Drew was visible, and however many questions I asked, I soon realised they were all foothills to the one central mountain of a question:

Was this believable?

More personally, but the same question: Did *I* believe it?

I wanted to understand and accept Dru for what she now said she was, but the main obstacle was the possibility that at some level deeper than appearance her new incarnation was simply *not true*. It was an elaborate charade, a deception, a jape.

It was Bugs Bunny.

No one wants to be fuddled and duped by the cheeky

wabbit, and the popular depiction of transgendered people as performers probably made me wary. That's how most of us have previously encountered the idea, in high-octane novels like Gore Vidal's *Myra Breckinridge* ('you crazy, mixed-up chick!'), or in films like *Transamerica*. In fiction there seems to be a limiting sense that transsexualism is, by its very nature, a bravura performance. And, of course, broadly comic.

Caroline Cossey, the model and Bond girl harried by the British tabloids in the seventies and eighties, recognised that she was always treated as if 'transsexuality was some vast joke made at the expense of an unsuspecting public.'

Not much has changed. Contemporary television, trapped in the same how-low-can-you-go limbo as the tabloids, recently tweaked the joke by inviting transsexual Nadia Almada to join the cast of *Big Brother* series five. The viewers were in on the secret but the contestants in the house were not. What a hoot! In fact it's so good it's worth telling more than once.

There's Something About Miriam, on UK Sky 1, was a reality dating programme with a twist (!). You guessed it. Miriam was a gorgeous, available, pre-op transsexual babe. After the programme was broadcast, with the viewers aware of the conspiracy throughout, the unknowing male contestants sued for defamation and personal injury. They each received £100,000 in damages, and one of the lads punched the producer. Now that's reality, but it wasn't included in the film.

Was Dru another trick? Did I believe in her as a woman?

Compare it to asking whether you believe in somebody's marriage, or career. Yes, I'm a human being admitting to

11

judging another, but the question to be answered is one of sincerity and good faith. Does a life, in this case Dru's life, result from honest intentions and choices, or is it a sham, inspired by motives that are at best delusional and at worst rather sinister?

She was my friend. I was doing my best to believe her, to not judge her, though I wasn't alone among her friends in finding this difficult. Dru showed me an e-mail she received shortly after she came out which elegantly summarises the non-believer's position:

> We don't want to hurt your feelings more than we can help, but the nub of the problem is that it all seems like a tragic charade, because you didn't ever seem like the sort of person with whom nature had made a mistake.

However loyal I wanted to be, I could sympathise with this carefully worded view. I tried to remember what we had actually talked about, when we were out camping and cycling and walking. Everything. But then again obviously nothing, as I had no idea what was coming. Dru's conversation was full of the scaffolding of facts, the operational adventures of HMS *Cavalier*, the flight patterns of RAF Tornados, the differences between jackdaws and ravens and rooks. I was only ever half-listening, distracted by my he-man musings on being alive and not long now until the pub.

Now that I thought about it (having thought too little at the time) I remembered we never talked about sport, because Dru wasn't interested. Also, we rarely had conversations about women, at least not in the Boy Scout sense, collecting and comparing badges. I used to *think* that way, and assumed that Dru was thinking it too, but we were both married and I assumed the camping was partly about the absence of women. I remember on one trip, after her daughter was born, Dru's relief at finally being able to walk at a normal pace.

Not talking was hardly unusual. We were men, and could tramp long distances without saying a word, the silences unremarkable as male reticence. In any case, we had other ways to express ourselves. When I got married, Dru gave us a stockpile of burnable wood that filled a flatbed truck. It was my favourite wedding present.

Another clear memory from Bristol: here she is in the road outside our house, climbing off her MZ motorbike. On the black fuel tank there's a stencil of the Uffington white horse above, in Welsh, *The Flying Pig*. She is wearing blue overalls, come to fix the sink. Helmet off, readjust glasses. Out of the top box she pulls a very large hammer, but no other tools: the best of British engineering.

I wasn't *looking* for anything else. I was taking people as I found them, suspecting it may even have been bad form to look any further, with a view to making a judgement. When I first met Dru I liked her immediately. I was jobless and doubtful about writing as a career and here was a real man with a motorbike and a real man's job, in the engine room of the Channel Island ferry. That was her appearance and I was happy to accept it. She was a manual worker, a member of the working class! I was slightly in awe. She also liked her drink, as I did, as well as books and camping. She was so straightforward.

I can see now that this was a bad time for Dru, and the drink was a factor. I wonder what else I should have seen.

There was our sudden impulse, early one summer, to canoe

across the Bristol Channel. It would be an adventure to paddle between the old Severn Bridge and the recently completed new one, a kind of personalised welcome to the second crossing. Dru claimed they wanted to call the new bridge Serena, or Sabrina, but it never caught on. Was that a hint? (Another time at the top of Snowdon, we noticed that the train that tugs up the other side is called *Enid*. We had a pint of lager in the café and then walked back down, and until now *Enid* hadn't seemed important.)

I wasn't sure about that canoe trip. I'd never canoed before and had never seen a canoe on the Channel. Dru phoned the coastguard, but they refused to confirm it was a sensible thing to do.

'As long as you take all the right precautions, we don't see why there should be a problem.'

Which roughly translated in my lexicon of timidity as: it's not our fault if you drown. With Dru in charge the plan soon had momentum, and by then I couldn't back down because that would have been unmanly. Twenty-four hours later, a paid-up believer in acting tough, I found myself in the front half of a flimsy two-man canoe, the only vessel afloat on the famously treacherous waters of the Bristol Channel. We taped emergency flares to our biceps and then lunged the paddles urgently at the muddy water, racing the tide before it turned and drowned us in Lundy or Fastnet. That's what I was thinking. I realise I have no idea what Dru was thinking, except that I'd always believed she was naturally hardy and knew what she was about.

Maybe she was feeling suicidal. Didn't think of that, not at the time.

That was the day, in the back half of the canoe, she started softly to sing a song once made popular by the Royal Flying Corps, '. . . a drink to the dead already, Hurrah for the next man who dies.'

This was entirely in character. It never once entered my mind that Dru could be a woman in a man's body, but if she'd come out of the closet as a time traveller from 1948 I'd have nodded and checked my fingernails. That was her natural habitat, making do and mending under a supportive socialist government, pickling vegetables and banging together some scran, living an ideal of practical self-reliance as the highest form of virtue.

Dru was a scavenger and a fixer, a person with a talent for the ad hoc solution, thinking nothing of stopping by the roadside for some ingenious amateur mechanics, often involving her sidecar. And if the repairs didn't always last, then she'd happily mend the repair. She was a maker of her own jams and wine, a great cook and a complete no-hoper when it came to cleaning – she could lose heavy engineering projects down the back of the sofa. Which came from a skip. *All* her furniture came from skips, including the wardrobes and the hi-fi and every interesting pickle jar on the home-made shelves in the kitchen, each with one of Dru's hand-illustrated labels in gorgeous Indian inks. I think the canoe in which we crossed the Bristol Channel came from a skip. We definitely had to borrow a paddle.

Over half a lifetime of living like this, and by the time I met her, Dru had become like one of the characters in *Catch-22*, possessing 'a thousand useful skills that would keep her in a low-income bracket for the rest of her life.'

If Dru was different, not like the other boys, it was also because she was nicer. She used to make regular visits to a former friend who was sectioned in the Barrow Hospital. She took in the girl's mail and offered practical and moral support. On the day I went, in the sidecar, I stole the girl's self-inflicted injuries for a novel ('the backs of her hands were large brown blister-bubbles, over-doming the bones, the skin tight but also wrinkled, like the skin on milk. She also had a bandaged foot, and stitches in her neck.') Then I chatted up the psychiatric nurse.

So what did we have in common? Not sport, that's for sure. In Dru's flat I've watched Wales against England at rugby while in the kitchen she did something more interesting, like cleaning out the compost bucket. Motorbikes, and a fondness for history and provincial Britain. Romantic notions about books and sleeping under the stars. More importantly, we were both free during weekdays because Dru worked two weeks on, two weeks off with the ferries and I was writing. Or not writing, because I was spending lunchtimes at the Highbury Vaults before swooping the hills of Bristol in Dru's sidecar, an experience both crazy and serene, a cross between dreams of flying and a high-mortality video game. Later, when we both had a family, we shared an interest in wood-burning stoves (Dru installed hers herself). Outside my house near Shepton Mallet there was an unattended copse. Dru owned a chainsaw. How could we not be friends?

How could I miss her churning desire to appear to the world as she really was?

It felt like a failure in our friendship. Perhaps the British trust too much that appearance is reality, our traditional method of emotional evasion:

'Hi, Dru, how are you?'

'Fine.'

'Dru?'

'Keeping my head below water.'

So that's alright then – we want to believe in brave faces. But when Dru put in the earrings I think there was a sense of disappointment on both sides. She let me down because she never told me. I let her down because I never guessed. I'm a writer. I'm supposed to be in tune with other people. Jesus.

I go over it again and again. Were there any clues, any feminine traits that should have alerted me? There were contradictions, certainly, some of which I noted down at the time, like this diary entry from one of the early camping trips: *'He knows the names of flowers but has no sense of smell. He's an insomniac who falls instantly asleep. He decided to travel light and is carrying two bottles of pickled fish.'*

Camping is supposed to be a good way to get to know someone. I noticed she always took care to be impeccably shaved, and she assured me that cold water provided the only reliable protection against shaving rash. She's right. Also, looking back, it's important not to fall for the stereotypes, the familiar Bubba to Biba storyline.

Christine Jorgensen was the first transsexual woman to attract the hysteria of the popular press, at the beginning of the fifties, and her story had the necessary basic ingredients – **'GI to Blonde Bombshell'**. The fact that these ingredients turned out to be exaggerated – George Jorgensen had worked as a secretary when drafted into the army – barely mattered.

Stereotyping isn't only for transsexual women; it also applies to GI Joes and merchant seamen. Dru was never the bum, belly and tattoos gibbon from the car deck. She doesn't have any tattoos. Many seafarers don't. She's always been in good shape, and sometimes she spent the evenings in her cabin reading Wyatt's *Old English Grammar* ('All a bit alien as yet,' reports her 1989 diary. 'No doubt I'll get used to it.')

I'm particularly interested in Dru's diaries, such as they are, from this period when we first met, but when I get my hands on them I find no mention or evidence of the agony of gender repression. Nothing at all. The diaries accurately reflect my original impression of Dru, and what I liked about her. She records a life of alcohol and outdoor pursuits and cheery self-reliance.

In one way this is good. If she was hiding it from herself she wasn't consciously deceiving anyone else. It's also, possibly, bad: if it wasn't always there, then where did it suddenly come from?

Her diaries express no explicit urge to the feminine, and a typically unfussed diary entry is something like this from January 1991:

> *The engine room was in a bit of a state this morning. A non-return valve on the sewage discharge line is not functioning, and the shit was pouring out of the top of the tank where a macerator should be, but isn't because it's fucked.*

This is the same Dru who in 2001 decided to take to the streets of Bristol in a dress. She had no idea what she was doing – she went out looking like a transsexual. I remember an occasion when she joined us at the Bristol Old Vic, walking the same, talking the same, but wearing a sleeveless brown corduroy dress, black stack-heeled zip-up boots, and a blonde wig. The full Oxfam rig. In the dark of the theatre, not distracted for a moment by *The Beggar's Opera*, I realised that I had no intrinsic objection to any of these bits and pieces. I just didn't want to see them on Dru.

She went to her endocrinologist and to Topshop and to the shrinks in the Claybrook Centre at Charing Cross. I went to live in Tokyo, and being so far away was like turning my back. I didn't have to watch the awkwardness of Dru learning a new role, or register the physical changes provoked by jolting doses of female hormone. I knew little about Dru's in-between life except for isolated details: that she changed her name by statutory declaration to Drusilla Philippa Marland, and was still working in the engine room of a P&O ferry, the ear defenders infecting her newly pierced ears.

We exchanged e-mails, but only perverts insist on gender over e-mail. It's true that Dru had previously spelt herself Drew, but I couldn't get flustered over a spelling change so small it could have been a typo. She kept her messages brief and jaunty:

Just coming to the end of my second week on board. The run to Spain was eventful for several reasons; there was some considerable rowdiness and violence, which I was slightly mixed up in . . . More personally, I was flashed at. Goes like this: there's me doing my safety rounds at o3ooish, and I encounter this bloke standing there in boxer shorts of a rather unhygienic shade of grey. He puts his hands behind his head and makes gross pelvic thrusts in my direction, saying, 'I've got something in me boxers fer you, doll.' There's this THING flopping around down there. Quite sick-making. But I am equally struck by the look of contempt and hatred in his face. It's one thing to know about misogyny, and another to be on the receiving end of such an extreme example. Not that I think ALL men are bastards, you know . . .

And the next night, I get my tits groped. By a woman who wants to know if they're real. Well, really. The pills are obviously working.

When I was in the country we'd sometimes see each other, and when we met we'd kiss, cheek to cheek. On my part it was a self-conscious kindness, to show I was kind, but I kiss men all the time. I kiss my father-in-law, my sons. I once kissed a short French aristocrat on his bald head as consolation for not wanting to sleep with him, and then when I tried to push him away, also by his bald head, I was amazed at how the skin moved but left the skull behind. I claim no special sensitivity, but I'm not against learning to be sensitive, even if it tends to be through the blunt methods of trial and error, of practice makes perfect.

I made a big effort to say 'she', not always successfully. 'She' was like a lie that told often enough might come true, and I did wonder if it was so important to Dru because she was thinking the same thing. 'He' and 'she' now carried more weight than pronouns felt designed to bear. They were the keys to an elaborate and disturbing deception, elaborate because it involved so many of us pretending that Dru was she, and disturbing because the lie was possibly the truth.

That was a long time ago, at the beginning, and saying 'she' was difficult because it didn't seem like the complete picture. I'd met Dru when I was twenty-three and she was thirty-two – that was thirty-two years of the picture incomplete, and for Dru it hadn't started that day in the doorway of her flat with the earrings, nor even in the black velvet dress on the Weymouth seafront. The narrative arc of biography always goes back further than that, to young adulthood, adolescence, childhood, to parents, antecedents. We start before we're born.

Whenever we met, I'd vow not to ask too many questions and then ask them anyway. It was as if I wanted as much information as a biographer, and suddenly there it was again: my weakness for a ludicrous idea. I could research Dru's story and write it down: a biography. Writing a biography would soothe my writer's vanity (didn't see *that* coming) and also give me an excuse to go back as the inquisitor, and this time do it right. Inhibited by manly reticence, I didn't feel I could just ask. At least not the more direct questions, the ones for which I really wanted answers.

- Wasn't it worth trying homosexuality first?
- How often did you dress up, when, where, at six, eight, twelve years old, as a student? What happened when you first saw a naked woman and when did you start wearing women's underwear?
- Was it sexually exciting?

I flew over from Japan to spend the weekend in Bristol, to see if Dru was interested in the idea of a book. Her life, my words. She had to realise that I'd be taking on a role. I'd be laying traps, probing, trying to capture both her and her life on the page. As a minor act of revenge I didn't say that this would also be an investigation for fraud. I wanted to find out if Drusilla was true, even though there she was in the doorway again, and the good news was that her hair had grown out and she'd stopped modelling her look on Audrey Hepburn.

'Hah!' she said, 'Blame the hormones. I had all the sense of a teenager. You should have heard me natter.'

I did hear her, though she's forgotten – she used to witter

on about shops and make-up like a flushed fourteen-year-old, and blush when other women took the trouble to say they liked her shoes. It was no one's fault – the hormones couldn't know they were in the body of a 45-year-old mechanic.

On the day we first discuss this book, though, Dru is in flat-soled shoes with red laces and a calf-length denim dress obscured by wraps and shawls. She looks eccentric but convincing, a confirmed individualist as a man finding an identity as an individualist woman.

We do most of our talking in her battered Sierra estate, parked on the kerb outside the flat.

'I've given up the motorbike,' she says, 'for the time being. It doesn't really suit a skirt.'

It is early evening, nearly dark, and inside the rusting blue Ford the electrics hang in the footwell because the car needs hot-wiring if Dru can't find the key. The boot is stacked with trays of Lidl baked beans – I don't know why. I do know that we're in the car because Dru's ten-year-old daughter is in the flat, mashing up paper to make suns painted gold for Mother's Day. The operation is still several months away, but Dru prefers to spare her daughter too much chat about blood and hospitals.

Dru likes the idea of sharing the story of her life, 'except if I die in surgery, obviously.'

'Right. Don't want to ruin the heart-warming ending.'

She's prepared, she says, for however I might try to provoke her and her memories. 'I'm anxious about lots of things,' Dru says, 'but not about this.' She's less shy than she used to be, I decide, and there's no trace of her stutter, though mostly she used to stutter with strangers, and only then when there was money involved. I remind myself it's important not to over-interpret, but it's true that her eyes remain still for longer. She has less to hide. That's what I want to believe.

'I'll need documents,' I say, like any cheap investigator. I feel shifty, making deals in battered parked cars in the dark. 'Diaries, school reports, whatever you've got.'

She looks away. 'I wasn't always paying attention.'

'And I wouldn't mind seeing your psychiatric reports.'

I want to be fair: that's what friends are for, and the stakes are very high. If Drusilla is not true, then in her place sits a fizzing combination of modern afflictions. She's probably psychotic, possibly sexually deviant, certainly attention-seeking, and conceivably a secret special agent of the patriarchy. No wonder candidates for surgery have to see so many psychiatrists.

That evening after dinner we play some games with Dru's daughter and Dru's latest flatmate, a large woman somewhere in her late twenties, early thirties. We start with Twenty Questions, which amounts to *How To Write a Biography* in miniature. The idea is to write the name of someone famous on a Post-it note, and stick that to someone else's forehead. The person hosting the Post-it note then has twenty questions to work out one of life's great conundrums: who am I? I write 'Dru', and thumb the Post-it note on to her daughter's smooth forehead.

'Am I alive or dead?' she asks cheerfully. She is a very beautiful, open-faced, bright-eyed, blonde-haired ten-year-old girl making a good game-playing start. Alive or dead is indeed an important consideration when getting to know a stranger.

'Am I real or fictional?' She must have played this game before: she knows what counts in how we decide who we are, and then abruptly, with a little stab of horror, I see where this has to go next. I think I blush, and I hate myself for writing Dru's name, her new name.

Inevitably, the third question is precise, universally defining, clearly one of the first facts any one person needs to know about another.

'Have I ever been on television?'

It is only a brief respite.

'Am I a man or a woman?'

I look down. I don't know the answer. There's a pause – Dru notices, but won't give her own reply, then the flatmate steps in and answers defiantly: you're a woman. It's only later, when she's telling me over wine how much she loves Thailand, in particular Bangkok, and the gentle and caring nurses on midnight call in private Bangkok clinics, that I realise Dru's flatmate isn't just talking about her holidays.

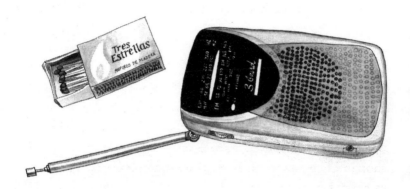

II

In the oak's shadow
The sheltering sheep tell the time
– too hot to go out.

It is May 2007, nearly seven months since Dru came out of Ward 4 South at Charing Cross Hospital. We're going walking, like in the good old days, but the complications begin before we've even started, in S. E. R. Beard's electrical shop in Chepstow High Street. Dru assures me that a radio is essential kit for camping.

'It wasn't on the list,' I say. 'Do we really want to carry a radio?'

'For the news, and the weather.'

'What news are you expecting?'

'We need to know the Russians aren't attacking.'

Dru is forty-nine years old. We used to worry about global calamities like nuclear conflagration, though these days senility seems the bigger danger. Dru forgot to note down the radio as something to pack, then forgot to pack the radio she had ready in any case.

'It's a necessary item,' she insists. 'Don't worry. I'll carry it.'

From behind the counter, middle-aged Mr Beard with his Chepstow combover shows us a three-band tranny. Long wave in addition to AM and FM.

So far, so good. Mr Beard is treating us like a couple of springtime hikers at the start of a National Trail who have forgotten to pack their radio. Why should he treat us as anything else?

'I used to have one of those in the North Sea,' Dru tells Mr Beard. She's being friendly, making conversation, and the pitch of her voice on this occasion is neutral to low. 'But we were over the horizon and could never get reception.'

She decides to buy it anyway, because of the Russians.

'Thank you, sir, and would you like batteries with that?'

Dru is wearing an attractive necklace made of household buttons in purple, pink and white. On her wrist is a bracelet of brightly coloured cubes. She has a low-cut, half-sleeved grey top that is tight over her evident breasts, mascara, lip gloss, shoulder-length hair highlighted and dyed the same copper colour as her eyes. And Mr Beard from Beard's Electricals in Chepstow High Street says:

'Would you like that in a bag, sir?'

Mr Beard is a non-believer. No flies on him. It must be important to Mr Beard, towards the end of an ordered life in Chepstow, to make it known, however quietly, that he's no one's fool. He can see the bunny ears beside the bonnet, and I can hardly blame him for this. We share the same name. He reminds me of an unconvinced version of myself, already in evidence the day before at Blacks The Outdoor Experts in the Broadmead Shopping Mall in Bristol.

I'd never bothered to notice before now, but nearly every item in a camping shop comes in Men's or Women's. We both need new boots, and because Dru takes size ten she selects from the Men's shelf. A sign says **Men's** in big black letters. Wearing a white dress emblazoned with deep red petals and a black cloche hat with a red trim, Dru surveys the racks in a characteristic pose: pursed lips, hips pushed forward, hands crossed one on each shoulder the better to swing her body from side to side. She shows no sign of feeling out of place; she's just a woman with big feet. I am looking at the size nines. The salesman, badged as Simon (but who can tell these days?), serves Dru first.

In the rucksack section, Dru goes for **Women's**, because the straps are cut away to make room for breasts. She doesn't like the colour, pale blue, but they're out of pink and you can't have everything. Dru tries a couple on for size and comfort – she's proud of her breasts, they're all hers. Sleeping bags also divide into Men's and Women's. I have to ask why. Apparently women's sleeping bags are shorter and narrower, with added padding around the feet and torso, for metabolic reasons. That's what Simon says.

Dru shuttles between Men's and Women's, making unimaginable calculations, and I'm with Dru, but also occasionally *not* with her. I find I'm a coward in the face of a thousand potential embarrassments. I slink off and find a basic insulated mug. One size fits all.

Alternative lifestyles are fine, it seems, except in so far as they make me personally uncomfortable. I squirm and wriggle, justify and defend – is the fault in me, or am I just being human? Perhaps it's *natural* to flinch.

Partly, I blame the nightmares. In mine, the characters and

locations vary, but the sickener is always the same. Someone familiar or who appears friendly is shockingly revealed as monstrous. I doubt very much this nightmare is mine alone, because it's the basic premise of most horror stories. The werewolf is a good example. Most of the time the person is normal (with werewolves it's usually a man), but come the full moon . . . and today the public space on the second floor of Blacks is our full moon. The twist in this tale is that I'm the one who changes – I feel exactly the same towards Dru and most of the time act quite normally, until the moment we venture into the world outside.

Back at her flat, everything is fine again.

In the seven months since her routine NHS operation, Dru seems to have made a perfect recovery. We sit at her kitchen table, drinking tea, and it's just like old times. I wonder what has changed. No sign of feather boas or tiaras, no matchbooks casually filched from the little-known torch-song bars of Bristol. Dru's pre-operative past is still in evidence, very much so in fact, because most of it is scattered randomly about the flat.

I'm looking at the flat as a biographer, and a cheap investigator, but now also as a naturalist. The best way to get an idea of Dru's natural habitat is to throw a metre square at random and see what it ends up enclosing.

The kitchen table, for example. On the kitchen table there is a repair folder for Morris cars, a box of organic Dath Mesa Sunrise Flakes, the picture book *Wales* by Jan Morris and Paul Wakefield, a pair of knitted leg warmers, a letter to the DVLA, *The Spark* magazine, a roll of kitchen paper, a jar of Hellman's mayonnaise, half a bottle of Villa Belvedere Frascati with a plastic stopper, a roll of pressure sensitive industrial duct tape, a jar of *cipolle borettane* (pickled onions), a tub of Toni and Guy Shine Addiction, an OS map of Dorset, a pair of grey socks, a yellow waterproof Filofax, a bag of Ugandan red hot chillies, a tin of travel sweets, a glass bowl containing corkscrews/Rennies/bicycle lights/Strepsils/scissors/Lockets and a stapler; a plastic measuring jug, a packet of neutral henna, a beret, two carving knives, the fascia of a car stereo, a tube of Miso Pretty Deep Tube bodywash, a pile of Sainsbury's Active Kids vouchers, a packet of upmarket chocolate ginger biscuits, a pestle and mortar, a tin of vegetable hotpot, two candles, the Girl Guides Association 1933 edition of *Hiking and Lightweight Camping*, a tester bottle of Weleda citrus deodorant, two pairs of women's underpants (black), some Ella Fitzgerald CDs, some empty wine bottles, a bottle of Quella, a compass and a tea towel. And a sleeping white cat.

It is not a big table.

This could be another biographical game: make sense of the woman who has these objects on her kitchen table. But the results would be unreliable because Dru shares the flat and therefore the table. I'm also discovering that biography is never that easy.

We've already sat down and tried to establish the basic past-life Freudiana: family, dates, places.

Dru's father was born in 1936 and her mother in 1933. Neither are still alive. Her great-grandfather was a stoker on a steam lorry, in Lancashire. Her great-grandmother, so the story goes, was the stronger of the two and founded the family building company.

'I know what you're doing.'

'I'm looking back through the family. It's standard procedure.'

'Mmm. For any other nonconformity.'

'Or whatever.'

'These are just half-remembered family stories,' Dru tells me, 'but you might be right. Current thinking is that it does run in families.'

She cites a recent example from her favourite Internet support group. After the original shock, a father stands by his son as she starts the difficult process of transition. Then starts to wonder if, all things considered, he wouldn't like to do much the same kind of thing himself.

Dru's grandfather, son of the great-grandmother builder, set his cap at a girl from a family of farmers who lived on the banks of the Wyre near Garstang. He courted her by wheeling barrows of sand up from the river, and taking her for rides in a part-shared Trojan car. The building company his mother founded still exists, Marland Brothers, in Leyland, but Dru's grandfather did not follow in his mother's footsteps. He worked his way up to chief clerk in the Leyland and Birmingham Rubber Company, and was employed by the same company his entire career, from leaving school until the day he retired.

'They gave him a clock and he lost his marbles.'

We think about this for a moment, out of respect. I focus on the Miso Pretty artwork and try to imagine a lifetime on the straight and narrow to be rewarded at the end with a clock and forgetfulness. Aged sixty-five, he probably already had a clock. His son, Dru's dad, must have come to a similar conclusion, because early in his life he decided against the straight and narrow. Unmarried, he and Dru's mum came to live in his parents' house, with Granddad leaving promptly every morning for another day's work at the rubber company.

'They had separate rooms,' Dru is quick to add. 'You can be sure of that.'

'How did your parents meet?'

Dru doesn't know. 'My Aunt Mary would know.'

The women always know, I think. In which case, why hasn't Dru taken the same kind of interest as Aunt Mary? Maybe she would have done if she'd been brought up differently. That's what I hope to find out, but already I can taste the sourness of making everything a test, of investigating every word Dru says, looking for the kinks in every aspect of her upbringing.

Dru's father was a grammar-school boy who went to art college.

'In Manchester, I think. I think so.' Dru digs out some faded 1952 photographs. Her dad looks very old, for a boy of sixteen.

'Maybe I'm wrong about Father's date of birth.'

This isn't a promising start – the biographical past was supposed to be reliable. I soon learn that Dru's uncertainty extends further than dates and ages. Whenever I make a suggestion about her motivations or reasons the answer she gives is the same: 'Up to a point,' she'll say. Occasionally I get an 'I suppose so,' or the equally non-committal 'Might be.' It's as if she's wary of fixing the details of her life.

'Is that because the past is too painful to remember?'

'Might be.'

'Or because you have something to hide?'

'I suppose so, or used to have.'

'Or is it just because that's the way you are?'

'Up to a point.'

Calming myself down, I reach for the bottle of orange juice but struggle with the top. Dru absent-mindedly offers to help. She then deflects some more questions while applying Clinique mascara, and keeps me quiet by pushing across the chocolate ginger biscuits.

I eat one. Dru does her make-up. I eat another one. Some time later I ask if I can have another.

'Fill your boots,' she says, fluttering her eyelashes.

I'm prepared to disregard the dates. It's the bubbling Freudian soup I'm after. Dru's dad was a silversmith, but his first job was as a woodwork and metalwork teacher in a school. Dru isn't sure where. In Salford maybe. Then her parents married, then another job.

'Somewhere up Burnley way. My brother was born in Preston.' That would be her older brother, by seventeen months.

In a school that may have been in Salford, at an unspecified date in the fifties, Dru's dad had to fight the classroom bully. Along with other teachers he clubbed together to buy shoes for the poorest kids, so that in the family folklore Dru's dad is physically brave and emotionally generous, even though in the Salford lanes the other dads, the bad dads, grabbed the shoes off their children's feet and sold them for drink on the market. How could Dru hope to live up to that?

These are the bones: marriage, a first son, various teaching jobs, a period of moving back and forth across the border of the rose counties, until finally Dru is born at home in Yorkshire. A snowdrift is covering the cottage at the end of a narrow lane.

The birth certificate, dated 7 February 1958, confirms Dru's existence.

	REGISTRATION DISTRICT				
	BIRTH in the Sub-district of			Saddleworth	
Columns:-	1	2	3	4	5
No.	When and where born	Name, if any	Sex	Name and surname of father	Name, surname and maiden surname of mother
171	First February 1958 Hillcrest Thorpe Lane Scouthead	Drusilla Philippa	Girl	Henry Booth MARLAND	Barbara Jean MARLAND formerly ELLISON

That's what the birth certificate, issued on 21 August 2007, officially says. When Dru was seven, her dad found a job at a teacher training college in Caerleon and the family moved to South Wales.

'And then a lot of things happened in a very short space of time.'

Dru makes a hand gesture, a bit like a washing machine, a bit like a dismissal. She has a headache and doesn't want to talk about this any more.

'It was a complete . . .'

She leaves the room.

*

We're in Wales walking along the B4228 to the north of Chepstow, looking for the path. The one we're after is the

Offa's Dyke National Trail, the 187-mile walk that loosely shadows the English-Welsh border from here to the North Wales coastal town of Prestatyn.

This isn't new territory for either of us. On our own, we've both walked the whole thing, and the two of us did various stretches in the days before everything changed. I like this first part especially. The lowland countryside appeals to me because it's safe and signposted, a gentle introduction to the great outdoors.

We find the path, waymarked at stiles and gates with the National Trail acorn, and now that we're off the road I see birds, trees, grass, more trees. Trees really need some help with their branding. They don't make themselves distinct enough, not like flowers. Though I don't know the names of many flowers, either.

Left to me, the green countryside of the Welsh borders would remain generalised, open to allegory: fruitfulness, fallowness, forests (beware!), rivers (of life), cultivated fields, native woodlands, blasted heaths, and sometimes a close-up of the path and its astonishing range of shits. To prove that I'm not completely blind to the realities of everyday existence.

Dru is having none of it. She knows the names of everything, but is mostly interested in the birds, the blue tit and the blackbird and the chaffinch. All I can recognise is a distant car alarm.

'Pavement warbler,' Dru says.

She has an eye for the nature we're passing through. She points out a dead shrew, and in a short stretch of lane a swallow's nest in the rafters of a bus shelter. I hadn't seen it because I was reading the graffiti: *Mikey Dee Dee and Babies*

To Be. It is springtime, a blowy and bright day in late May. On a woodland section Dru spots a trail of snail shells smashed by a thrush, and instead of conversation she constantly identifies places, birds, farm machinery, animals, rivers. I see cows and Dru will say:

'Mmm. Welsh Black cattle.'

This naming is a way of putting everything in its proper place, perhaps as a counterbalance to uncertainties about her own proper place. Not now, necessarily, but before, when anxieties about her true nature may have subsided before the authority of *Complete British Wildlife*.

'Would you say that was right, Dru?'

'Maybe. Up to a point.'

Dru is swinging her new alpine walking poles, and she swears they make a difference. I can't have poles because I need my hands free to build fires and kill the edible mammals. We're walking through lush green fields dotted with yellow and white, with sheep in the shade under trees.

'Ash,' Dru says. 'Each sprig has a number of leaves on it. See? There's a cluster of leaves.'

So thanks to Dru, I nearly always know what I'm seeing: Welsh Mountain sheep in the shade under ash trees in a field of dandelion clocks and buttercups. The dandelions are already past their best, apparently, because for winemaking they need to be picked on St George's Day.

Back on Offa's Dyke we're about to ignore many other fascinating geographical and historical sites. The bleached ruins of Tintern Abbey, for example, have something strange in the field behind them. At the Devil's Pulpit, a natural viewpoint, we get out the binoculars. The strange object is a giant fibreglass shoe. We pass on by, with nothing much to add because this book is not intended as a guide to the Offa's Dyke path, for reasons that will soon become clear. Having said that, the Dyke is the best, because most varied, National Trail in Britain, a barrier that intersects some of the most beautiful and occasionally depressing borderlands between England and Wales.

There is no intended pun. I didn't choose this route to suggest that Dru was an obdurate middle-aged dyke. If she was, I would say so. Like this: until recently, Dru was a middle-aged lesbian. That may now be changing, because sexually she finds men increasingly interesting, though it's really too early to tell.

As for obduracy, we have already had the saga of the Tilley hat. When we were packing I realised I had nothing to wear on my head. Dru has always been generous and immediately offered me her best trekking hat, in fact the best of its kind in the world. We know this because it says so on a label inside the crown:

THIS IS THE
TILLEY HAT

IT IS THE BEST OUTDOOR HAT IN THE WORLD.

IT FLOATS, TIES ON, REPELS RAIN AND MILDEW, WON'T SHRINK, AND WILL BE REPLACED FREE IF IT WEARS OUT. (YES, PUT IT IN YOUR WILL.)

Dru found it in a skip. This was several years ago, when Tilley hats were only available in white, so Tilley hat mavericks liked to find ways to customise them. Dru remembers a work-experience student at the Canadian cemetery in Beaumont Hamel. His Tilley hat was supplemented by a maple leaf enamel badge, as worn by travelling Canadians everywhere to stop anyone mistaking them for Americans.

Dru can be equally optimistic about making life-saving distinctions. She has dyed the Tilley hat pink.

'It's pink,' I say.

'It's the best outdoor hat in the world.'

Why, in need of a hat, would I refuse to wear the best outdoor hat in the world?

'It's pink.'

'What's wrong with that?'

Nothing. In theory. 'I don't think it's me.'

'You aren't what you wear, you know.'

'Of course not. No one would be that superficial.'

'It's the best outdoor hat in the blinking world.'

Dru can be very stubborn, and she knows exactly what the pink Tilley hat means: she's an expert at signifiers. Her purple spinster glasses, over which she can peer inquisitively while arching her shaped eyebrows, are an excellent signifier. They signify her femininity. As does wearing a dress. Dru usually wears dresses, although our walking trip means that today she's in calf-length black clamdiggers.

'They're just cropped pants.'

'Capri pants?'

'If you like.'

Even so, she does have a creaseless Rohan summer dress in her new pale-blue women's rucksack. For any special occasions we might encounter.

I am in Wales wearing a pink Tilley hat. It is not the hat of an investigator, though I can fasten the poppers at the sides to make it look a bit like a trilby. In pink. There's no mistaking the colour, and this is definitely a pink hat, and not a white hat dyed pink. Perhaps walking wasn't the best way to approach this book.

Gender transition is nearly always called a journey. In Britain if you're lucky, as Dru was, you'll get on the NHS pathway. That's what the health professionals call it. The official Charing Cross Gender Reassignment Surgery booklet is titled *The Whole Journey*. Jan Morris described herself as 'a lost traveller finding the right road at last.' In the literature this image comes up so invariably that I couldn't avoid the obvious question: why not? We could make a real journey, with a tent and muddy boots.

'Quite,' Dru said. 'Why not?'

'Well, I thought camping would be out of the question.'

She did that thing with her eyebrows.

It's late afternoon and we've walked about twelve miles, carrying our packs. This is not a superhuman distance but people get sponsored for less, and I know exactly how heavy Dru's women's rucksack must be feeling: it weighs exactly the same as mine.

This wasn't the idea when we laid out the equipment, after first making a space in the front room where I'd been sleeping on the floor. We cleared away a fridge, a microwave, two vacuum cleaners, a bottle of Kahlua and a violin case, a bicycle with a fruit-box on the back, a bucket full of empty Coke bottles, a stand-up fan, an electric power sander, a dusty computer and screen, three boxes full of dismantled boxes, a futon, LPs, two full-size axes, a jerrycan, a gramophone with speaker-trumpet, a fireguard, a metal watering can, wicker baskets, saucepans, frying pans, and a mirror with a sticker saying 'You Are Beautiful'.

What kind of a woman would keep these objects in her

front room? Maybe I should just ask.

'One with a lot of stuff,' Dru answers, 'and with no attic or garage. Now let's get cracking.'

She has made a list of camping essentials:

Tent
Sleeping bag
Sleeping mat

Maps
Compass
Knife

Camera
Notebook/pens/drawing gear

Towel
Toothbrush/paste
Shower gel
Shampoo/conditioner
Razor/shaving oil
Mirror

Dilating gear

Stove
Fuel
Mug
Teaspoon
Tea bags
Condensed milk

Other items go without saying, like a flask of Powers whiskey. In fact, as it turns out, *many* other items go without saying, the radio among them. As always, we end up with far more stuff than we'd intended. I insist on carrying both the tent and the cooker because Dru has recently had major invasive surgery, but when we weigh the rucksacks they both come out at fifteen kilos. This isn't right.

'Not because you're a woman,' I add quickly, meaning, honestly, not being *sexist*, of course not, but . . . 'you're responsible for the tea bags,' I say, covering up, 'and the matches. Have you remembered the tea bags?'

'Yes,' she says, 'and the radio.'

We've been lucky with our first day outside. The clouds have been full of high-altitude huff and bustle, leaving the sun to do its shining, strewing the earth of the path through ancient woods with lozenges of sunlight, like litter. Treading carefully, I've had my eyes on the side of the track finding meanings for tree roots and moss, holly, ivy, and great green floods of stinking wild garlic.

'Ramsons,' Dru tells me, 'that's the Anglo-Saxon name.'

Sometimes I don't bother to ask, like in an open field where Dru has to go first because there are three horses, all the kinds that exist: small, medium and large; black, brown and white.

'The secret is to show no fear,' Dru says cheerily, and strides forward as if horses weren't mean, feckless, sly beasts with no respect for human life. 'I'm grateful to animals like this for teaching me not to show fear. It worked at P&O.'

We haven't come across any other walkers on the path today, not one person, and this simple existence out in the open is easier than I'd expected. In these fields and woods, on a brief detour to the Moravian church at Brockweir, along the floodplain of the slow brown Wye, we are what we claim we are. We're two friends out for a walk – no one's looking and it's like coming home.

Behind me, unfolding over yet another of the Dyke's many stiles, Dru says 'Ow.' I worry for her.

'Ow feet, ow legs, or ow . . . elsewhere?'

'It's nothing. I'm fine.'

The afternoon has grown long and our legs are weary and we decide to call it a day a few miles up the path at Redbrook. Dru knows a pub there, the Boat. This means there's just time for Dru to explain that white dog shit, high in calcium, was once highly valued by leather tanners. This can be differentiated from fox shit, which for dietary reasons is more likely to have hair in it. At some stage today I also knew the names of the three culturally and geographically crucial rivers of Wales, and retained this information for minutes on end. It's easy to learn such things, just difficult to remember them, but one of the important rivers is the Wye, which we have been intermittently following, and which we will cross once more to reach the pub.

There will be people there, and suddenly it's like Blacks in Bristol. The moon! I can feel myself changing.

Our last public encounter was with Mr Beard in Chepstow, which is not a reassuring precedent. In the Boat at Redbrook I have no idea what to expect, but even as we walk I'm trying to work out if Dru passes.

I don't know. It's a question I find difficult to answer because I feel overqualified. To me Dru is Dru. I talk to her and see her face and it's Dru's face – I don't have to place her by gender. Now come on, I chivvy, be honest. Does she pass? As what? Not as a sex bomb, no. She is forty-nine years old.

Then again, as Redbrook gets closer, I can appreciate that Dru has some favourable genetic assets. She always had the cheekbones, but now the hormones have softened her complexion and rounded her face. She's added a few other touches – delicate eyebrows and copper highlights and this evening a definite rosy-cheeked bloom from a day's mild sunburn.

I try to put myself in Dru's shoes. Walking may have made this imaginative leap easier: size ten low-cut KSBs, in brown Gore-tex and suede. I'm in Dru's shoes, with room to spare, and I instantly know what she's thinking. I'll bet every mile we've walked and every adventure we've ever had that I know precisely what at this exact moment she's feeling.

She's thirsty.

Apart from the sex-change thing, we're pretty much alike.

III

Standing on the Kymin
My shadow's mostly English
But its head's in Wales.

At Redbrook, we cross the old latticed bridge across the lazy brown river.

'Dru, any poetic images come to mind, feel free to share them.'

She does. The names of birds are themselves a kind of poetry, at this time of day the evening swallows giving way to rapid horseshoe bats. The locals at the Boat are sitting outside, either on the small veranda facing the river or in the terraced garden with its waterfall and scattered collection of gnomes.

We go inside. There is a young man behind the pumps.

'A pint of Beck's, please.'

Then Dru seems to realise.

'Beck's Vier,' she says, concentrating very obviously on the metal label screwed to the pump. Her eyebrows go up and her voice alarmingly hinges and brackets. 'Is that the low alcohol version?'

'It is,' says the man behind the bar, 'half a pint?'

'Pint please.'

'Come on, Dru,' I say, after we've gone outside and found a table. The waterfall gushes from a grey plastic pipe. 'Don't you ever make concessions, help people out?'

'Normally I would,' she says, taking the head gracefully off the Beck's. 'But I really needed a pint.'

And after that one and another one, I've forgotten what it was that worried me. Either no one notices or no one cares, because none of the Boat's other customers look at us twice. A man in the garden, a chummy thirtyish bloke in the pub, like in pubs everywhere, says he once walked Offa's Dyke with his wife and when they got to the end he threw her into the sea.

'All the usual stuff,' he laughs. 'Everyone does it. We're divorced now.'

'How was Prestatyn?'

He gets a faraway look, one of nature's cheeky optimists in a sudden clinch with reality.

'It has the largest pub curry house I've ever seen.'

We go inside to eat and, speaking for myself, to watch the Champions League final on the television. As usual in pubs, Dru and I enjoy sharing the vast territories that we don't have in common. I tell her about Kenny Dalglish and she claims, absurdly, never to have heard of Kenny Dalglish. In revenge I get a detailed profile of Albert Tatlock. Never heard of him. Dru can't believe it.

We have one eye on the open doorway because we'll need the last of the daylight to pitch the tent, but even then we only leave the Boat when it's clear that Liverpool aren't going to win. Outside the bats do their dusky flit as we walk half a mile downstream on the pub side of the river. We find a spot in the long grass which isn't overlooked from any side. My long grass is Dru's Himalayan Balsam, though it's too early in the year for their flowers or seed pods, which Dru makes sound highly exciting by describing how they explode when touched.

Nobody can see us, which is important if we want to avoid being beaten up and/or run off the land. This is therefore going to be fine. We've done it many times before. Assemble tent. Peg. Throw over the flysheet. Peg. Lay out sleeping gear, walk into the Himalayan Balsam, come back, wriggle into sleeping bags, watch the darkening Welsh greys become night. Probably, as we get comfortable, we bump against each other in the dark. We forget about it and Dru goes to sleep.

The authorised version of the modern world, in which I've been thoroughly educated, has it that I should treat a woman the same as I would a man. Or in Dru's case as I used to treat her, only with changed pronouns. Dru has made this easier by not choosing a dramatically different name. Drew to Dru. Easy. Say it aloud and there's no change at all, as if she's rejecting that mainstay of the conventional transition narrative: reinvention. (I imagine asking her, come the morning: 'Is that right, Dru?' 'Up to a point,' she'll reply.) But then there's the problem of Drusilla.

Dru always uses the name Dru, except on official documents because on her statutory declaration she decided officially on the full Drusilla. I'll have to ask her about that. As it is, Dru was luckier than some because there aren't many names that look both ways. Toni, Andi, Terri, Alex, Jo. Dru. At least she had the choice. She wasn't an Arnold or a Kenneth.

I asked Dru to research the names that transgendered women most commonly choose, and she did a trawl through the Internet sites. The most popular names, by some distance, are Becky, Claire, Alison and Jennifer. The undisputed winner, however, is Kate. Life starts anew, and to keep in touch with the past a transsexual woman can need her own cast list, like an all-in-one Tolstoy novel: Kate, formerly Derek, ex-husband to Charlotte, now wife to Ian.

Dru is Dru.

'I've *always* been Dru,' she says, and this conviction of continuity reassures me: it makes a multiple personality disorder seem much less likely. In Dru's case, even the standard double-life approach of Before and After feels wrong, or as Dru once reproached me, 'You mean before I went weird.'

As far as I can tell, Dru never went weird. I'm lying in a tent beside her and she's sleeping. I can hear an occasional car on the road beyond the trees on the other side of the river. I wonder what kind of trees they are. I think I can hear an owl.

It's all so familiar, yet *she* is asleep beside me. I repeat it to myself, at the risk of forgetting. She is asleep, she is snoring, she is exhausted, hardly surprising because seven months ago she had her testicles and penis removed and a week recovering in hospital. She has another long day ahead of her tomorrow, but I want everyone to know it was hard for me, too. I risked getting my pronouns wrong. I have had, and occasionally still do have, severe outbreaks of pronoun anxiety.

There are gender radicals who suggest replacing him and her with 'shim'. The subject of the verb will be 'heesh', while 'hir' identity will be strictly kept to 'hirself'. These proposals come from the warrior caste at the transsexual fringe, and the

American writer Helen Boyd reports that 'some Genderqueer activists use these terms exclusively, basically just to tell anyone who comes along that their gender will not be made clear . . . and if you need to know that badly you shouldn't know hir, anyway.'

I can see the logic in this. But it's not logic, it's Dru. I once asked shim what heesh made of it.

'I think it's bogus.'

So that was the end of that.

The form commonly respected in memoirs is to use 'he' before the transition and 'she' afterwards. This is the method employed by Jan Morris in *Conundrum*, and also by consultant psychiatrists in diagnostic reports – 'He grew up in a mining village in South Wales and went to local schools and co-ed grammar school where he was bright but underperformed . . . I will see her again in three months.' It seems a sensible approach, and was originally the style I intended to follow, because after forty-odd years another few 'he's surely can't matter that much.

They can.

Dru is clear about how she wants to be seen. She's a woman who once suffered more obviously than now from an unusual medical condition. There is no he in this story (apart from me, and I'm not a he, I'm a me). The lingering 'he' is a fundamental misunderstanding of Dru's condition, a false representation of who this person is. That's a fairly unforgivable crime, in a biography. If Dru is right, if she's real, this is what the rest of us have to acknowledge and appreciate.

One side effect is the occasional breakdown of grammatical orthodoxy:

Drusilla Marland was born the second of four brothers.

She is on good terms with both of her ex-wives.

She was thrilled to become a dad.

These sentences read like test exercises for first-year TEFL students: identify the basic wrongness in each of the sample phrases. Fortunately, TEFL students don't arbitrate the use of English, and neither should grammar pedants. These sentences are unusual but not incomprehensible, and it's for this level of difference that I'm hoping to learn to allow. An amiable grammatical tolerance mirrors the process of accepting that Dru is not that different: unusual, not incomprehensible.

But what kind of biographer would simply take Dru's word for it?

If Dru is a woman and always has been, however she once acted and appeared, I'd like to know when she first became aware of this. The way the transgender story is usually told, both to readers and psychiatrists, makes this moment and the beginning of consciousness one and the same. It's a knowledge that is always there, from the dawning awareness of the self. Jan Morris wrote the guidebook:

> I was three or perhaps four years old when I realised that I had been born into the wrong body, and should really be a girl. I remember the moment well, and it is the earliest memory of my life.

Dru has no such narrative certainty. I asked her for an early memory, any early memory, though preferably the first.

'When the time came for me to go to school we were in

Lancashire, at New Longton. In the village primary school there was a Wendy house at the back of the classroom. We had the idea that if we could get into the Wendy house the teacher wouldn't know we were there, and the lesson would go on without us.'

The Wendy house was a frame and canvas tent, somewhere safe to hide, a first and flimsy closet.

Perhaps. I'm extrapolating.

More worryingly, interpreting it in a different way, it's the sign that Dru has always associated tents with going missing and not being found out. Maybe camping is going to be counterproductive. We had to do something though: it was obvious to both of us during that first session over tea and chocolate ginger biscuits that we couldn't simply sit down either side of a table and talk this through. It wasn't our way, and ended up with Dru getting a headache and leaving the room. We wanted some cover – physical exertion, movement, camouflage.

So we left the flat and went on a road trip. This was a few months before the walk, a bright March Sunday morning at eight. Dru had been awake for four hours. I had not, but I was keen to take a ride in Dru's new car – since the operation she'd dumped the rusty Sierra and bought a 1971 K-reg Morris Traveller, old enough to carry us back to her childhood.

A Morris Traveller is the estate version of the Morris Minor, and Dru's is in shiny, reconditioned racing green with an olive plastic interior. It has the characteristic half-timbered back end, now with Dru's added red and yellow sticker: 'Nuclear Power No Thanks'. Irresistibly, I think of Dru's new old car as a Jan Morris Traveller, and though I try my hardest to get Dru to call it Jan, she sticks with her original name of Trav.

That morning Dru put Benny Goodman on the glove compartment CD player, and we travelled at fifty-one miles per hour along the M4 towards Wales, cruising the open road. There was nothing in the world that could hold us up.

We're off to visit Dru's childhood houses, her homes, and I have my notebook on my knee, a scavenger of scraps. First stop is Nash Cottage in the small village of Llanfrechfa, not far from the Newport junction. This was the family's first home when they landed in Wales from the north, and where Dru was living when 'lots of things happened in a very short space of time'.

They settled in.

Dru started at the village school.

Another brother was born.

Then another.

Her mother died of leukaemia.

It was 1968. Dru was ten, and this is what she'd rather not talk about. Before that – and she would love to be able to remember more about before that – everything in Nash Cottage was 'very nice'.

We drive into the village, past a field in which stand a couple of llamas and a steamroller. We park by the church where Dru was once happy, a high-voiced chorister, but now on a Sunday morning the church is locked. It has a fine grey-blocked medieval tower.

'I always wanted to go up the tower.'

'They didn't let you?'

'I never asked.'

The churchyard is full of tombstones for people who have

died in Llanfrechfa in the time since Dru and her family left. There are daffodils.

The old house, small Nash Cottage, is on the main road opposite the pub, formerly the Gate, now the Raj Gate, Free House Indian Restaurant and Takeaway. The front door of the cottage is in a narrow lane across from the village school. The school has been demolished, but the empty space not yet developed. A sign on the chain-link fence says it's for sale. All that's left is the grey concrete of the playground and an imprint of L-shaped grass where the classrooms used to be. The village's old red phone box is right outside the cottage, and next to this is a rotting wooden stump which used to support the old parish noticeboard. It was made by Dru's dad. Nash Cottage is therefore a house genuinely convenient for all village amenities: the school, the phone box, the pub, the road.

For Dru, this is the place of happy memories and bob-a-job, wolf cubs, a mummified dog in a basket and the time her elder brother blew his fingers off with a shotgun.

Dru points out where the post office used to be, but then on the other side of the road we see a house with the sign 'Old Post Office Cottage'. Dru frowns. She has also lost the vicarage, but is adamant she's right about the post office.

It's a mystery, but we speculate that classic village name-plates go up for sale at auction and can be attached to the highest bidder's house. They're like private number plates – they can't be duplicated, only bought and sold. The Old Post Office. The Rectory. The Old Village Stores. The School-house. The Old Forge.

Dru is remembering the days when all male children wore shorts, and she remembers her first long trousers, aged nine or ten. 'They felt awful,' but it's a bit extreme to blame itchy trousers for what happened later. There was a freedom in those days, happiness in these high-hedged lanes, innocence. Children lived out heroic afternoon epics, running go-carts down suicidal hills before walking home the long way via Ponthir to stop at Mr Saunders's shop for sweets and fizzy orange.

Walking, the outdoors life, it all goes back. I ask Dru to tell me more about the family camping holidays.

'They were nice.'

I want much more than that. I want to intrude more.

'We once owned a caravan. That wasn't particularly nice.'

The camping Dru remembers best was wild, and wild camping was easier then. The most idyllic memory comes from somewhere in North Wales, in a sailcloth tent designed by Dru's dad and made by her mum on a sewing machine. They set up camp beside a shallow-sided lake, the occasional fish leaping, and cooked over an open fire. It could have been in the Cambrian Mountains, but Dru isn't sure.

In Llanfrechfa Dru remembers a bully, if pushed. A farmer's boy named Preece who kept a fox cub in a derelict car. Dru used to play with him until Preece turned nasty, but I can't honestly fit this up as an oppressed childhood, blighted by a mistaken identity. I press the point, wanting to make sure, and even at this distance Dru can recall a sense of displacement.

'I always felt that Lancashire was my home and I'd go back there.'

She continued thinking so until her late teens, but she never did go back.

'How do you remember your mother?'

'She was full of life, active, creative.'

'And what about your life before she died?'

'It was just happy, mostly.'

I want more detail.

'It was my brother becoming progressively a hard nut and me being arty. I liked drawing pictures.'

'Did you have friends who were girls?'

'Not close friends, no. Didn't really have boys as close friends, either.'

Dru remembers helping in the dairy; riding a pony. Sunlit memories like those we all have, and which we hold close as protection against fading. Dru had a poem published in a local magazine, lost now, but she remembers the subject was cavemen. She had a new brother, born at Christmas, and started looking forward to her tenth birthday on 1 February. Mum would be home from hospital by then.

We don't talk much in the lane up to the church where we parked the car. We get it started, and in our spinsters-and-widows car we pull out just as the spinsters and widows arrive for morning service. These days they drive Renault Clios.

I've been prodding at the other big Before and After question, the one about Dru's mother, and to be kind, to be sympathetic, this would be a good moment to leave them both alone. I sip some water from a bottle, watch the slow blur of reflected hedges in the quarter-light.

'Were you already dressing up at Nash Cottage, either before or after your mother died?'

What a snake, but I won't be cheated out of a gender-dysphoric childhood.

'I used to play in the wardrobe, certainly.'

'But did you dress up as a woman before, or was it only after?'

'I remember the first time,' Dru says.

A fat youngster in a yellow breakdown truck overtakes us on a corner. He shakes his razored head, as if to say 'Women drivers!'

'I know what that headshake means,' I say.

'So do I,' Dru replies. 'It means he's a dumb fuck.' She checks the rear-view mirror. 'It was after.'

*

Dru is listening to the 6 a.m. news on her new transistor radio. It is the *Today* programme on Radio 4. Outside the tent the sun is struggling, and the mist from the steaming river joins the mist rolling down from the hills. In camping terms it hasn't been a bad night, but no one adapts immediately and I seem to have slept on my cheekbone.

The Russians haven't invaded, but the 6.15 a.m. press review brings us the latest news from Cambridge. In last night's council elections the people of the city of Cambridge elected what the BBC calls the 'UK's first transgender mayor'.

Dru looks at me and I look at Dru.

Dru shrugs. 'We're everywhere.'

We're now fully awake, and would have brewed some tea only Dru has forgotten the matches.

'Didn't I remind you about the matches?'

'You did. Maybe I lost them.'

If Dru messes up it's because she's a ditzy woman. If I do, it's because I'm creative, and inside the tent I show huge reserves of creativity by making a complete hash of rolling up my Therm-a-Rest. I'm sprawled full length trying to subdue it while Dru kneels and calmly inspects her face in her compact. She shaves. Despite the hormone treatment and electrolysis, it's always worth checking. She cuts herself, on the right side of her chin. She then does her mascara and eyeliner, takes her hormone pill, fastens her button necklace below her Adam's apple, her cube bracelet around her mechanic's wrist, and makes sure her silver flower earrings are securely inserted in her ears.

These accessories are important because the more of them she can assemble the more likely she is to pass. Passing means that no one will call her 'sir', swear at her, or spit at her, as once happened by the ticket barriers at Temple Meads station in Bristol. This explains why Dru has acquired a lively interest in hairbands, scarves, necklaces, glasses, brooches and bracelets. These are signifiers, the immediate signals read by strangers as meaning male or female. As natural signifiers she also pays close attention to lips, eyebrows and eyelashes. Deploying all these accessories at once is what can occasionally give the impression of overdoing it, like in the early photos of transgendered pioneers like Christine Jorgensen, nearly all accessory and no Christine. For the same reason, many wealthy European women in their forties look like they've recently had a sex change. I don't imagine this is the intended effect.

As for me, I have my pink Tilley hat. It's the only camp item on our camping trip. As with the Dyke/dyke thing, there are enough double meanings in life without unwelcome extras.

The transsexual experience, as lived by Dru and many

others, is not a camp subject. In her famous essay 'Notes on "Camp"', Susan Sontag was the first to point out that 'Camp is playful, anti-serious.' In the transgender story, especially if the change comes late, it's sometimes difficult to find the frivolity. Sontag goes on to define as camp everything that Dru is not. 'It is the love of the exaggerated, the "off", of things-being-what-they-are-not.'

Dru is intent on being exactly what she is.

Camp sees everything in quotation marks, says Sontag. 'It's not a lamp, but a "lamp"; not a woman but a "woman".' Dru spits on those quotation marks, though not literally, because that's not the kind of woman she is.

So we're definitely not camping it up, even if despite my best efforts I sometimes can't help rambling. Susan Sontag namechecks Tiffany Lamps and Flash Gordon. What we have in mind is a full English breakfast in Monmouth.

Before setting off Dru takes out her phone and checks the signal. She needs a minute to do 'comms', and then we're away. Back past the Boat, over the river and into the trees on the Offa's Dyke path to the Kymin, the last big hill before Monmouth. On the way up the wooded slope Dru stops, and we listen to the intriguing fax-receiving calls of a skylark, Dru's favourite bird. We can hear it but we can't see it.

A small bird dips and flits past. 'Is that a skylark?'

'Nearly. It's a wren.'

'Is that the same thing?'

'Just about. They both have wings.'

At the top of the Kymin, a naval temple commemorates the greatest of the late-eighteenth-century admirals, many of whose names (as it happens) are now also first names: Duncan, Rodney, Warren, Keith, Vincent, Mitchell and

Nelson. From their privileged viewpoint we can see the huge panorama of where we're about to go, across the Monmouthshire lowlands and into the farness of the mountains. I like the idea of just trogging along, following the path, letting the regular acorn waymarks take the strain. The National Trail gives us a direction, and eliminates all risk of getting lost. We have a sure destination in Prestatyn, so we know where we're going and can get a sense of achievement and satisfaction by getting there. What's not to love?

Monmouth is laid out below us, and its ancient school catches the eye above a green spread of straight-lined games pitches. Arriving in a built-up area at eight in the morning seems more daunting than a friendly pub at half past seven at night. There won't be any Beck's to soften the edges, and Chepstow's Mr Beard was definitely a morning person.

Dru, like me, is a little edgy. Naturally, or so it seems after so many years' camping, neither of us brings this sense of unease into the open. Instead, Dru has already seen and named hemp-nettle, dog rose, wild strawberry, vetch, nipplewort, celandine, honeysuckle and forget-me-not. I've seen *loads* of flowers. She's also finding views and taking photographs with me in the foreground. I'm not sure I'm keen on this.

'Keep clicking and eventually we'll find one which is passable.'

Must have the word on my mind. I too want to pass, in the photo at least, for rugged yet caring, tough yet tender. And I hope my knobbly knees don't show. We're all trying to pass as something.

'Dru.'

'Yes.'

'Why the name Drusilla?'

'I really didn't give it much thought,' Dru says.

'Don't believe you.'

'Women my age wouldn't have been christened Dru. They'd have shortened their name later.'

Good thinking. It also presents a total lack of ambiguity in the documents. Drusilla is a name, on forms and applications, that passes. No real need to circle the M or F. It's a kind of statement, even if in daily life Dru never intended to use the full three syllables.

'Is that right?'

'Up to a point,' Dru says.

Drusilla is from the faraway planet Illa, an exotic import like chinchillas, sarsaparilla, Godzilla, and I don't know how we'd get on, me and a being I could only call Drusilla. Dru is still Dru, and like lots of people, being chummy, wanting to be liked, I see a virtue in repeating someone's name while talking to them. It shows you're concentrating just on that person, and reinforces a sense of friendly connection. You can leave the name out, but then a closeness has gone, or an illusion of closeness.

On training days junior salesmen probably learn this by heart, but the continuity of the 'Dru' sound is a big help for Dru's long-term friends. Though harder, in some ways, for Dru. When I say Dru this, Dru that, communicating close-ness, she doesn't know whether I'm welcoming the new short-form Dru, or just confirming to myself that underneath the warpaint it's still my harmless old pal Drew. And neither do I, really. If she'd become a Kate, I might much earlier have had to accept her Kateness.

We're now descending fast towards Monmouth, and I ask Dru directly if as a woman she feels any different.

'To what?'

'To how you were before.'

'I feel the same but in a different body minus testosterone.'

What does *that* mean? How can that be the same?

'Less anger,' Dru explains, 'less lust.'

I don't quite see how this connects to forgetting the radio and the matches (and enough tea bags, as we later discover). For me that's a more immediately obvious difference.

'I always had to hate someone,' Dru says. 'Usually someone on ship.'

I suggest everyone feels this, and by everyone I mean me. I'm always hating someone. I've spent months of Sundays killing the upstairs neighbours, but I've always thought the best way of eliminating that feeling would be to move flat. Not, you know, the other. As usual, Dru backs away from taking too extreme a position. It's as if she doesn't trust any statement that makes her seem intemperate, unusual, emotionally distinctive.

'It wasn't really hate,' she says.

'So not hating isn't that big a change?'

'Not really. My feeling about my body is a huge change. Huge, huge, huge.'

Well thank goodness for that, I think uncharitably. Dru is clodding along and farts loudly. We're nearing a *town*, for God's sake. Come on Dru, do yourself a favour.

Then I have to work out what I mean. *Act more like a woman.*

That's what I mean, and bang go my good intentions. So far I've been modern and soft, treating the female Dru the same as if she was Drew, which in fact is the easiest option. It's not Drusilla, it's Dru, which is an abbreviated way of saying good old Drew in a frock, as if only superficial items like clothes and pronouns have changed. I used to congratulate myself on this narrow broad-mindedness: I treat my friend Dru as if nothing has changed. Look at me. I'm not shocked. I don't see a freak in a dress, I still see Drew.

But this is making no effort, is refusing to be challenged. The truth is that I often used the wrong pronoun because I hadn't made any profound adjustment. And this is also the truth: Dru *is* the same as she always was, it was what she was *before* that we got all wrong.

'Do you want to be treated the same, or differently?'

'I want to be treated like a woman.'

I don't know what that means. This is when she goes Drusilla, when I feel I don't understand her because she comes from a different planet.

'I want people to treat me as the same person *and* as a woman.'

The same person I can do, but I struggle to work out how best to behave with a woman after a night's camping, heading into Monmouth for a fried breakfast. Presumably I'd just *be*, if I was with a woman who wasn't Dru, and wouldn't even have to think about it. In other words not like now, in the outskirts of Monmouth, where I'm trying to think which side of the pavement to take. Even in these gentlemanly basics I remember potentially conflicting advice. The man walks on the outside, to protect the lady from wheel splash. Or the man walks on the left, keeping his scabbard clear, ready at any moment safely to draw his sword and defend the lady's honour. Or is that the right, freeing his sword arm?

'I know what you're thinking,' Dru says.

'Bet you don't.'

'I may not be an oil painting, but I'm not alone in that, either.'

I walk on the outside of the pavement as far as Wye Bridge and across the river. Then in the subway under the Monmouth bypass I walk on the left, and in Monmouth's St Mary's Street I honestly can't remember. The pressure of civilisation is making the pitch of Dru's voice rise as she tries to blend in. The same happened when she was ordering her pint in the Boat, and although I'm relieved she's making the effort, she also becomes slightly distant to me. She is almost Drusilla.

Without mishap, we buy some pasties for lunch in a bakery with a 'Rick Stein Recommended' sticker. But we can't find the café which used to sell amazing breakfasts. We're down the High Street and through the town before we know it, and have to backtrack.

I refuse to ask the early shoppers if there's anywhere in Monmouth we can get breakfast. That would be demeaning. Dru stops to ask two girls sitting on a bench in Agincourt Square, but in problem-solving mode I'm already heading down a narrow street towards an outside table I can see in a courtyard. It's more of a tea shop than a greasy spoon, but the blackboard advertises 'Breakfasts'.

Dru comes through with a knowing smile that wasn't there before. She shrugs off her pack and leans it against some railings, pulls out the chair opposite, sits down and crosses her hands smugly on the tabletop. Still smiling like something has made her day.

'What?'

'One of those girls was TS.'

'How do you know?'

'It was her voice.'

'No.'

I grab my notebook and trot back up the street to the square. The two girls have gone. I walk back and sit down.

'You wouldn't have, would you?' Dru is appalled.

'I don't know.'

The friendly Indian man who owns the tea shop comes out to take our order.

'Everything alright, gents?'

Dru is totally miffed. She's deflated, also angry, but purses her lips and nods while I order breakfast, saving her reaction until the man goes away. 'It's the watch,' she decides, the Timex Explorer she wanted to bring because it's a good sturdy watch. 'It's a signifier. It's off.' And off it is, stuffed somewhere deep in Dru's rucksack and never seen again. There is a pale band on Dru's smooth wrist where the watch strap blocked yesterday's sun, and I think it's going to be tough if for the rest of her life she's obsessed by what people make of her. Though as another woman friend of mine pointed out, that would be a genuine and authentic female experience.

As soon as we've finished breakfast Dru is up and flinging on her rucksack.

'I'm going to look in some clothes shops.'

Treating Dru exactly as I would a woman, I leave her to it. I do my own supporting of the local economy, buying matches, half a pound of Brays fruit drops, some tea bags. And then I wait. I admire the medieval bridge and gate, and I'm glad we didn't go walking in Spain, or Antarctica. I don't feel any pressure to discover the 'real' Monmouth. Oh, and then I wait some more.

Dru is in Hawkshead looking for tops. Specifically, tops that signify her gender more clearly than the two tight V-necked numbers that have so far let her down.

I wander back to Agincourt Square, just in case Dru's TS friend comes back, but she doesn't, so I admire the statues of Henry Rolls (of Rolls-Royce) and Henry V (of Agincourt). These are just two of the lives that intersect with the Dyke and that I could have chosen to write instead of Dru's. I could have researched Raymond Williams (invented Cultural Studies), Eric Gill (slept with his dog), William Spooner (slandered by a lack of pies), or the lesbian ladies of Llangollen, Sarah Ponsonby and Eleanor Butler (periodically dressed as men). A biographer could find as many potential subjects on a straight line of similar length anywhere in Britain, because ours is a nation rich in interesting people.

But I'm writing a biography of my friend Dru Marland (in Hawkshead looking for tops). The difficulty with this choice is that Dru's life goes on, and she isn't always a great help in working out what it means. All the dates are 'by my reckoning', and nothing is true except 'up to a point'.

She comes out of Hawkshead wearing a low-cut top, half-length sleeves. It is a much brighter colour than the other two, in thin stripes of lime green, grey and orange. It squashes nice shapes out of her breasts, and the cheerier colours in lightweight cotton *are* more feminine.

'Looking good,' I say. 'Onwards and upwards?'

'Unless you want to hunt down and persecute the other TS.'

I give her a glance. I probably wouldn't have done it. Probably not. If it's not true, no one wants to be asked. If it is true, no one wants to be asked. All women are the same.

IV

A distant jet plane
And a blackbird chipping chinks
From the dawn's silence.

'Hospitality has always been a boast of the Welsh,' writes Jan Morris in *Wales: Epic Views of a Small Country*. She may be right, but then it's the boast of every people on earth. Not even the French admit to thinking 'we're miserable bastards and wish you were gone.' The landlord and chef of the Hunter's Moon in Llangattock Lingoed may also think he can cook.

We've been walking for seventeen miles, and approaching the village up a steep grassy hill we're very hungry and hoping for some kind of comfort food.

'All British food is comfort food,' Dru says optimistically, as if in the history of this country, at the end of most days, we've all done something that merits an arm round the shoulder and a plate of potato and gravy. This is not what we find at the Hunter's Moon. The food is awful, both ambitious and clueless. It's *stupid* food.

On the plus side, no one calls us gents and we've spent the early evening having a pleasant chat with the formidable ladies of the Raglan History Society. They've been on a private tour of an eighteenth-century cider-house, and after asking our advice they decide to eat elsewhere. They have cars.

Dru's new top seems to make the difference.

We escape the pub, and my first idea is to put up the tent in the village churchyard. It's flat and not overlooked and the grass is invitingly short. Dru refuses point blank to camp on hallowed ground. We keep on walking, picking up the path at the far end of the village's straggle of houses.

'Are you baptised?'

'No,' Dru says.

That's interesting, I think. She refuses to camp in a churchyard yet isn't baptised, and these small facts, in a biographer's mind, might lead to a telling conclusion. Dru's family were freethinkers ahead of their time, prepared at the end of the fifties to disregard the Church in what was an altogether more conformist era. From her earliest years, then, Dru was surrounded by a quiet preference for individualism.

'Oh hang on. I think I was.'

This is a typical exchange.

A mile or so further on we find a hidden flat spot in front of a row of oaks at the bottom of a cultivated field. There's a busy crow's nest nearby; this has been another winning day for nature. Dru saw her first yellowhammer, and there were goldfinches among the thistles. Proudly, I identified the call of the cuckoo, and in a sunken lane a buzzard dropped and flew down the path in front of us, filling the available space with its wings. All day the clouds were high and hurried, and after a lunchtime Rick Stein pasty I slept beside a stream while Dru kept tabs on a greater spotted woodpecker in the trees. She told me all about it, the male making its clacking alarm call while the female brought food to the chicks. Woodpeckers know what's what.

Lying in the tent beyond Llangattock, night is falling and a dog is barking, but far away. Dru has taken her hormones and she's close to sleep.

'You know what?' she turns away from me, fusses for a good position. 'I'm much more comfortable sharing the tent than I used to be.'

It's like a bump in the night. What does she mean by *that*?

After the change of clothes in Monmouth, we've been worrying away for most of the day at what can be said to make a woman.

'I don't think I'm very feminine,' Dru says at one point. We're crossing a series of open fields and I walk buoyantly through the waist-high barley, arms out hands down, taking the adulation from the sticky tops. I'm getting Dru to talk – so far so good. We pass stacks of silage stuffed tight into white and black plastic like giant overripe fruit, and in every field left fallow there is rusting farm machinery and usually an ageing bathtub. I'm patient; try not to rush her.

'I want people to treat me differently, but not as a freak.'

I suggest that the way people treat her differently will probably connect to some idea of her femininity, if she wants to be treated like a woman. That's what she said she wanted, if she can remember. It was only earlier on today.

'Yes.'

I think of the pints of lager, the fried breakfast, the farting. We pass some lambs in a field, and then some calves. The lucky ones are female, destined for a longer life. The males are doomed, except for the biggest and strongest, for whom in compensation there is a kind of gender reparation, and life will be truly sweet.

'Putting gender aside for a moment, in what ways would you say you *were* feminine?'

'I wouldn't.'

'You mean no ways at all? Even now?'

'What kind of things?'

'I don't know. Being scared of spiders.'

'I don't like mice very much. But those other things that are supposed to separate masculine and feminine I find bogus.'

Even so, if we're looking (I'm looking), Dru has, for example, certainly allowed her interest in clothes to surface. We've already had the new top in Monmouth, when I know as a fact that as a man Dru went to renew her ten-year passport and was wearing the same German Army shirt in both photos.

'You used to be so thoughtless about clothes.'

'But they weren't worn thoughtlessly.'

'Yes, I can see that now.'

The baggy trousers and long sleeves and shapeless coats hid the body inside. 'But what have you changed *consciously*?'

'There's the walk.'

'*This* walk?'

'The way I walk.'

Elbows in and a bounce, as distinct as possible from the stewards' walk she despised on the ships, legs splayed wide to allow for the enormity of their big stewards' bollocks.

'I read somewhere that men and women hold beer bottles differently,' I say, remembering something to do with the bottle's neck or the body, and how many fingers touch the glass. This may be a prompt, or a hint, thinking ahead to the many more pubs between here and the end of the road at Prestatyn.

Dru looks puzzled.

'I shall hold a beer bottle as nature intended.'

*

Ah, nature and nurture. Our walk along the borders has already raised the question of appearance versus reality. Add an identity crisis and in Dru alone we have years' worth of undergraduate late-night chats. I'd have liked to take us back to those heady days, but we're in our forties and it's gone ten o'clock. Dru is already asleep, but thinking those words together, nurture and nature, has made me feel eighteen again. I remember what it was like to feel confused.

The service-industry people of Chepstow and Monmouth did not believe that Dru was sufficiently womanly. In their eyes she failed to pass because gender is determined at birth, and cannot be changed like clothes. Or alternatively she failed because gender is shaped by cultural and social conditioning, and Dru lacks the training.

Nobody knows which of the two is more important. These days we're generally agreed that gender is not decided by appearance: paratroop boots are unisex. Nor is it decided by behaviour, because everyone knows girls who like boy things and boys who like girl things. It's not sexual orientation, nor is it any other fixed range of preferences or skills, despite the many tests designed as if it were. There's the Moir-Jessel Brain Sex Test and the Guilford-Zimmerman Temperament

Survey and the Bem Sex Test and COGIATI and the *Guardian* newspaper's 'Essential Difference' questionnaire. This measures an individual's Empathy Quotient against their Systematising Quotient, and like all the other tests it's rubbish, the results inconclusive and unusable.

Do you enjoy being the centre of attention at any social gathering? To any sane mind of either gender the answer is always the same. *That depends.* It always depends.

Can you appreciate someone else's viewpoint, even if you don't agree with it?

Poor Drusilla. Her womanhood is examined, considered and criticised much more relentlessly than that of other women, despite the fact that science is on her side. In *Woman: An Intimate Geography*, Pulitzer Prizewinner Natalie Angier sets out to tackle the question 'What makes a woman?'

At a basic level, looking for absolute differences, there are the chromosomes. All human beings have twenty-three pairs, which are the same except for pair twenty-three, the sex chromosomes. Women are XX. Men are XY. Nature, however, is rarely, if ever, conclusive. There are women with a Y chromosome who have what's called androgen insensitivity syndrome, or AIS. This is a rare condition where testes may bud in the foetus but the X chromosome has no androgen receptors. The penis and testicles fail to develop, and the woman has a vagina and clitoris but no uterus or Fallopian tubes. Due to other factors related to androgen, she will tend to have great skin, great hair, large breasts and will probably be tall. A woman with AIS and XY chromosomes is definitely a woman, and often a total stun-gun.

Looking further along Angier's checklist the news, for Dru, is good:

In a basic biological sense, the female is the physical prototype for an effective living being . . . foetuses are pretty much primed to become female unless the female program is disrupted by gestational exposure to androgens.

It gets better. Angier is careful to avoid the trap of 'womb worship': 'The womb does not define a woman, philosophically, biologically, or even etymologically. A woman does not need to be born with a uterus to be a woman, nor does she have to keep her uterus to remain a woman.' This is exactly as Dru would have it, because she, like many other women, doesn't have one of those.

She does have breasts, 'engines of pleasure, great treasures of the human race'. Tick. Angier then relishes the challenge of communicating the magnificence of the vagina – 'the vagina is its own ecosystem'. Yup, got one of those too, tick. Dru also has a functioning clitoris and no lingering penis envy – or as Angier puts it, 'who would want a shotgun when you can have a semi-automatic?'

The fact that Dru wasn't born with this equipment doesn't necessarily count against her. Writing about hysterectomies, though this could equally apply to the transsexual experience, the exemplary Angier concludes: 'The naturalistic fallacy warns us against elevating the presumed innate to the presumed optimum.' If human beings had always believed that what is, is best, we'd never as a species have managed to progress.

Biologically, Angier is constantly struck by how 'the line between maleness and femaleness is thin'. Slosh aside the organs and hormones and chromosomes to seek out what's important. What makes Dru Dru? Or Dru Drew? If beyond the body it's the soul, then the last time anyone checked the soul had no conspicuous gender.

So nature makes small distinctions, which are then exaggerated by nurture. I never met a girl who grew up as a boy before. It's like meeting a girl who grew up alone in the forest. She isn't going to be like the other girls, but she's still a girl.

I want so much for Dru to be on the right track, to have made a correct decision. I therefore keep reminding myself that it's some time since girls were expected to act in specific, authorised ways. Not so long ago, feminine behaviour was easier to recognise, and Jan Morris, as an example, had a clear idea of the version of femininity she wished to live: 'my own notion of the female principle was one of gentleness against force, forgiveness rather than punishment, give more than take, helping more than leading.'

Morris understands that her sex change is subversive and exciting, but she's also seduced by a simpler world of wide-brimmed hats, pleated skirts and spinsters on country bicycles. 'Her frailty is her strength, her inferiority is her privilege.'

This vision of femininity has not dated well, idealising the rare type of woman who is submissive, dependent, softly spoken. She does not eat fried breakfasts or drink pints or break wind in public places. Even at the time, or at least once the critical praise had died down, there were women uneasy with *Conundrum* and Jan Morris's passive idea of what it meant to be female. In 1984 the feminist Nora Ephron wrote:

[I was] no good at being a girl; on the other hand I am

not half bad at being a woman. In contrast, Jan Morris is perfectly awful at being a woman; what she has become instead is exactly what James Morris wanted to become those many years ago. A girl. And worse, a 47-year-old girl. And worst of all, a 47-year-old *Cosmopolitan* girl.

This is not unfair, though it's worth noting that there is little residue of the *Cosmo* girl in any of Jan Morris's subsequent writing, and this contradiction reminds me of something Dru said right at the beginning. She was a woman and she wanted to dress as a woman. At the same time it had shocked her to see, looking back from the mirror, such a *middle-aged* woman.

With no agreed definition of womanly behaviour (nurture), it's hardly surprising that many transgendered people feel an urgent need for some incontestable biological evidence (nature). Men are different from women, and transsexual women would like to see this scientifically proven. The fact that no one has yet found a definitive biological connection between transsexual and genetic women hasn't stopped the search, and the yearning for a 'natural' explanation can sometimes go to extremes. At different times, US studies (that great euphemism for flawed science) have shown that transsexuals are taller, or three times more likely to be left-handed.

'The finger thing,' Dru says.

'What's that?'

'If you have one finger bigger than the other, index or middle, or perhaps the other way round, then you're in the wrong body.'

Dru says that trans-people invariably dismiss these theories then rush somewhere private to check. Most sufferers of gender dysphoria would welcome a physical sign, anything to lance the uncertainty, and the autobiographers I've read often claim intersex status before deciding on the operation. Their dubious assurances range from 'I was growing breasts anyway', to 'I'd always had long eyelashes'. I ask Dru for any physical characteristics that might have suggested her body wasn't right. She comes up with two: she never had much body hair and puberty arrived late. It's not much to go on.

'Also, I have a vestigial second set of nipples.'

Christ alive, I think, why didn't she tell me earlier? Didn't she imagine I'd be interested?

'Or they might be moles. They're the same distance apart but just below. The diagnosis is just so flimsy,' Dru adds, sounding a bit peeved at her condition. 'If you say so, then you are.'

There has in fact been some progress on the biological side. We now know that the human brain has a hundred billion neurons connected by a hundred trillion synapses. The permutations make numbers so big I don't know the numbers, but in any of these connections there may be an answer. Dick Swaab in the Netherlands has, over a twelve-year period, dissected eight male-to-female transsexual brains. Every one had identifiable female patterns. In science-speak this translates from 'the interstitial nuclei in the anterior hypothalamus, and a nucleus of the stria terminalis, also in the hypothalamus, are larger in mass.' Men have larger brains and more neurons, but women have a higher percentage of grey matter. No one knows why, or what this means, but Swaab's problem has been to accumulate a big enough sample to make his results stick. Fresh transsexual brains are not that easy to come by.

In the meantime, there are others who continue to look for the causes not in what the brain is, but in what it has suffered. It is the psychoanalytic approach. Look back. Look behind you. The subject over-identifies with the mother or mother-surrogate, and therefore wants to dress like her. The subject's father is absent and the subject is making the mother happy. The mother is absent so the subject is replacing her to please the father. The mother is too dominant; the father is too dominant. The mother is under-involved, or the father is. Cross-gender identification was under-encouraged by the subject's ever-blameable parents, or encouraged too strongly – Renée Richards, the transsexual American doctor who tried to join the women's LTA tennis tour in the seventies, was born Richard but her mother always called her Renée. Just as she called Renée's sister Jonathan. Why did she do that? The therapists would find the answer by forming opinions about pre-existing family pathology. It's not what you are; it's what someone did.

Which is where biography comes in. If characteristics and outcomes are not inherent, then events and accidents make us what we are, what we will one day become.

I keep thinking of Dru's mother. It's where everyone else looks: there's an instinct (nature) that says mother is always the place to start. Dru remembers her mother suffering no periods of illness apart from the pregnancy. She was 'lively and busy', and then she was dead of leukaemia. Dru never talked about the exact chronology of the disaster with her dad, or with anyone else in the family.

'We didn't talk about big things. We had a low-key emotional way of dealing with life. We were just hiding from things.'

'Have you always been hiding from things?'

'I think so.'

Dru knows what I'm getting at.

'The big gender issue,' she adds. 'Finding ways to deal with it.'

But the gender issue comes later, and I led Dru into tagging this on. Must stop doing that.

In total, Dru owns less than a dozen photographs of her mum, and three of these are formal wedding photos (big white dress – nurture). Of the others, six are in black and white and roughly photocopied on to a single sheet of A4 office paper. They were sent by Dru's stepmother after her father died. In one of these, at the 1952 Leyland show, Dru's mother is aged nineteen, in a skirt and jacket, standing beside a brassed-up shire horse. Three more are from a family trip to the seaside, on the front at Fleetwood in about 1960 when Dru is two and a bit. The granddad whose lifetime was worth a clock is wearing a white shirt with the sleeves rolled up, braces and a tie. As the man of the family, he is making a comedy bicep. The boys, Dru and her older brother, are sitting in swimsuits on a tartan travel rug eating ice lollies. The women, Grandma and Mum, are in floral-print sundresses buttering bread.

Grandma is wearing sensible black lace-up shoes, but Dru's mum is barefoot. She has short hair, a strong rectangular face, and powerful forearms and hands.

There are other photos from slightly later of the boys on their own, in short trousers and wellington boots, sitting on a windowsill, the bleached mid-sixties sunlight brightening just one side of Dru's plump little boy's face.

She remembers helping with the cooking. 'I didn't have the kind of parents who made me do boy things.'

Sewing, too.

But she also did boy things. There's a photo in which she's wearing a tin helmet, a tommy gun slung casually over her shoulder, defending the nation in a Lancashire garden.

Dru fondly remembers the brothers sitting down to needlework.

'But,' I protest, 'you didn't shy away from . . .' I gesture at the photo, the hard hat, the replica M1A1 Thompson sub-machine gun with a .45 calibre thirty-round magazine. Dru is a little exasperated.

'I've always done exactly what I bloody well wanted to.'

This is not true, because it never is, for anyone.

*

Dru doesn't know the exact date her mother died. It was sometime in the first week of February, 1968. She has her mother's last diary, and inserted inside it a short poem written by her dad.

'She must have died by the 7th because that's when the poem is dated.'

Her funeral was on the 14th, as reported in a cutting from the *Lancashire Evening Post*, also inside the book, and Dru knows her mother was alive on 1 February because that's the day she last saw her, 1 February 1968. It was Dru's tenth birthday. She visited her mum in hospital taking along her favourite present, an Airfix plane she'd received that morning and had already glued together, painted, applied the RAF roundel transfers top and bottom to the wings. She proudly held up the plane for her mum to see, flying it one way, flying it the other.

Dru has this final memory, the A4 sheet of copied photos, and the desk diary. Inside the diary, along with the newspaper cutting and the poem, there is a flattened blackened rose from the wreath, but the entries her mother made are not expansive expressions of the self. It isn't that type of diary; or she wasn't that type of woman. There are birthdays and hospital appointments. These look ominous in hindsight but might have been for the pregnancy. The handwriting itself is the memorial, the relic, all that's left behind.

Her death came as a complete shock, and then the many things that 'happened in a very short space of time' kept on happening. A year later Dru's dad remarried, to a widow with two children, a boy and a girl. They all moved into Nash Cottage in Llanfrechfa. Dru dressed as a woman for the first time.

In the summer of 1969 it was decided that the two families now combined as one should go on a family honeymoon. Naturally Dru remembers the ship – the P&O SS *Iberia* – and also the itinerary: Southampton-Lisbon-Ceuta-Southampton.

At that time there were eight of them crowded into the three-bedroomed cottage but Dru's dad, a novice at making things right, told them to ready themselves for the holiday of a lifetime. Deck quoits, bingo, dancing. Slap-up dinners, party games, fancy dress. Eleven-year-old Dru was already thinking ahead: she'd need to find a costume. She went upstairs, put on a pince-nez and a dress, and came downstairs again.

'Was this your mother's dress?'

'My memory's vague. I think it was. It was my first real outing.'

'How did the family react?'

'I don't remember. They were pretty relaxed. I think it's only people with gender issues who tend to get all bothered by that sort of thing. Allegedly of course.'

Dru's impersonation of an old lady, in her dead mum's dress, would later win her a prize on the SS *Iberia*. It also echoes the plot of an Alfred Hitchcock film. That film is *Psycho*.

*

So there you have it. The evidence requires a verdict, and in the film *Psycho* Anthony Perkins dresses up as his dead mother to alleviate his grief and loneliness. As an unfortunate side effect, the dressing up provides an alter ego who stabs Janet Leigh in the shower.

Dru, however, is not a psychopath. I have her psychiatric reports. Dr Russell W. Reid, MBChB, FRCPsych, is of the opinion that 'she is not depressed or mentally ill and is mentally competent to make decisions for herself with regards to her gender role.' Dr Penny Lenihan, BSc (Hons), MSc, PsyD, Couns CPsychol, has sat down in a professional capacity with Dru and decided that 'Ms Marland appears to be functioning well in the female gender role.' Dr A. Chalu, MB, BS, MRCPsych, agrees: 'she appeared relaxed, appropriate and passed very well in a female role.'

So why should I think my conclusion will be any different? Well, for a start, these psychiatric reports are not infallible –

'drinks moderate alcohol'. They go on to suggest, if gently, a self-harming or self-destructive factor in risky activities like climbing and motorcycling. I'm fairly sure Dru simply used to enjoy them. Also, I have another advantage because Dru can't search the Internet for what to say to friends (moderate drinking!) and none of her psychiatrists, as far as I know, have gone walking with Dru both before and after and shared the same tiny tent.

Even Dru concedes that there are nutters about.

'I've seen some pretty loony people in the Claybrook Centre.'

This is because gender can be the 2+2=5 answer to more basic confusions between causes and symptoms. Are you socially clumsy because you were born into the wrong body? Or does your social clumsiness make you think you must have something wrong with you, like being born into the wrong body?

The condition now known as gender dysphoria may be unique in requiring self-diagnosis. No doctor is going to listen patiently to a list of baffling symptoms, reflect carefully for a moment chin on hand, and then suggest a sex change. You have to make up your own mind, then visit your GP and announce what it is you believe you need, that gender dysphoria is the condition you think you have.

Self-diagnosis is also a classic symptom of insanity. In the comedy nuthouse everyone has decided they're something they're not: a fruit-loop Napoleon shouting furious orders to a man who listens patiently because of course he's convinced he's the doctor.

'Yes, I've met some very eccentric people, really,' Dru says. 'Where the hell is their sense of reality?'

I don't know, Drusilla.

The clinical possibilities are well documented. The most common mental illnesses that can resemble gender dysphoria include schizophrenia, dissociative disorder and narcissistic personality disorder. These are all forms of psychosis.

Alfred Hitchcock is not alone in finding psychotic behaviour deliciously dramatic, and I too am always looking for my shower scene. I'm hoping to uncover the one pivotal moment in Dru's life. This will be (da-dah!) the moment when she flipped her lid (clash! – cymbals). Although, as we're friends, I'd prefer it to be the exact moment she received, once and for all, for sure, definitely, without any doubt, perhaps with a tear in her eye, the certain sign that she was unquestionably, in her heart, a woman (strings, heavenly music). Failing that, I'd settle for the one moment, above all others, when she finally decided, after years of pain and hesitation, to act (silver trumpet?).

I'm going to be disappointed.

Life just seems to happen. Dru wins a cruise-ship prize in her mother's dress, but dressing up doesn't become a habit. The reconstituted family returns from the SS *Iberia* and moves from Llanfrechfa to the nearby pithead village of Newbridge. The new family home – Ty Celyn, Holly House – is much bigger and was once reserved for the colliery manager, though recently no one has lived there and the house is semi-derelict. Dru has the room in the attic beneath the dripping roof.

'It was surrounded by big holly trees,' Dru says, 'and gloomy things they are too.'

The colliery manager had lived higher up the hill than the miners in their terraced streets down in the town. No one in

Newbridge, though, could avoid the slag heap – the manager just had a better view of it.

After our visit to Llanfrechfa and Nash Cottage, we drove across to Newbridge, the Morris Traveller puttering away happily as it eased into a familiar era. Dru lived in the town from 1969 until 1974, a time when the coal mine was fully operational. Now the railway station is the Somerfield car park, and in the streets where Dru delivered papers the youngsters wear Manchester United shirts. Newbridge is only ten miles from the fields and lanes of Llanfrechfa, but Wales is so changeable that before Newbridge Dru had never seen a pithead.

'It was much more obviously industrial then. There was the winding gear, and the aerial ropeway taking the slag up the mountain. That was until the miners' strike.'

There is coal rubble beside the new cycle path, and although the former slag heap is disguised by grass and shrubs it continues to leak rust. The short cut to the grammar school was over the shoulder of the slag heap, then along a pipe suspended across the river. There's a new road bridge which we stand underneath, contemplating the pipe and beneath our feet the litter: crisp bags, beer cans, fag packets, from lives of crisps, beer and fags. The valley is still cleaner than it used to be: the once black and red water of the Ebbw now so clear you can see the sofa lying upside down on the riverbed.

We walk round the sensible way to have a look at the school. Dru tells me that Newbridge Grammar had two entrances, with uncomplicated instructions carved in stone above each doorway – BOYS or GIRLS. When we get there the space above both doors has been covered by yellow and blue plastic signs saying Newbridge Comprehensive School.

'How was it, the two families in one?'

'I think my dad built a wall around himself. If it was anything important we didn't talk about it, except when we did something wrong. Then we'd get a good telling off.'

'Were you effeminate as a boy?'

'Yes.'

'Were you teased, bullied?'

'No. Because I didn't act effeminately.'

'Eh?'

I bite my lip. I feel like I'm looking for explanations that don't exist, to straighten a line that was never bent.

'Since I wasn't a girl,' Dru explains patiently, 'there was no point doing girly things or dressing like one.'

This is a no nonsense, pragmatic approach, of the kind that once saw memsahibs walk halfway across the world, whatever obstacles stood against them.

As far as I can tell, Dru is a young boy thriving in her early years at the local grammar school. 'A very good beginning,' say the end of year school reports, 'Keep it up! Most satisfactory.' There is no outward sign that she desperately wants to be anything other than a schoolboy who excels in class. But she did. She wanted to be something else as strongly as she ever wanted anything in her life. Yes, I think, anything. She wanted to be a fighter pilot.

*

At 6 a.m., in one of the rare moments I'm actually asleep, Dru offers me the radio so I can listen to the news. She's already heard it, an hour earlier.

'No thanks,' I say, pulling the top of the bag over my head, 'it's all war and transsexuals.'

'Taking over the world,' Dru sighs, and keeps it on as if the next hour might somehow prove decisive.

Dru makes the tea, but now we've also run out of condensed milk in a tube. This is a brilliant invention available in the Clifton Down Sainsbury's in Bristol, but as we are about to discover, nowhere on the borders or in the foreign shops and supermarkets of Wales.

'Never mind,' Dru says cheerfully, because the day is dawning bright and she's looking on the bright side, a morning person. I climb out of the tent and she hands me my mug of black tea. 'Condensed milk is just around the corner. Some medieval tinkers will soon be coming up the lane. I wonder what they'll make of us.'

I take a good look at the tight curves of the tent, the miracle of modern nylon, the colour mauve, our self-inflating Therm-a-Rests and the foolproof methylated-spirit stove.

'They'd bow down and worship us. Or they'd burn us. They'd definitely burn *you*.'

Dru disagrees. She already knows what she'll say:

'I come from the future, where women are differently beautiful and have deep voices.'

I'm growing a beard. No question of gender anxiety in *my* family, at least I don't think so. But then maybe there are questions that need to be asked, like why exactly did those Saxon ancestors grow beards so extravagant they became known and recognised by them? Perhaps they were covering up, generation after generation, a profound ambivalence about their gender identity.

I'm rarely ambivalent, but in this situation I do find it one of life's unfunnier jokes that in some ways I'm more feminine than Dru. I drink from the Sigg water bottle in a far more ladylike way than she does. I use its broad mouth like the rim of a cup, and sip. Dru surrounds the spout like a beer bottle, and glugs. There's also the way in which Dru sees a contraption and wants to know how it works. I just want to know what it does, and in the case of her catheter on Ward 4 South at Charing Cross, not even that. Not that I'm effeminate. The only perfume I use is a bit of Vicks in the winter.

We pack up camp, leaving no trace of ourselves behind, and have high expectations for the day's walking, because we're heading to Pandy, then crossing the railway and the river and taking the route over the tops to Llanthony Abbey. This is a ruined Augustinian abbey founded in 1103, and you can find out all about it in other books. For our purposes, it is a very beautiful Gothic ruin with a pub in the former crypt.

We shall be going by way of the Black Mountains. These hills, at the eastern end of the Brecon Beacons National Park, have a bad reputation, where SAS men from the Hereford base go on training marches to die. Even Jan Morris, who loves almost everywhere in Wales, confesses 'it is a queer part of the world, and queer dark things happen there.'

What happened to us was that we sometimes didn't talk about gender for hours. The path up to the Hatterrall Ridge, the start of the Black Mountains, is cropped grass through bracken still curly at the ends, unfurling like fiddleheads. We settle in for a long climb, a slow tramp up a hill stamped with the ancient clopped tracks of horses. Dru tells me about rhino shit. Sheep have their tails cut off so that the shit doesn't stick, because stuck sheep shit is an open invitation to blowflies and, surely as night follows day, maggot infestation. Rhinos, on the other hand, whirl their tails around so their shit goes everywhere.

'"Hey!" they're saying,' Dru elaborates, '"I'm full of shit!"'

This is a very attractive quality, in a rhino.

'Or it might be hippos,' Dru muses, stopping to catch her breath. 'I think it's hippos.'

So more uncertainty to add to the details from her past, and the particular vagueness she has about dates. She doesn't remember the date of her wedding day, neither the first time round nor the second.

'Last time it was the season of the dog rose. We had them as a bouquet.'

'So what dates *do* you remember?'

Her daughter's birthday.

The day she made the statutory declaration changing her name to Drusilla Philippa Marland, 30 May 2002.

'At least I think it was.'

She has even forgotten the exact date of the operation, which was less than a year ago. 'I think it was October.'

Her life becomes a kind of GCSE version of history. Dates aren't important, because Dru was never self-obsessed. She never made a habit of ordering her life for posterity, just in case one day someone like me should come along and ask.

'What other dates do you remember? Not personal ones, any dates at all?'

'6 June – D-Day.'

Out in the open, Dru's fuzzy memory makes me worry there must be something else she's hiding, like the something else I failed to notice every other time we were supposedly out in the open. I sidle, I stalk, I belly-down in the grass.

'Give me your favourite TV programmes, when you were a child.'

Even Dru must have watched television, and I want her to be like everyone else, as far as possible.

'*Play for Today*. Anything by Alan Plater.'

'I mean really.'

'*Alias Smith and Jones*.'

'Ah! You see, they're not who they seem to be either, are they?'

Dru looks at me blankly. 'You're really ringing the changes, aren't you?'

'I didn't pick *Alias Smith and Jones*. You did. Were you thinking about it all the time?'

'About what?'

'Being a girl. How often did you think about it?'

'I've read that men think about their thingies every nine minutes.'

I'm shocked, astonished.

'Can't you say penis?'

'I can,' Dru says, 'but there are some people coming this way.'

And so there are, but they veer off to look for their dogs, which we can see further up the hill towards the lip of the ridge. Among our traveller's tales are many mini-dramas that never quite happen. Two escaped black dogs on the hillside fail to worry any sheep.

'Think of it more like a dodgy hip,' Dru says, once we're on our way again.

'What, your penis?'

'No, being a girl when I seemed to be a boy. Sometimes the knowledge aches more than others, but always it's a bit of a nuisance.'

'Can you give me some more explicit examples?'

She gives it some thought, perhaps while looking through the binoculars at the puffs of hawthorns on the valley flanks below us. I want examples of feeling like a girl. How it affected her relationships with her father and brothers. Examples of it being less 'a bit of a nuisance', and more a horrible, inexorable, unbearable, irrepressible yearning which if she didn't escape she would die.

'Not really.'

'Christ, Dru.'

'I'm not good value for money, am I?'

As soon as we make the top, the clouds close in and sweep over the side of the ridge like theatrical dry ice. I can't see much, but I can see why you wouldn't want to get lost up here. Stick to the path. I can see the sand in the ruts where we're walking, but not the severe drop on either side. The mist is more like a soft rain, like an Evian spray.

'Good for the complexion!' I yell at Dru, and then worry why I knew that.

We follow the path towards Llanthony and eventually it takes us on a steep descent off the ridge and down towards the treeline in the direction of the abbey. Dru is murmuring about a bird she saw earlier that she hasn't been able to identify, though we stop so she can write down its song – 'lurk chick chick tsk tsk'. Apparently the wittering we can hear now is from swallows, but when the tiredness gets into my legs and shoulders I reach a point in every day when I'm profoundly uninterested in what mountain is where, or the name of the bird behind the birdsong, or what animals live in any particular hole.

We drop through the cloud base and Llanthony Abbey appears in Gothic glory in the cradle of the valley ahead. 'That's the great thing about walking,' Dru says. 'You never know what's round the next corner.'

We trudge on, thinking of ways to pep each other up as the day grows weary and the view stays largely the same.

'And you carry on not knowing for ages.'

We enter the woods and something flies overhead as I climb over a stile.

'What's that? A duck?'

'A low-flying buzzard. Ow!'

It's Dru at the stile, at the same stage of the day as yesterday. I turn and she's halfway over the fence, her head turned as if she's listening closely to the greenery that arches above. For Christ's sake, I think, I don't want to know what it is, where it comes from, or what noise it makes.

'My earring's caught on the bloody ivy.'

I have to laugh. I'm still giggling as I set Dru free. Whatever happened to the story of triumphant reincarnation? 'I felt resplendent in my liberation!' That's Jan Morris but she can't speak for everyone – 'I shone! I was Ariel!'

Below the ruins we can now see the field that serves as the campsite, and unusually there are many big cars. This isn't part of the plan. I'd been looking forward to a night out without the pressure of strangers that had made itself felt in Chepstow and Monmouth. We've been here several times before and normally it's quiet, as if the secret still hasn't got out that it was here St David grew the original Welsh leek. Hold back the coachloads! Also, the campsite may be in a beautiful spot, but you have to wash from a cold-water standpipe.

We set up our tiny tent, no car. The 4x4s parked beside massive three-bedroomed canvas mansions bring out the worst in Dru.

'Slightly larger than the average bedsit,' she sniffs, and many years of achieved nonconformism have made her a terrible snob, in an alternative kind of way. As well as tent-and-car combinations, she despises horse magazines and misspelt butchers' signs. Caravanners bring on a bad case of misanthropy and she can always find it in her heart to criticise the artwork on the walls of local tea shops.

'I *am* intolerant,' Dru admits, as we throw in the mats and the sleeping bags, as she rolls her eyes at a gang of young men next to us sitting on the tailgate of their Subaru, drinking beer and having a belching competition. 'It comes from self-loathing and insecurity.'

She once planned an illustrated book called *Pond Life in Modern Britain*. As well as all the types already mentioned, it would include businesswomen on phones in quiet train carriages, French schoolchildren at TEFL centres, and journalists outside employment tribunals.

'Need to wash,' I say, and at the standpipe I get chatting to a single man who arrived in a large car with a large tent. Apparently the activity in the campsite can be explained by half-term and the Hay-on-Wye books festival. The man lives in Australia but is taking a roundabout route to visit his mother's grave in Ludlow.

'We're walking to Prestatyn,' I say.

He nods seriously. 'Used to go there on family holidays. Don't have to do that any more.'

V

We drink tea and watch
The sun slowly light its way
Down to this valley.

The next day over morning tea Dru is visibly, physically nervous. When she's consciously trying to pass, she adopts contrived facial expressions: scrunched up rabbity nose (I had a girlfriend who used to do that), a pout, a shake of the head to bring the hair forward and smother the hairline. With quick fingers she then makes sure her fringe has no gaps, anxious and fidgety like a self-conscious adolescent. When she gets really riled, or if I overcook the teasing, she can do the double teapot, pushing her hips forward and flaring her nostrils.

We have been outside for four days. She glances round the packed campsite and plays with her hair again, keeps her chin tucked into her neck.

'I feel vulnerable. Signifiers down.'

We haven't washed properly since Bristol, and we've had a bad night. The campsite was overflowing before dark and then a school party from Birmingham arrived at midnight. I had to ask their male teachers to be quiet at about one in the morning. In my longjohns.

The temperature has dropped sharply and neither of us had much sleep. Which is strange, because whenever I was awake Dru was snoring, and she said it was the same the other way round. Even stranger, neither of us snore, or we each snore less than the other, depending on who's telling the story. For the last time: Dru snores more.

By the middle of the afternoon we should be in Hay-on-Wye, where in the course of a fortnight the book festival attracts 60,000 visitors. Whatever else happens, we'll be seeing more people in one place than anywhere else on the Dyke.

This explains Dru's nervousness, though before we get to Hay we have to climb back into the Black Mountains and make the spectacular trek over Hay Bluff. The day is cold and blowy but also brilliantly sunny. The views will be truly magnificent.

'We could take the road,' Dru says.

There's a local road that runs up the valley past Capel-y-Ffin, and then threads its way through the Gospel Pass, the lowest point between the ridges. If we take the valley road we can skip the climb into the hills and take a short cut to our campsite beyond Hay, avoiding the extra distance into the town and out again.

'The path is up in the mountains,' I say. 'And today it's Hay Bluff. It's going to be fantastic.'

'Will we get there in time?' Dru mumbles. She's squashing air out of her Therm-a-Rest, is unhappy with the result, is doing it again. She knows that the tickets I bought in advance are for the historian Eric Hobsbawm. He's on at half past five, and we'll get there easily.

'I have a sore hip.'

The walk back to the ridge will be steep but brief: it looks a lot worse than it is. I'm happy being tough and thinking nothing of it. I also want to stay on the path because to my mind the point of a National Trail is to walk all of it, no cheating, to the bitter end. I suspect Dru of not wanting to climb the hill. Simple as that.

'The valley road is still pretty high up,' she offers. 'It's what we did last time.'

That's because last time we were wrecked, feet cut to pieces. We'd overdone it from Chepstow in the wet, and by Llanthony I had blisters on the inside of the big toes, along the bone, on the little toes, on both balls of my feet, and on my heels. I suspect Dru did too, but by that time we'd stopped talking. Apart from shooting lame horses, there was nothing to talk about. We arrived in Hay in the rain, shuffling, mincing, tottering along. We caught a bus back to Bristol. We were defeated.

'And also,' Dru adds, 'if we take the road we'll get to see that bit on the Gospel Pass where they filmed *American Werewolf in London*.'

'Did they?' I'm interested, but not persuaded.

'The bit on the moor. Where they say "Don't go off the path."'

'I see,' I stop folding the tent just to make sure I'm clear about this. 'So you want us to go off the path to see the path where they were told not to go off the path?' In *American Werewolf in London* the two friends leave the path. One is killed outright by a werewolf. The other is only injured, but one month later will end up dead in a London alleyway.

'I've run out of Nurofen,' Dru adds, after searching her bag. She means her hip is very sore, although she hasn't mentioned it before now. She means she doesn't want to be late for our date at the festival.

'We won't be late,' I say. 'And besides, we only have the strip maps that follow the path.'

'Have you added on the time we'll need to get ready?'

No time at all, I think, but this is already Dru's third excuse; she's really not keen on climbing up to the Bluff. I could ignore this. I could insist on sticking to the path, but as a general rule I try not to be an insensitive tonker. I tag along as Dru shoulders her pack (no tent, no cooker) and heads for the Llanthony Abbey car park. There's an ornamental car-park-style map in there, which may or may not give us approximate directions for our short cut, but if the leading explorers of the world have learnt one simple lesson it is this: car-park maps are not a reliable system of navigation.

'Okay,' I say. 'Let's take the road.'

I feel like I've been outmanoeuvred.

Dru is so happy with this decision that she does voice practice most of the way to Capel-y-Ffinn. In the shadow of the Black Hill she recites 'Home-Thoughts, from Abroad' by Robert Browning – 'O, to be in England/Now that April's there . . . The buttercups, the little children's dower,/—Far brighter than this gaudy melon-flower'. The voice and the poem and the poem in the voice sound absurd, and because I'm often an insensitive tonker I let my tetchiness spill out.

'C'mon Dru, you can do better than that.'

Since we started in Chepstow Dru has been talking in

strange two-tone sentences, up and down like the terrain. The pitch of her voice has fluctuated like this for years, especially over the phone. Whenever I ring up, Dru answers with a noticeable rise, in a light and feminine voice – 'Hello, Dru speaking.' Then the voice tends to lapse, to relax and slip back downwards. I don't know if this is for everyone, or just for me, but I've always taken it as a kind of compliment, a recognition of the past, hers and ours. Dru doesn't have to make an effort.

Now I wish she would, at least when there are people about, and she's not the only one who's worried about what happens when we get to Hay-on-Wye. I want us to pass better than we did for Mr Beard.

I therefore pay close attention and hear that some words nearly always go Drusilla:

'Yes', which falls from an initial syrupy high.

'Thank you', two clear syllables but breathy on both, sounding contrived and forced, like an Anglican flirt.

'Gosh'. The expletive from the planet Illa – Don't mind me, I'm just a girl!

'Hmm?' rising like a spinster disturbed at her knitting.

The removal of testicles doesn't instantly raise the pitch of a voice, as it always does in cartoons. Testosterone ('T' to those who talk about it often or have a low syllable threshold) alters the vocal cords irreversibly. This is one of the few ways in which it's easier to go Female to Male – the voice changes in a matter of months, once the T gets to work in the throat.

'I always feel very growly in the morning,' Dru says, in a growly voice.

It's the voice, I decide. Not the Timex Explorer, or the strong hands, or ill-judged references to previous employment in the North Sea. As we march along the road I reach the unilateral conclusion that Dru's voice has undermined her efforts to pass as a woman. It also provides evidence, far more so than climbing or motorcycling, of lingering self-destructive urges. She knew her voice wasn't going to change with the operation, and she's been living full-time in a female role since 2001. Dru has had six years to work on this. You can learn Mandarin Chinese in six years.

'I know,' she says, giving up completely. 'I should have made more of an effort.'

'Can't you get your vocal cords done?'

'It's not the Holy Grail.'

Surgeons can perform an operation called a cricothyroid approximation. Sutures are placed through the two main cartilages of the voice box. They are then tightened to remove lower pitches from the voice, and the patient will be asked to talk during the surgery, which is why the procedure is carried out under local anaesthetic only. Quite apart from that, there are potentially chronic complications that can jeopardise the ability to sing, and more importantly, to swallow. This is why Dru visits a speech therapist and can now recite Browning's 'Home-Thoughts, from Abroad' like a female impersonator. I find the high fake vowels hugely irritating.

Also, I don't understand why she practises on fake-sounding texts (look at the vocab! – 'rapture'!, 'Hark'!, 'hoary'!) when sounding fake is a part of the problem. How much of her life, exactly, is she planning to live in Victorian verse? She'll do a couple of lines, 'Lest you should think he never could recapture/The first fine careless rapture!' and then interrupt with a basso profundo, 'Oh God. Oh no. Bloody hell.'

'Not good enough,' I say. 'See if you can do the voice for ten minutes without stopping.'

I have a fat black watch precisely for occasions like these. I press the stopwatch button. 'Ten minutes. No lapses. Go.'

Which means that Dru has to talk for ten whole minutes. She tells me in her finest lilting tone about camping grounds close to where we are, points out on the side of the Honddu Valley the farm described by Bruce Chatwin in *On the Black Hill*. Her voice becomes more convincing when she describes the youth hostel and the campsite at Grange Farm – 'a great place for children.' It's as though the female voice is more comfortable with children, animals, and all that is furry and fluffy.

Dru seems surprised. 'If you've picked up on that you may be right.' We walk on, through sunken lanes with hedges three times our height. 'And you may be mistaken.'

Drusilla trills out the honeysuckle and wild strawberries. With great and affectionate care, rolling the R: herb Robert. The wayfaring tree in blossom, like elder but more compact. Jack-by-the-hedge.

'And there,' Dru says, pointing at the tarmac, 'is a black-bird egg smashed by a magpie. Gosh!'

She's investigating a badger sett in a bank above a stream. I tap my watch.

'Slugs is to badgers,' says the elegant, eloquent Drusilla, 'as rice is to the Chinese.'

I'd rather be up on the tops in the buffeting sunshine than here in the windless shade, discussing slugs.

'In that voice,' I say, meaning the exasperating Drusilla voice of Browning and flowers and badger food, 'are there words you won't be able to say? What about sump? Or carburettor?'

Dru concentrates, chin up, voice high and controlled. She says, in note-perfect Drusilla:

'The Redrupp reactionless coaxial rotary engine.'

*

I blame Biggles. That's how Dru was first drawn to the RAF, through books.

'Any particular favourites?'

'*Biggles Fails to Return*.'

That's brilliant. Dru then corrects herself.

'*Biggles Sweeps the Desert*. That's the one I kept when I threw everything else out.'

'Not *Biggles Fails to Return*?'

'I might have kept that one as well.'

What I never knew until Dru told me was that W. E. Johns, the author of Biggles, also created a heroine. Her name was Worrals, and her first book *Worrals of the WAAF*.

'You didn't *know* this?'

I didn't.

Worrals of the WAAF had her own adventures, her own books, but she wasn't allowed to fly missions in fighters, because she was a girl. Dru is still shocked by my ignorance, though she tries to make allowances.

'I'm sure there are lots of people who haven't heard of Worrals. Probably haven't even heard of Biggles, not these days.'

Unlike in 1972, when Biggles and Worrals offered Dru a solution. She hadn't yet named her feelings of otherness: there had been no epiphany, no orchestral manoeuvres. But if these feelings were gathering, if they were seeking expression, if she *was* a girl, then she was a girl who liked boy things who had been born as a boy. Not ideal, but she'd make the best of this unlikely situation by flying the missions Worrals of the WAAF was denied. She will be happy.

This is a brilliant QED, both by me now and by Dru's subconscious mind way back then, at the time it was actually happening.

At the age of thirteen and three-quarters, the earliest possible age, Dru joins the Air Cadets.

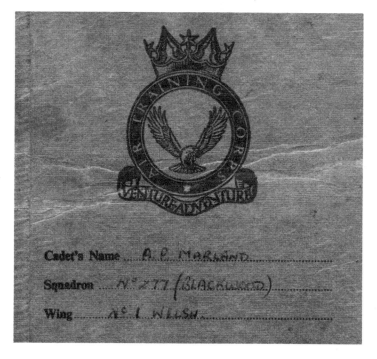

Cadet's Name ... A. P. Marchand ...

Squadron ... Nº 277 (Blackwood) ...

Wing ... Nº 1 Welsh ...

Dru still has the RAF blue cadet book, which sparks memories of Monday and Friday cadet nights at 277 Squadron ATC.

'We used to go shooting, and flying.'

There were thirty cadets aged between thirteen and three-quarters and eighteen. All boys, because the girls were in the Girls Venture Corps, where Dru had a friend, Mandy, who also wanted to be a Spitfire pilot. Theirs was a romantic, nostalgic vision of the Royal Air Force, even in the early seventies, but the romance was nonetheless genuine.

With a clear objective in mind – to become a fighter pilot – school for Dru seems to have been a breeze. 'He is a very capable boy who will do well if he sustains the effort.' Pronouns, headmaster. The teachers obviously weren't seeing straight, and should have paid more attention to what was happening in PE.

'I did play some soccer,' Dru admits. 'At primary school. That wasn't too bad. Get the ball to the other end. Kick, kick.'

Then there was rugby. Drusilla was a boy at a grammar school in Wales. A collision was inevitable.

'I hated it. It was never explained because it was assumed you knew. I hated everything about it. EVERYTHING!'

Personally, I like rugby very much – a forty-year-old trying and failing to give it up. 'But what is there to hate?'

'If you had the ball, someone would hurt you to get it. Or you'd get hurt trying to get the ball. I was set to tackle two lads who had the ball. There was no way I was going to grab their legs, so I grabbed one of them around the waist. He kept running. Everyone laughed. A lot.'

I suddenly see my own early rugby coaches in a new light. Anyone who flinches from rugby, they used to say, is a girl. If only these PE teachers would take their prejudices more seriously. Then girls like Dru could be saved a lot of time and heartache.

'I escaped it by going cross-country running. That's how I got out of rugby. Jog along and chat, and run long distances just for the heck of it.'

Compared to the other boys, puberty came late for Dru, but it did arrive eventually, and when it did I was ready to hear that this was it, this was the defining moment (cymbals, strings, the kitchen sink).

It wasn't.

'I had an unusually quiet adolescence, I think. Not much rebellion. I took the keys and crashed my dad's MG in the drive. It was a mistake. I cried.'

Dru's first physical transformation involves traumas that most boys will recognise, at whatever age puberty struck. There is the universal pubescent horror of changing rooms and communal showers.

'I didn't want to share the same space as naked boys.'

There was 'horseplay'. For women readers, this means physical cruelty between boys not wearing clothes, and Dru would time her unsupervised cross-country runs to get in early or late. She wouldn't have wanted to be singled out as four-nipples Marland. Boys, eh. Will be boys, so I've heard.

But she wasn't mixing with girls, either.

'Did you want to?'

'Yes. Not hugely.'

She speaks about her early gender doubts in a vague, perhaps even hopeful way. On being a boy: 'I had an idea it was wrong and uncomfortable, and that it would be nice to be a girl. Yes. I sometimes dressed up.'

'Did you ever dress as a cowboy?'

'I remember in particular a swimming costume. I'd play

alone in the attic and if I tucked away my genitals I could make it disappear.'

Then, aged sixteen, she read the serialisation of Jan Morris's *Conundrum* in the *Sunday Times*. If this provided an epiphany, it was a muted one. There were no trumpets amongst the Sunday morning church bells, but I have a sense, talking about this now, that Dru is rather hoping that the trumpets were in there somewhere.

She devoured the extracts, but never considered buying the book, or so she says.

'Why not? If it meant so much to you didn't you want to own it?'

'Of course I did, but I never dared. Someone might have seen me holding it in the bookshop and thought "Ah! A transsexual!"'

Dru remembers identifying closely with the serialised *Conundrum*, while at the same time feeling unconvinced that Morris had done the right thing. She recognised similar emotions and sensations but assumed everyone had these gender issues. It was just that the other boys were better at containing them, and Jan Morris, too, should have made more of an effort. Thought Dru Marland, sixteen-year-old air cadet, about the actions of Jan Morris, 47-year-old international celebrity writer.

'You were just in control of them,' she says.

Me? Leave me out of this, I think. At that age I wanted to play cricket for England. No issues. I am not being facetious.

'I thought it was wrong. I didn't see it as a viable solution for me. And I didn't feel unique. I thought all boys had similar feelings but there was something wrong with me for being so worried about it.'

And anyway, she was going to be a fighter pilot. Her path had been mapped by a different type of book – Biggles was the bible, not Jan Morris.

*

Hay-on-Wye, home to Britain's most prestigious books festival and over thirty bookshops, turns out to have its own place in the literary history of the transsexual experience. Iain Sinclair, an expert on the psychogeography of London, once forced himself to the Welsh borders to write about somewhere else. In his book *Landor's Tower* (another name for Llanthony Abbey) his main character becomes obsessed with the notion of Hay-on-Wye as the national capital of 'Casablanca snip jobs' and 'the gender-reassignment mob'.

This is very odd. Sinclair has it on the brain, looking out for hands that 'give away a gender-jumper' from the 'old can opener and bulldog-clip days'. Another of his characters, considering a quick bounce with the transsexual 'Averil Astaire' thinks: 'Why not? I've done worse.' I don't think this means 'I've had sex with worse-looking women.' I think it means 'I've behaved worse.' Sinclair's an inspired writer – he probably means both.

> Some of the Hay transsexuals were exotic, others were dumpy, twinset and sensible-shoes matrons who thought that changing gender allowed them to reinvent their ancestry and come out as thoroughbred Welsh cobs.

Sinclair seems to be founding his generalisations on two real individuals: the former showgirl and model April Ashley

('Averil Astaire') and Jan Morris. Both had their operation in Casablanca and Morris set up home in Wales and became an active Welsh Nationalist, despite her upbringing on the wrong side of the Bristol Channel. She is therefore the reinvented 'thoroughbred Welsh cob'.

April Ashley is the 'exotic'. In the sixties she was Britain's first celebrity transsexual, working as a *Vogue* underwear model and flitting from Soho drinking dens to society weekends in Paris and Rome. Down on her luck after stints as a Malaga nightclub hostess and a Chelsea restaurant owner, by the early eighties Ashley was licking her wounds in Hay-on-Wye. The bookshop king Richard Booth admired her eccentricity, and conferred on her the title 'First Lady, Duchess of Hay and Offa's Dyke'. You can read all about it in either of April Ashley's autobiographies, although the second was pulped because the ghostwriter had plagiarised the ghostwriter of the first.

In both books Ashley is honest about looking for clues in her past, and the smoking gun seems at first to be her mother. Mothers: you can't live without them. 'One of my mother's favourite tricks was to pick me up by my ankles and bang my head on the ground like a workman with a pneumatic drill.'

This is not conclusive evidence, and neither Morris nor Ashley can satisfactorily answer the question 'Why?' The answer they both give is essentially 'Because I'm me, and that's the way I am.'

In this sense Dru was probably right, even aged sixteen in 1974, not to take Jan Morris as her model. *Conundrum* can read like a guidebook from a different era, and Morris had started out from a very different place. She admits she was influenced by her background, an upper class 'shot through with bisexual instinct'. I take this to mean fondling in the dorms and, later, the officer-class flair it takes to spurn Charing Cross in favour of a clinic in sultry North Africa. As a symbolic farewell to masculinity, Morris threw away her dinner jacket and made her hard decisions while driving an open-top Rolls-Royce to the South of France.

Conundrum is an excellent book, but it wasn't much help to Dru. What the two women did eventually have in common is perfectly summed up in my favourite of all Jan Morris's lines: 'Heavens, I was a jumble!'

To find the recurring patterns in these autobiographical accounts, it's worth turning to *Sexual Metamorphosis: An Anthology of Transsexual Memoirs*. This is a very useful book edited by the Brooklyn essayist Jonathan Ames, who has read enough transsexual memoirs to identify a pattern they invariably follow:

Act 1: Gender-dysphoric childhood
Act 2: Move to big city and transformation
Act 3: Aftermath of sex change

The old three-act trick, so beloved of story editors and, indeed, anyone who loves a story. Unfortunately, Dru's life is refusing to follow the structure. In fact we're stuck as early as Act 1, because Dru's childhood reveals no obvious sign of chronic gender dysphoria.

At school, she was the only boy with short hair in her class, which was hardly surprising given that she was going to join the RAF as a fighter pilot. There is a picture of her from this time in her uniform: she looks like a doomed youth before the

First World War, sad and very beautiful. She knows how she looks – 'Good God, if only I'd started on the pills back then' – it's the only photo of herself she's ever volunteered to show me.

So Dru was destined for a life in the RAF. She had read and rejected Jan Morris. She was doing well in school with positive reports and excellent results in O levels.

'I got lots,' she says.

She is passing, not just in exams but in life, passing with flying colours. Just to check that everything is in order before the next step forward to a healthy and productive adult existence, the school organises a medical for all students when they turn sixteen. Dru is in excellent health from daily cross-country running. The only small problem she has, until now undiagnosed, is the almost amusing handicap of colour blindness.

'Will that effect what job I can get?' Dru asks.

'Only if you want to be a pilot.'

*

We have turned off the Gospel Pass on to narrow lanes that descend into the valley. We are lost, and the soles of my feet are aching from the tarmac roads I never intended to walk in the first place. I wanted to be up on the soft cropped grass and the sand of the high Black Mountains.

The Gospel Pass has taken us along that exposed ribbon of road famous for its film role illustrating the common-sense caution of not diverging from the path. *Don't go off the road.* That's what they say in the film. If you do, then don't blame anyone else for the consequences. We take a left and drop

112

into another valley to the west of Hay. Perhaps south-west. Our directions for this short cut are based entirely on a map in a car park and Dru's instincts.

Does it show that I'm feeling irritable? In any friendship people get bad-tempered, but sharing a tent is a foolproof way of hurrying the process up. I'm furious at not sticking to the path, in a rage about getting lost, and absolutely speechless that Dru isn't even mildly annoyed about either.

'We could always ask someone,' she suggests.

'That's pathetic. We are not asking strangers for directions.'

I am not in a generous mood. We should have been up with the angels high on Hay Bluff, but instead we're on the B4350 or the B4348 or an unmarked lane, and I am without pity, wondering whether castration is a kind of emotional lobotomy. No anger, no lust. Let's ask someone. Gosh. Where is Dru's compelling male fury, the same fury I'm hating myself for feeling?

At this time of year, thanks to the book festival, campsites and bed and breakfasts for miles around are fully booked months in advance. We had to phone ahead, and the only place with space for a tent was a pub called the Three Cocks. Dru knows the pub and she arranged it, and she thinks we're probably on the wrong road but possibly in the rightish area when she at last finds someone to ask. I stride on ahead to make it clear that asking has nothing to do with me. Read me: I am a long-distance expeditioner and not a feeble dilettante rambler who stops to ask strangers for directions. Oh no.

The Three Cocks is several miles down the lane, apparently, on to the main road and turn left.

We reach the main road. Dru seems doubtful. 'I'm fairly sure . . .'

'The lady said left.'

'I thought you disapproved of asking?'

Dru squints left along the road, then right. She looks puzzled.

'Actually, I'm wondering whether I've got the name of the pub wrong.'

'The Three Cocks. I don't think you'd make that up.'

Through my teeth I suggest we turn right, because a sign tells us that Hay-on-Wye is two and a half miles away. It might be better to arrive *somewhere* identifiable before the T that is now coursing through my bloodstream demands an aggressive exit. I quick march, head down, chuntering. It's a main road and we have to walk on the verge but still we nearly die every time a car passes, over and over again.

By the time we reach Hay we are recognisably a couple, me many yards ahead with steam leaking from my ears. Dru lags behind, jauntily swinging her alpine poles, pretending nothing is wrong, sometimes checking out habitat in the hedgerows.

The noises she makes while walking behind me are doing my head in. All of them start high and fade away.

'Wooo . . .'

'Oooo . . . oh . . .'

'Mmmm.'

These are noises made by presenters on children's television. Silence, then a 'Wooo . . .' and I take this to mean, every time, 'I've had a splendid thought but I'm not sharing it unless you ask.' I don't ask, and then the swooping noises start to follow selected words.

'Spotted woodpecker . . . Oooh.'

'Chaffinch . . . Mmmm.'

The suffixed noise is like an abbreviation of all the knowledge assumed in the silence, knowledge Dru knows I don't have, and which she knows I'm not going to get unless I ask. I sulk instead, thereby learning nothing. That'll teach her. Then when I do eventually crack and ask what it is she's noticed, she replies in a sing-song voice, up and down to the high note on the middle word.

'Can't hear you . . .'

I decide never to speak to her ever again.

In Hay, we discover our mistake. The Three Cocks, to which we were directed by a kindly local, is a pub in the village of Glasbury. The pub we want, where Dru reserved a place for the tent, is the Hollybush in the village of Three Cocks. It could happen to anyone. The Hollybush not the Three Cocks, about 300 yards to the left on the main road where I made the executive decision to turn right.

We still have a couple of hours, but I want to go straight to the festival site. Dru disagrees. She prefers to act like a madwoman in Hay town centre. She falls off the kerb, drops a new tin of condensed milk on her foot, stops abruptly to look with total concentration at the clothes in the window of a ladies' boutique.

'It's the people,' Dru says. 'They're making me nervous.'

She needs to wash and brush up, so we call for a taxi. All the taxis are busy.

*

Much has been written on several continents about the challenges of changing sex, and it quickly becomes clear on this afternoon in Hay that books have all the answers. Like what to wear to a major literature festival after spending four days and three nights outside. The creaseless Rohan summer dress, as mentioned earlier in this book. Out it comes from the bottom of Dru's rucksack, preserved for special occasions. The dress is sleeveless, with a low square neckline. It is floral and feminine in orange and beige, but April Ashley in Dior and cockfeathers this is not.

We have finally succeeded in getting a taxi to the Hollybush pub, which is like a Wild West frontier town run by the Indians. We've admired the cannabis plants by the toilet block. I've found a place for the tent in a crowded field, and after a shower Dru reappears much prettier and happier. Her face is cherry-reddened by sun and wind so she looks like a healthy schoolmarm. I like her looking like that. I don't think I can hide it. I calm down a bit.

Dru puts on her make-up, checks her necklace and bangles, no watch. Since stuffing the watch out of sight, she keeps the time from her phone, which has an alarm set every morning and every evening for eight. The alarm is Sounds of the Amazon Jungle, a reminder to take her hormone pills, but she always remembers. Usually several hours before the insects start creaking and the monkeys shriek.

I shave off my beard. This is a decision based on a British application of self-knowledge. Since the Greeks, self-knowledge has been a prized philosophical commodity, but whereas other cultures understand it as a tool of enlightenment, in Britain it's an early-warning system. The value of self-knowledge is that it allows us to see what needs repressing, before it's too late.

In this instance, my self-knowledge tells me that I haven't

been shaving because I'm having doubts about my masculinity, and need to project obvious external signals to counter the messages of the pink Tilley hat and walking across Wales with Dru. Knowing this, I can use self-knowledge as a practical rather than spiritual device to make sure nothing gets out of hand. Instead of dealing with the problem, I will shave off my beard so that no one will suspect what my problem actually is.

Perhaps, in the past, Dru used self-knowledge in a similar way. She knew herself well enough to understand that she genuinely wanted to live as a woman. 'I had an idea being a boy was wrong and uncomfortable, and it would be nice to be a girl. Yes.' But she's British. Self-knowledge was a way of discovering what she needed to hide, self-knowledge as secret police, to detect and destroy.

So I shave off my beard, but avoid dealing with what the facial hair is trying to say – I feel uncomfortable going out with Dru. Still, the Hay festival attracts people from all over, and art is an excuse for many different kinds of flakiness, thankfully. We probably won't stand out.

We're at the main road outside the Hollybush waiting for another taxi to take us the three miles back to the festival site. Dru is looking fine in her flat red-laced black shoes and her Rohan dress. The pattern of beige petals on a dark orange ground is not unlike the dress worn by her mother in the photos at Fleetwood. Unfortunately, the effect is smudged by the weather, very cold with rain not that far away, so Dru's dress is mostly covered by her yellow cagoule, which she will be wearing for the rest of the evening. I am clean-shaven and in my dry trousers, but not wearing my anorak, even though it's cold. That wouldn't look good.

It is shortly before five when at last we enter the festival site, both in our separate ways obsessed with our appearance, and both of us fully aware that appearances are unimportant. Only reality matters; we know this from books, in particular from fiction. Here in Hay-on-Wye if I was to present myself as a writer (suit and polo-neck sweater, perhaps a corduroy shirt) that wouldn't make me what I'm not. I'm just a twerp who probably went to UEA.

We wander about, get a drink, are impressed by the security for Gordon Brown, check out the women. I'm not sure that before Drew became Dru I appreciated the range of female appearance. I think I truly saw only pretty girls and my mum. At the age when women complain of becoming invisible, I didn't see them.

Now I've started looking, the genders are closer than I thought. Lots of these women could have started out as men, and the older people get, the vaguer the facial distinctions become. Amy Bloom, novelist and psychotherapist, calls age 'the great androgyniser; the skin softens and sags, the secondary sex characteristics shrink and fade, slacken and thin.' Our ambitions also merge, simply to stay alive and read only good books, until the difference between men and women is mostly obvious only in the clothes.

The Hay festival website boasts a gathering of the 'most socially attractive people in the country'. Initially I took this to mean that everyone here must be ugly, but the organising committee should relax. The festival is full of pretty boys and handsome women, but there are so many people about that people barely matter. They become crowds, and we're happily lost among a crowd of lively, well-dressed men and women whose genetic origins are impossible to know.

In our seats in the huge tent for Professor Eric Hobsbawm, eighty-year-old Marxist historian, we listen to the great man make a very simple point. Things change. They don't always improve, nor were they always better beforehand.

He focuses his discussion on the rise and fall of global empires, but if his conclusions weren't applicable to individuals nobody would be interested in history. As for the future, Professor Hobsbawm points out that the Internet encourages 'communities of nutcases'. He enjoys the laugh. 'An enormous variety of nutters!' he rephrases cheerfully. More! 'You get 50,000 people who also believe the moon is made of green cheese, and then there's a community!'

No need to go overboard. For scattered, socially hesitant groups like the transgendered, the Internet has been a blessing. Virtual contacts ease the sense of isolation, while also providing discreet access to catalogues of stilettos in size eleven, ordered by Frank in Reading under the name of Melanie. Less innocently, female hormones are also available, as are post-operative blogs that include intimate photographic evidence. Never Before and After, just After. Some people are so proud.

With Professor Hobsbawm in a tent in Wales we're sharing another sense of community, and we relax into the unmistakable smugness that envelops the Hay festival. Nothing can touch us. We and thousands of otherwise meek bookish people have successfully colonised an entire town, and it feels good. Hobsbawm has been introduced by the historian Simon Schama, who now chairs the Q and A. He calls for a question from a lady near the front.

'Oh, I'm sorry! It's a gentleman!'

Titters. Schama elaborates. 'That sexually ambiguous person with a beard.'

Ho ho. How everyone laughs. Schama then digresses to tell a story about mistaking a Welshman for a Scotsman, as if it's the same thing. I have a lot of time for Simon Schama. I wonder if he's right.

After Hobsbawm, we eat in the Blas Cymru tent, an attempt to persuade people who have no experience of travelling in Wales that Welsh cooking is edible. The tent is packed, and most of the food has gone. We end up with sausages and mash, and wander around with our trays until we find a place on a table next to another couple. They politely make some room and then in true British fashion we ignore them and they ignore us. That is, until they hear us (me) pursuing the exact trigonometries by which Dru managed to get us lost on roads we never should have taken in the first place.

Our neighbours at the table join in.

'You've been to Bickering, then,' they say. 'Can't miss it. Look at the map. Just this side of Sulking.'

They have instantly assumed we fit the standard pattern: woman can't navigate, man is a tit. We must therefore be a couple like any other. This is the first totally unambiguous encounter we have had with . . . people. Dru is very happy. I am very happy. We talk to our friendly neighbours for a decent amount of time. We find out where they come from and what they do. We discover they're living a strange *ménage à trois* in a caravan that started its journey in Essex, and the other woman is saving her energy for tomorrow and Wole Soyinka. The man raises his eyebrows:

'You know what women are like.'

Dru can forget the bangles and the necklaces and the Miso Pretty facials. She can even stop worrying about the watch, because the significant accessory is me. Drag along a grumpy bloke and everyone knows what you're going through, feels pity for you, as a woman. This is quite a discovery: until now, I'm the one who's been causing the problems. Somehow I've not been giving out the signals that we're man and woman, and people have been reading us as a pair, an imperfect pair. I've been letting Dru down.

We finish the evening in a tent watching a female comedian. A little distracted, in fact, because rain is drumming the canvas roof and we still have three miles to get back to our very small tent. The comedian is Australian and suffers from no obvious gender confusion. She is young and funny and sometimes a bit overwrought, but she leaves our minority group alone and tells some excellent jokes at the expense of midgets.

She's then off on a jaunty riff about boredom. 'I've been here thirty-one years, and, frankly, it's growing a little bit thin.' That's her hook for some more crazy-girl gags, the sameness of day after day provoking any sane person into all sorts of bird-brained stunts.

That's what she says, and no one would laugh if it wasn't also the truth.

VI

The ridge's hawthorns
Fling spindrift of white blossom,
Roll to the storm's swell.

Maybe Dru was just bored. She appeared in the doorway wearing a dress at the age of forty-three, a difficult age. Is this it? Is that all there is? If these questions hurt enough then do something stupid – it makes life worth living. And when asked why, point to the usual suspects: unhappiness, disappointment, the midlife crisis. Maybe, in Dru's case, that's what this is.

Not quite, because with hindsight we can identify patterns.

Dru is an outsider. English in Wales, a stepchild in her stepmother's home, a lonely long-distance runner in a school of teamed-up rugger-buggers. The only place she feels she belongs is the Air Cadets, and when she learns about the colour blindness she ignores the diagnosis, hoping it goes away. This may sound familiar. With epic stubbornness she holds on, sticks at the Air Cadets, as if at some later point her physical abnormality will magically put itself right. She is promoted to cadet flight sergeant by 1976, gets her glider permit.

In 1977, eager and eighteen years old, she attends the Officers and Aircrew Selection Centre at RAF Biggin Hill. She passes the exams for the pilot-training scholarship, to be taken up at the university of her choice. All she needs now is the A levels for university entrance, and to pass the formality of an RAF medical.

The A levels shouldn't have been a problem, but in retrospect some wrong turnings seem obvious. We regret having left the path without always knowing when or how that happened. In Dru's case, the false turning isn't hard to find. At O level, she consistently excels at Art ('Tries hard. Has original ideas') and English ('very pleasing work, good material and stylish writing'). At A level she finds herself studying Maths and Physics.

'I wasn't interested in the subjects. I wasn't at all interested! My fucking father! I went along with what he wanted me to do.'

So, despite what she said earlier, here is Dru not doing exactly what she wanted, once again.

By now the family have moved out of Ty Celyn because Dru's dad, still employed as a teacher, has bought a thirty-seven-acre sheep farm. It must have seemed a good idea at the time. Newbridge is the closest town, and by car these are easy distances.

We therefore take the car, the racing-green Jan Morris Time Traveller, and leaving Newbridge we strain in third gear up the steep hill through the Pant Estate, unlikely municipal birthplace of New Romantic pop icon Steve Strange. Perhaps it's something in the water.

At the top there's moorland and a single-track road, and Dru tells me about car crashes and the dramas of a family childhood as the Morris pootles over Mynydd Maen Common, an exposed stretch of blank heath. Mynydd Maen means Stone Mountain, and it's not a place you'd choose to live for healthy adolescent interaction. At best, it might be a good place on a sunny day to bring a kite and a Thermos.

Beyond the isolated moor, the road slopes gently downhill and there's an old wooden sign planted in the verge and painted long ago by Dru's dad. Hafod Fach, the name of the farm. We turn down a grass track that winds round the side of the hill. It is potholed and unruly hawthorns scratch loudly at the windows.

'Are you sure about this?'

I'm worried about whoever lives at the farm now, and don't think we should be driving uninvited down their unkempt road. Anyone who lives up here and neglects their track is probably unstable. It's certainly not a universal indicator meaning Strangers Welcome! Dru seems unperturbed, happily bouncing the Morris over the bumps.

The track ends at a wooden gate. It is locked with a padlock and chain. The house is just around the corner.

We climb the stile beside the gate, turn the corner, and in front of us is the end of the world. Dru knew what to expect, because her dad sold the house and land to a quarry. Me, I was hoping for clues and teenage scene-setting, but where the house once stood there is now empty space, sky, air, the Pennant sandstone exploded and hauled away. There's simply nothing there, nothing to see, nothing to walk on.

Dru's past has been savaged. She looks over the edge into the gape of the quarry, the bitten earth.

'The Romans didn't even do that to Carthage,' she says.

There is a white leather armchair overlooking the void. All that's left standing, slightly uphill from the gate, is a ruined stone barn in which we find a decomposing sheep. On the wall behind it is a whitewashed souvenir of *Cen + Lucy*.

You wouldn't want to live here with a wicked stepmother. Dru's stepmother was from Preston, the widow of a merchant seaman. For Dru, no more chip butties and no more camping holidays, the highlights of life before the fall. I feel a little sorry for the wicked stepmother. In Dru's version of the story she has her unchanging role, and her function is limited to nagging and cooking badly and not going camping while Dru and her brothers doubled after school as farm labourers.

'The haymaking was good,' Dru says. 'Helping to pull dead lambs out of sheep was, however, bad.'

If any of the children wanted to walk to Newbridge they were welcome. It is 1,000 feet down in the valley, yet still they would sometimes walk it. No surprise that as soon as they reached legal age, or perhaps a little earlier, they fixed up their own mopeds and motorbikes and developed a genuine interest in keeping the engines running.

I wonder if Dru's dad regretted the move to the farm. He had presumably acted on an urge to change, transform, live a new and hopefully better life, but it doesn't seem to have worked out as planned. He started to drink heavily, got a drink-driving conviction, and would move house twice more before he died; another reinventing leap to central Scotland and then an ageing limp home to Lancashire. It's almost as if the last move cancels out the others. He'd gone looking. He'd found nothing better. He'd come home.

By that time Dru would be long gone, but the farm at Hafod Fach, where her father and the wicked stepmother lived from 1975 until 1989, was her last real family home.

It was also where the disappointments started. At RAF Biggin Hill, after securing the pilot scholarship, she failed the medical. It was the eye test: colour-blind, just as she had been two years previously. She would never make a pilot.

By way of consolation she was offered a cadetship as an RAF engineer, an award that was also conditional on finding a place at university. She didn't get the grades. At her first attempt in Maths, Physics and Geography, she was given FFF. This amounts to some serious backsliding in Newbridge Grammar with the Welsh rugby shirts on the wall at the back of the Assembly Hall. At the farm Dru is successfully persuading the family to call her Drew, making a start at moving away from a given name, a given self, but in her school reports it's Andrew does this, Andrew does that, Andrew 'must seek to raise his standards'. They didn't have a clue what was ailing her.

She stayed another year for a second attempt at the A levels. EFF. For someone with eleven O levels, these paper results are barmy. You could call them a cry for help, and I will. There is a hollow at this point in her life, a sinking.

'I had no great life plans after the RAF fell through.'

Instead of life plans, Dru had the same vague ambition as most people her age. She wanted to get off the farm and see the world, to get experience, to 'find out what life was all about'. There is no mention of exploring her feminine side, just a powerful nineteen-year-old sense that life could improve dramatically on what she'd seen so far. She'd been reading Aldous Huxley.

'I very much wanted to use drugs to find out what was in my head.'

*

We have our Hay-on-Wye breakfast in the Granary, the first people through the door when the café opens at nine o'clock. Dru orders a bacon butty. I could slap her sometimes.

In books, progress is made – it's called the narrative arc, but between the two of us we're not making much progress. We scored a great success with our shared table in Blas Cymru, but we're now back in the familiar demi-monde of avoidable embarrassments and confusions.

The Granary is a small place with a lot of echoing wood, and this morning Dru's two-tone speech seems especially pronounced. In a pre-coffee baritone, she is telling me about her recent work in a Gloucester tricycle factory. It involves much welding and discussions about the provision of a women's toilet.

The schoolgirl waitress passes by. Dru stands up, and in full Drusilla she breathes:

'Oh. Where are the loos?'

The girl looks confused, but like so many other good eggs she computes, composes herself and points Dru upstairs.

'Very good loos,' Dru says when she comes back, at an approvingly deep pitch.

'Aren't we doing the voice today?'

Dru pouts, and folds her hands on the table. She shakes her hair forward, adjusts the fringe.

'I want to avoid nasal, which happens when I go high.'

The T is in me this morning – I hate the old voice, I hate the new voice. 'You could always practise.' (Who do I think I am? Henry Higgins?)

'Yes,' Dru says, lowering her chin and keeping eye contact, 'after the last few days I feel duly admonished.'

That's telling me. The look in her copper-brown eyes is easy to read. It says just you wait, Enry Iggins, just you wait.

Dru and the waitress have a conversation about the weather. Cheery, friendly (so what am I *worried* about?) the waitress is the one person in Hay-on-Wye who thinks the weather might brighten by the day after tomorrow. But like everyone else this side of Calais she concedes that today is all set to be a wet, chill, wintry bastard.

It was raining when we went to sleep. It was raining when we were supposed to be sleeping. It was raining at first light. It may well be raining now, but the windows of the Granary have steamed over.

The night before, confident that books improve readers as human beings, we had stood outside the festival car park and tried to hitch a lift. It was raining hard and we were wet, but obviously solid festival folk – we were all dressed up. Not once, not twice, but three times a car crawled up to the car-park exit and indicated right, the direction we were going, and where I was standing less than a metre away on the drenched verge, thumb out, smiling harmlessly. The driver (each time a man) studiously ignored us, even when I peered in the window, then drove off leaving us to drown. The fourth car picked us up. This is proof that literature is a good thing, but it only works on about a quarter of the people who read it.

Dru has another coffee. At the next table a youngish, financial-services-type chap is explaining the etiquette of caught-behinds at cricket. To his girlfriend. She can barely sit still.

'You can walk, or not walk,' he says earnestly, making the point by turning his hands one way then the other. 'It all depends.'

And out we go, thin-eyed and tired, into the gruel of a damp, grey-black Welsh morning. We walk, because that's what we do. Even when it's not raining we're getting soaked from the ground up, tramping through long sodden grass. In the fields and lanes we see animals, but today most of them are dead, memorably a crushed hedge warbler and a stiff roadside badger. There's a plastic bulb, like a long sea-buoy, sticking up behind a fence.

'It's a splice,' Dru tells me. 'It's where two underground cables are joined together. The splice is above ground so that sections can be isolated for the easier identification of faults.'

'Thanks, Dru.'

'Girls know these things, you know.'

I'm still regretting leaving the path after Llanthony Abbey. I wanted to do the Dyke correctly, following the official National Trail Guidebook and ticking the promised landmarks. Like Hay Bluff, from where I'd intended to contrive an overview, several days into our journey, from an elevated position, of how we were getting along. We stayed low and got lost, but that's non-fiction for you. You don't always get the metaphors you want.

With Dru I'm not sure what I'm getting instead. I haven't found the three-act structure as identified by Jonathan Ames. That fell apart at Act 1, when Dru's gender-dysphoric childhood turned out to be short on gender dysphoria. Nor are we following the reassuring and familiar plot line of a conventional transsexual biography, where the sex change provides a climax and a structure. What's the climax? We're walking just as we used to walk, and nothing seems to have changed except it's a challenge to eat, drink or talk in public places.

In one pre-walk daydream, I'd imagined our trip like Graham Greene's *Travels With My Aunt*. Dru would be wild and woolly but also warm-hearted, her fearlessness eventually offering both of us the chance of a better, funnier, more adventurous life. With a spot of impropriety on the side. My paperback edition has Maggie Smith on the cover as she appeared in the film, her hair dyed the same shade as Dru's, her cavernous face handsome above a broad black choker, of the kind that would elegantly hide an Adam's apple.

But not quite. Or not yet.

At another stage I was considering splitting Dru's life into four sections, a single life lived by four different people.

Book 1 – Andrew
Book 2 – Drew
Book 3 – Dru
Book 4 – Drusilla

I could have done that, if I'd surrendered to the comfort of boxes and categories. I may even have shuffled the sections around, for reasons of narrative tension and psychological veracity. 3, 2, 1, 4. But it's not true. Dru is one person, and her life one story. It's not even a double life.

Most of the memoirs tell a story of 'Sir, goodbye; *hello* Madam!' that I don't recognise in Dru. In the earliest account, *Man Into Woman* from 1933, Lili Elbe writes about herself as if the man Einar Wegener and the woman Lili Elbe were two separate people, when in fact they're one and the same – 'So Lili and I continued to live our double life'. This kind of plotting is still evident as late as 1999. Deirdre McCloskey says of her earlier self: 'Donald practised feminine ways of holding the steering wheel.' What happens to Donald after transition? He just disappears. These narratives end in transformation, not symbolically but really. They seem false, and fit too neatly with the approved rhetoric of the age, with rebirths and fresh beginnings.

We've found a dingle, at least that's what Dru and the map agree this sheltered place should be called. The Dyke has taken us into a thickly wooded area where the pine needles on the path's soft earth stay dry even though it's raining beyond the trees. We hear blackbirds chinking and watch an owl glide past. I ask Dru about the business of a double life.

'Part of me was saying, "Right. The new me is not going to be like the old me." '

We walk slowly, making very quiet progress past fungal growths shaped like giant seashells. Dru sighs, starting high and staying high, possibly trained to do it that way by the voice coach.

'In fact, the new me is rather like the old me.'

So why bother? Why go to so much trouble? I could always ask – that's what we're here for – so I ask how it felt to know she was a girl.

Dru gives this some thought.

'How would you feel,' she eventually replies, question to question, 'if you had to live like a monkey? And no one would believe you were a person?'

'Like a lower order of being? Is living as a man lower than a woman?'

I know this isn't what she means. It was just Dru's analogy. Having said that, it does seem that for many transsexuals the choice is transition or suicide, as if living as a man is worse than death. 'It was be a woman,' April Ashley declares, 'or be nothing – evaporate from the torment.' Perhaps as a man I find that a hard idea to stomach.

Then we're out of the dingle and beyond the trees and it's impossible to talk through the white noise of rain crackling on our rain-hoods. We don't uncover until we overtake some walkers struggling very slowly in the same direction. They are Swiss-Germans, older than we are and finding the hills hard going, so we attempt to jolly them along.

'Have you done this walk before?' they ask glumly. They're hoping we'll say it isn't worth it so they can stop, go back to their bed and breakfast, phone Zurich and tell their daughter she was right about the Welsh weather. They ask me the question, not Dru. This is another of those good signs which is bad – I'm the man, so only my opinion will have any value.

'Keep going!' I say. 'Offa's Dyke is fantastic!'

'Prestatyn must be a very special place.'

'Er. The path's nearly all good apart from the destination,' I say.

'A bit like life,' Dru adds cheerfully.

We outstrip them easily, but with hoods up we can't talk and this seems a good time to remember how it is to live without a roof. When it's raining: miserable. I can see the path clearly in front of me, and I'm following it because it's there, but I realise that without the three-act structure, without Mr Maggie Smith or the double life, I've lost sight of what I was after.

On our earlier trips we knew what we were looking for. We went to the French battlefields to feel some historical empathy, which once there is not that difficult to feel. We went to the Lleyn Peninsula to climb up Carn Fadrun where the experimental writer B. S. Johnson claimed to have encountered God. That was my idea. As a bonus, Dru went to touch the door of R. S. Thomas's church in Aberdaron. That trip was as rewarding as any, even though Johnson's mountain was so small we were up and down it in a couple of hours and still had time for a crack at Snowdon.

I knew what I was looking for, and I found it. Or more accurately, if God is what you're looking for, that's what you'll find on Carn Fadrun, in the form of a skylark waiting at the top. The skylark hopped about a bit, to make sure we'd seen him.

With Dru, this time round, I'm hoping we'll stay friends. Today we're enduring together, persevering together, and in my particular world view that's a good place to start. We can then share whatever good fortune comes our way, soaked and miserable but finding miraculous free tea inside the quaint village church of Newchurch. Coats off, shoes off, socks off to steam on the edge of the font. There's a CD-radio playing spirituals ('Get on Board!'), and a piece of paper stuck on the wall, almost hidden, with some lines from R. S. Thomas:

In cities that have outgrown their promise, people are becoming pilgrims again, if not to this place, then to the recreation of it in their own spirits.

This break cheers us up no end. It's still raining when eventually we set out again, but we tell ourselves it could be worse, mustn't grumble. There's more Blasted Heath up ahead, on Hergest Ridge, but ignore that for a moment and think of the album of the same name by Mike Oldfield. We think of it but neither of us has ever knowingly heard it, as opposed to Oldfield's *Tubular Bells*, which provides the music for *The Exorcist*. In that film, the characters physically transform because they're possessed by the devil. It could always be worse.

The rain gets heavier, and this rain is not like sprayed Evian, is not good for anyone's complexion. It is constant and pervasive, my coat giving up any attempt at water-proofing, so that exhausted nylon sticks slickly to my soaking clothes beneath. It's too wet for any birds except the ever-optimistic skylarks, chirruping away as if it's only weather. On Hergest Ridge the fierce wind shapes the cloudburst into my chest and shoulders as I go on ahead, pathfinding between sheep turds, divots, dags, bracken, gorse, humbled grass and tyre tracks in the mud. Scraps of wool snagged on wind-bent thistles.

Up here, no one cares what gender anybody is. We just care about getting down, all anyone has ever cared about on Hergest Ridge in weather like this. Gender would only matter if we wanted to build a hut and settle down and start a family up here, but in the thousands of years of Welsh history no one ever has and no one ever will.

The walking is hard and simple: this is one way that men make friends, by testing together the limits of the will. You can measure such things in physical discomfort, and as my waterproof leaks and sticks I tell myself I'd have gained nothing from coming properly equipped. The greater the suffering the more we're likely to learn, until one day the worst journey in the world will teach us all the lessons that endurance has to teach.

If only the worst journey in the world hadn't already been done. It's brilliantly documented in Apsley Cherry-Garrard's 1922 book, *The Worst Journey in the World*. This is Cherry's account of Scott's doomed 1912 expedition to the South Pole.

How bad was it? It was the worst journey in the world. The cold killed all the nerves in Cherry's teeth, and they 'split to pieces', yet 'the day's march was bliss compared to the night's rest, and both were awful.'

Survival, then as now, was a sign of manliness. At the same time, Gloria Gaynor's 'I Will Survive' is a girl anthem.

We all like survival. We're programmed that way, though the story of Scott in Antarctica glorifies endurance as a specifically male virtue. In the 600 pages of *The Worst Journey in the World*, women are mentioned nine times, never for more than a sentence. This may help to explain why it was the kind of journey it was.

Scott's expedition elevated the connection between travel and suffering for travellers ever after. Backpackers with their stolen moneybelts and amoebic dysentery feel they're doing something good, because adversity and discomfort are a test. Cherry is in no doubt that 'what pulled Scott through was character, sheer good grain, which ran over and under and through his weaker self and clamped it together.'

Trudging along in the rain, I feel like Scott. I'm discovering my grain (again). The storm is bad and getting worse but we plod on, because what else are we going to do? One foot then the other, through the black and green heather. It's not as if there's anywhere to stop and rest. We can't sit down, so we keep going, barely glancing from one edge of the path to the other.

I stop and turn and shout at Dru through the rain and the wind. I want to know why she didn't just carry on. She'd made it for more than forty years and she likes pints and bacon rolls. Why not just grin and bear it, keep on keeping on?

'Didn't blinking work!' she shouts. Her yellow coat is also wet through, bought on eBay from a hairdresser with a tanning salon. 'I tried to get on with being a husband and father! Drinking too much! I was in a horrible state!'

'But what about Scott? What about the glories of endurance?'

Dru is very close now. She hardly has to raise her voice, and we're talking hood to hood. 'Scott's incompetent leadership led his men to their deaths.'

Dru is off and moving again, swinging her arms and her sticks, dismissing the conversation: 'Anyway it's all bloke stuff! Intrepidity lies within!'

Until I read Sara Wheeler, I thought stiff-lipped male endurance was all it took to have a polar adventure. Sara Wheeler also went to Antarctica and tells her story in *Terra Incognita*. Hers was not the worst journey in the world. In fact, she has little patience with the notion of suffering as a virtue, and no doubt about where this absurdity originated.

'The people lighting my way had one thing in common. They were all men. It was male territory all right.' Wheeler talks to Mike Stroud, partner to Ranulph Fiennes on his famous walk across Antarctica, and he confesses that 'sometimes I think I didn't have time to stop and appreciate it. I walked across, but most of the time I was miserable.'

She calls Stroud a Frozen Beard, and whenever she comes across a man with this dispiriting attitude of keeping on for its own sake she calls them a Beard. I know what I am, and I find this strangely unsettling. 'The Beard was silent.' 'The Beard looked at me expectantly.'

This Beard trudged on and did not see the hawthorns rolling like storm waves in the wind on the descent from Hergest, which Dru later described to me. I'm wet and I'm walking, I'm miserable and there's nothing I stop to appreciate. I'm losing faith in my role models: don't want to be a Beard all my life.

I remind myself there are Girl Guides as well as Boy Scouts, and back in Bristol I'd flicked through Dru's 1933 Girl Guides Association *Hiking and Lightweight Camping*. She'd picked it up in a charity shop, a slim booklet for 'those who wish to leave the beaten track'. I'd wanted to have a laugh at this, and smirk at underpants improvised from brambles, but it's all interesting, sensible stuff, especially on the subject of getting lost – 'fear, not being lost, will be your undoing.'

I'm so entrenched in male territory that before now it hasn't occurred to me that Scott, the great survival hero of the Beards, did not survive. 'Add to this,' Cherry writes, 'that he was sensitive, femininely sensitive, to a degree which might be considered a fault.'

Dru and I can't expect, not any more, to bond our friendship by stratagems as simple as testing the limits of the will. Not because she's a woman, but because we both know her will is the stronger.

Testicle pain is invariably portrayed as the limit. That's where a man's will is most likely to break. In the film *Casino Royale*, Daniel Craig's first adventure as 007, James Bond is tortured. He is stripped naked and tied to a bottomless cane chair. The heartless scar-eyed villain then repeatedly swings a knotted rope up into Bond's exposed undercarriage. In an earlier film incarnation, as Sean Connery in *Goldfinger*, James Bond's testicles were threatened by laser. For a man like Bond, threatened testicles are an occupational hazard – this is because he isn't a normal man. Any non-fictional man would recognise the limits of the will, give in. Anything but the testicles. Dru was not a normal man.

I occasionally despair of ever understanding her. Dru has lived a series of states of mind and consequent decisions that are close to impossible for a man to compute. Beyond the limits of the will (I mean beyond the testicles) is an unreal place where empathy is sometimes difficult.

I'm trying to explain why I don't always have sympathy for her. It's because she makes my small vacational gestures at courage seem insignificant. Keep walking, ignore the rain, get to Prestatyn, receive the bloody clock.

Dru has survived this day better than me, and we're still several miles short of the municipal campsite at Kington, the rain raining rain and raining rain some more. On the way down to the town, I've forced myself to notice the blossom blotted along the glistening slate tracks, the sunken lanes and long, soggy hedgerows of dripping cow parsley.

We reach the riverside campsite and Dru has a shower. I have a shower too, and back at the tent Dru is irrepressibly cheery because the Ladies' had a free hairdryer.

'So has the Men's.'

'Breeding a generation of pansies,' she decides brightly.

We're starving, and we walk through more rain into Kington and straight into the chip shop. One of the windows has been put out, and there are three, maybe four very sullen dark-skinned, possibly Turkish, men working behind the counter. I sum up the situation, the broken feel of the town, and make sure Dru sits with her back to the window, so she can't be seen from the street. I have suffered, I have endured, I have learnt nothing.

Dru now gets stared at from behind the counter, where another man has appeared, five pairs of dark eyes watching a woman eat chips. I eat chips. No one cares about my chips, and I transpose on to the five, six staring chip-shop men the most basic of my stubborn prejudices. I am not innocent of what they're thinking because I'm imagining their thoughts.

'She's not *real*.'

Ever since we set out I've been watching to see if Dru is real, or whether she's some kind of trick. This has meant staying vigilant for evidence that her original gender, her chromosomal sex, affects the way she acts, the way she thinks, the way she is. This is unfair, because a definitive womanly technique for eating chips with your fingers from a styrene tray does not exist. I know that, but do the seven Kurdish men behind the counter know that? Is Dru squeezing out her ketchup packets like a man?

She's had a shower, washed and blow-dried her hair, and she's wearing her dress because eating out is a special occasion. She has make-up and a necklace but only one earring, because the other fell out in the festival entrance at Hay. She looks like Dru. She does not look like any man I've ever met.

Amy Bloom in *Normal* provides the best description. When Dru isn't looking her best she doesn't necessarily look like a man in drag, more like someone 'of indeterminate gender with whom something has gone wrong.' The something gone wrong could be mental or physical – but there's a sense of something not quite right.

There, I've said it. There's nothing the chip-shop men can think or say that I haven't thought myself, though for me it's worse because I'm supposed to be a friend. Dru is not alone in living with the something-gone-wrong look, in any gender, but this is the look that can sometimes come over her.

That's not what frightens me. And yet, I'm frightened. I'm sitting in a deserted chip shop in the desolate Welsh town of Kington, afraid I may not leave here alive. I take a deep breath. Think this through – and I have plenty of time for thinking because I'm not asking or answering questions and I don't want Dru to talk. Don't want her to give herself away.

I'm not transphobic.

I'm not frightened of Dru.

I know her too well, and I've found nothing in her past that makes me think anything genuinely went wrong, or that I'm sharing a tent with Norman Bates's mum. Nor am I frightened she'll try to convert me. Hers is a singular experience and she wouldn't wish it on anyone else, unlike, say, certain homosexuals or the Seventh-Day Adventist Church.

Maybe I'm frightened of myself. The brilliant, gunslinging sex writer Pat Califia says 'a fear of transsexuals is directly traceable to a fear of your own opposite-sex self.' I don't know what that is. I like cats more than dogs. I'm fond of bath salts and in other people's houses always use the most unctuous, possibly gender-inappropriate shower gel. If I concentrate hard I can get a woman's score on the Bem Sex Test. I like to be looked after – can I say that? Only because it's true, but it doesn't feel like an opposite-sex self, it just feels like me.

I look for other clues. My first published story was about a street hypnotist at Beaubourg in Paris who could make penises disappear. He'd take four volunteers, two girls and two boys, then hypnotise them so they couldn't move. Next he swapped their genitals around. It sounds crazy, but the outraged expressions on the boys' faces looked genuine. I watched most lunchtimes for a month. Why did I do that? It was good entertainment. For everybody, not just me.

I'm not the only man with long eyelashes and trans-sexuality isn't catching, so why, right back at the beginning, was that the very first question which entered my head? Why since then had I considered wearing my wife's clothes? Don't go off the path.

It's not as if I'm against dressing up. For about a year when I was six or seven, I dressed up as a cowboy every day after coming home from school. What a drag. I've twice been cast as a woman in plays, once in crinoline and the other time as a prostitute.

Maybe I *am* partly scared of my opposite-sex self, but only in the same way I'm scared of nuclear war. It would really fuck up my life to discover I was a woman. The thought makes me seasick, at the centre of a collapsing world, life breaking down with me underneath it. And as Dru once told me, the only proven cure for seasickness is to sit under a tree, and that's exactly what we've been doing.

Finally, making sure I've covered every angle, I am not frightened that Dru is going to jump me and I'm going to lose sexual control.

So what the hell am I frightened of? Why do I feel intimidated in a chip shop in the dismal town of Kington?

The men continue to stare. It's only two exhausted walkers eating your fish and chips, for Christ's sake. Dru jauntily fetches more ketchup from the counter. She makes it back, totally unconcerned, and although Dru may have abandoned her attempt to live as a man, the rest of us carry on. I'm suddenly overcome with a deep, rather pathetic sense of gender self-pity. It *is* difficult being a man. It's this sense of responsibility, and the design flaw which means there are tricky choices to make even between our deepest natural instincts: fight or flight. Why does life have to be so complicated? Why can't we just flee?

Fuck it. Or just fight. *I* go and get more ketchup.

I have a middle-class fear that someone, anyone, is not going to be kind. I should be able to deal with that, especially in a Kington chip shop, because what exactly are the seven Lebanese brothers going to say?

'You're with a *tranny*.' I know that.

'*You* fucking tranny.' I think not.

'She's *weird*.' Is she?

They're looking at Dru as if she's some kind of bug, and maybe I'm frightened of getting stuck in the wrong kind of story. In *Sexual Metamorphosis*, Jonathan Ames speculates that Franz Kafka was influenced by Case Study 129 in Richard von Krafft-Ebing's *Psychopathia Sexualis*.

But who could describe my fright when, on the next morning, I awoke and found myself as if completely changed into a woman.

Gregor Samsa in Kafka's story 'Metamorphosis' has the same shock on awakening, not as a woman but a gigantic insect ('What about sleeping a little longer and forgetting all this nonsense, he thought, but it could not be done').

But Dru is not a giant bug. She is not going to die under the sofa with an apple embedded in her glistening black-brown back. I am, however, getting warmer: I'm frightened because of the way Dru looks. I'm frightened that everybody *knows*, and once they know, that there's no limit to what they could be thinking, the stories they could be constructing.

I'm not transphobic. I'm not. I'm transphobicphobic. I fear what the transphobics are thinking, and what they might plan to do.

Act 1: Here is a gay man with a pink hat who is in such deep denial about his male lover that he's forcing him to change sex. Just as Nero did to marry his favourite slave (they might conceivably know that, if they're Italian).

Act 2: There is no development.

Act 3: A violently baroque climax. This deviant and dangerous couple, for the good of civilisation as we know it, will be fried limb by limb in vats of bubbling chip fat. In Kington High Street, no one can hear you scream.

Hold on, hold it there.

I'm thinking about Dru as a man, in this story of mine she's a man in hiding. If she's a woman we have nothing to worry about, but it seems Drusilla is still from another planet. I learnt nothing in Hay: when I interact with her as if she's a man this communicates itself to others, to the potentially violent transphobics I'm scared of. However I'd act with a woman, that's how I should be and that's how I'm not.

I haven't felt this self-conscious since adolescence.

144

Everyone's looking at us. What's *wrong* with us? I tell myself it's not good to be frightened like this. Being different shouldn't be so terrible, and remember lesson one from most novels ever written: be yourself. That's the fictional antidote.

'Let's get off the path,' I say. 'I don't want to go to Prestatyn. And let's get out of this chip shop.'

I hold open the door for Dru as we leave, and I walk along the pavement with my sword arm free. Dru spots a pub, and she immediately turns right when the sign to the campsite says left.

'Where are you going?'

'The pub,' she says, as if I'm an idiot.

'Absolutely not,' I say. I'm not going through that again.

VII

This room's full of stuff
– will it ever go back in
That little rucksack?

The day after our polar expedition I wake up in Kington. Dru has been out and about for hours and has rigged up a drying-line on the small pebbled beach in a curve of the river. She is singing 'Green Grow the Rushes-O', and knows all twelve verses.

She hears the tent unzip and cocks her head in a way that means 'Good morning, you look truly awful today.'

I groan and turn over, and it's several minutes before I remember: my name is Richard and I am transphobicphobic.

'Nil desperandum!' says Dru in full-sail Drusilla. 'Look!'

A kingfisher zaps along the river and splashes into the water. I pull the sleeping bag over my head.

The oestrogen alarm on Dru's phone goes off, ooh-ooh-ooh monkey noises and the screech and steam of the jungle. The phone is somewhere in the tent, as it was last night when we were in the chip shop, because in the mauve dusk of the tent Dru suddenly remembered her pills, and rustled about by torchlight to find the vital blister pack.

'I don't want to wake up with a beard,' she said cheerfully.

It's unseasonally cold, my breath visible in the open bell of the tent. The kingfisher makes another pass along the river, tracked all the way by Dru's finger. She's making the tea, describing the heron that flapped away at first light, opening the packet of Eccles cakes we have for breakfast. Dru is loving being alive this fine morning, with the added bonus of me being feeble. God is in her heaven.

'In the town of Eccles,' Dru says happily, handing me my tea, 'these are called Chorley cakes.'

As she's packing up she does her voice practice, delicately overdone both inside and outside the tent. This time it's Hopkins – 'In the Valley of the Elwy' – and eventually under the pressure of Dru's good humour I have to get up, convinced there are easier ways to get to know someone. There are. Forget the camping and the book-length biography. Read the teen magazines:

Drusilla Marland – The *Smash Hits* Life

What is your star sign?
Aquarius. Secretly relieved not something animally or spiky.

What time do you get up?
Four-ish.

What's your ringtone?
Ring-ring, ring-ring, ring-ring. It's quite stressful, but

just about any other ringtone is crap. I've tried to find the call of the great northern diver, without success. Sometimes modern life is a bit of a let-down.

What single person had the biggest influence on your life?
My mother, by her presence and then by her absence.

If you had one superpower, what would it be?
Once upon a time I'd have said shape-shifting. But then I had a hidden agenda. Being able to fly would be pretty super.

Favourite colour
Started as red, went to green, moved back to red.

Favourite animal
Okapi. Stepping through a shaft of light in a rainforest glade. Disappearing silently.

Favourite item of clothing
Skirt, making up for lost time and v. comfy. Used to be combat trousers with pockets full of stuff.

Favourite film
Torn between something by Frank Capra and The Battle of Britain, *for the Spitfires peeling off. Neeeeeeeeow.*

Favourite band
Academy of Ancient Music? – too precious? Hatfield and the North.

Favourite place
Somewhere in my memory. But I keep going back to Newport, Pembs.

Favourite food
Fish and chips, on a harbourside, with a bottle of tomato ketchup that I'd cleverly remembered to take along.

Job and knock, as they say in the merchant navy. Job done and knock off. Go back to sleep.

We leave Kington by way of the path, dutifully following the Offa's Dyke acorn waymarks. I tell myself I'm able and willing to leave the path, but getting the timing right is always important. Dru chats knowledgeably about abandoning ship.

A. Hold on to the shoulders of your lifejacket so that when you hit the water the lifejacket doesn't break your neck.

B. How to operate a lifeboat: whack the Senhouse slips with the flat of your hand – if you try to grasp them while disengaging you'll probably lose your thumb.

C. Women, children and merchant seamen first.

This explains everything. After too much rum and too many harrowing seas, Dru the ship's engineer has conceived the ultimate belt-and-braces method for saving herself in case of shipwreck. She's crew *and* she's a woman. It's a masterstroke. Come the day, the rest of us will wish we'd thought of that.

Not really. I need to stick to the facts and get out more, and I am out, on a blustery day with occasional sunshine. We

150

watch two men and two dogs doing what they used to do on *One Man and his Dog*, a programme decommissioned by the BBC years ago, but it's important not to fall into the trap of thinking that if it's not on TV it's not happening. We see working sheepdogs with our own eyes, in Wales, in May 2007.

Telling it as it is, and not as told on TV, I haven't seen in Dru's past a life of tortured and suppressed effeminacy.

Act 2: Dru was nineteen years old, arriving in the big city. She would not be instantly transformed. Or she would, but not across the genders. With a single A level – grade E in Maths – Dru found a place at Portsmouth Polytechnic to study Civil Engineering. She had little interest in the subject.

'It was a way of escaping from home.'

Many college adventures start like this, and in spite of the questionable motives, *because* of the questionable motives, become the remembered best days of our lives. At an age when most of us want to shift identities, move ourselves on, we find in wonder that we can.

Setting off for Portsmouth Dru had the idea that there was a 'major truth out there somehow'. Though not, at that stage, the major truth that later emerged. She was of an age and inclination to explore and examine the self, and I ask hopefully for some clear indication that she was already, preferably constantly, beset by gender repression and doubt.

'I was unhappy about it, but felt it was wrong to do anything.'

That's the best answer I can get upfront, so I decide to go round the back, to the hidden first principles of the British further-education experience. Sex and drugs. Dru dismisses sex.

'It was so unlikely it wasn't worth thinking about.'

Dru liked arty people, favoured the drama group over the speccy metalheads in Engineering. She was in a play, Stoppard's *Dirty Linen*, feeling 'creative and interested in the cultural stuff'. In particular, she was impressed by the cultural stuff as strutted by the play's director, a student who was always smoking. Even cooler: always wearing an overcoat. His name was Vernon, and he was taking a bachelor's in the art of rolling joints. Dru asked Vernon if he could get some dope for Dru. Vernon could.

'Did the drugs work?'

'It was interesting, but the major truth continued to elude me. I was also interested in taking LSD. So I did. That was on my shopping list before I arrived. As a psychological tool. Unlock your mind.'

'Did it?'

'Self-knowledge through drugs was a bit of a waste of time, really. In hindsight.'

You don't say. Though I've never encountered the evidence quite so plainly. Dru the woman was only a changed vowel and a dropped consonant away, and still the drugs couldn't find her. Truly, the narcotics and chemicals are blundering dimwits, and Dru confesses she never had a totally good drugs trip. It was always extremely good *and* extremely bad, the same with mushrooms.

'Anything else, while you're at it?'

'The heroin. But that came later.'

*

In case we became fed up with the close quarters of the tent, I'd always had in mind my friend Ian Marchant in Presteigne.

I didn't think a detour of a couple of miles would matter, and now we're close there's nothing I'd like more. The path has introduced us to Mr Beard and Monmouth and the Kington Seven, but from here it carries on and carries on, more of what we already know. Dru is under-impressed by today's flowers.

'Nothing much new, really. Tansy. Aaron's rod.'

The truth is beginning to dawn: there is not a major truth out there, not for us, not on Offa's Dyke. Sticking to the path is not the way to understand whatever happened to Dru.

Probably just tired. Need to dry out. I do believe in camping and the virtue of back to basics, but I fancy a night in a bed. Ordinary things, like sheets, and tea made in a pot, and maybe a nice piece of cake, seem like wonders of the civilised world. I'm all weathered out.

So about midday I give Ian a ring. He's in, but he'll soon be out. We take a right on to the next road we cross and walk quickly down the B4356 to catch him in. I like Ian very much, especially at this moment, because he's a man who lives in a house. What wisdom. What elan.

There's another excuse for dropping in on Ian Marchant, house-dweller.

'Before I went under the knife,' Dru once told me, 'thinking I might be dead in a few hours, I decided I should think elevated thoughts. In fact I thought sod it, and went back to reading *Parallel Lines*.'

Ian Marchant's *Parallel Lines* is not a book about how the two genders, stretching into the far distance, and despite an illusion of convergence, will never actually meet. It's a book about trains. Before this, I had recommended to Dru Ian's equally excellent *The Longest Crawl*. It's a book about pubs.

I'm also fond of his *Men and Models*. Not the female kind, the ones made with care and balsa.

Ian travels the length and breadth of Britain and writes about men and pubs, men and trains, men and models, men and women, men and children, men and drugs, men and gods, men and this historically vivid country we call home. He also writes about himself, and this keeps him honest.

I'm writing about Dru, but since I recognised my phobia of transphobia, I've lost some confidence in what I'm doing. Feeling frightened of going out with a friend isn't very friendly behaviour. And if I can't be friendly, or on the other hand if I can *only* be friendly, should I be writing a biography?

There's a great book called *Gender Outlaw*, by New Jersey transgender activist Kate Bornstein. She criticises the way in which minorities are exoticised by the dominant culture. I understand what she's saying, and realise it might apply to me. Maybe that's what I am, a snake-oil seller from the dominant cultural group.

ROLL UP! ROLL UP! *SEE* THE BEARDED LADY!!

Rarely fails. It's a perennial theme of the movies, and plots with cross-dressers, gender-benders and other gender travellers are always in with a shout: *Glen or Glenda*; *Some Like It Hot*; *Tootsie*; *Mrs Doubtfire*; *Priscilla Queen of the Desert*; *Ma Vie en Rose*. Those are films I've seen without trying, before Dru gave me a more personal interest, so I know how the story of the Bearded Lady always ends. Self-acceptance is the happy ending, even though in truth it's rarely the end.

The Bearded Lady (Roll Up! Roll Up!) features in *Coronation Street* and *Big Brother* and *Little Britain*, and you can't get more mainstream in Britain than that. These programmes, however, are not made by transsexual women, and according to Bornstein the worst type of exploitation involves the appropriation of the minority's voice.

When *Gender Outlaw* was published in the early nineties, Bornstein called on the hidden self-esteem of increasing numbers of transsexual men and women. Be out and proud, she told them, assert your claim to be the only people who can tell this story fairly. She invites transsexuals (not yet an adjective in 1994) to step clear of the 'shadows of passing and assimilation'.

Come clean, she's saying. You are not a woman. You are not a man. Glory be to a new third gender, to which it is your privilege to belong.

'I'm quite binary, really,' Dru says, but I can't stop to listen because Bornstein is swooning over the full rainbow that is gender outlawism, 'outside the binary, in some third space, a space that constantly shifts and changes.'

'You know where you stand with a fully confirmed, transitioned TS,' Dru tries again, 'just treat me like a woman. What's the problem?'

Dru struggles to sympathise with any intermediate diagnosis, or with 'dual role' transsexuals, or with Bornstein's third-gender transsexuals as fully in-between, special and spectacular beings. A member of this third gender is a shaman who has figuratively died and been reborn, and is therefore uniquely qualified to tell her own sensational story.

'Bornstein's a New York intellectual,' Dru says. 'She has her USP. Being out and proud is less of a selling point on a P&O ferry.'

There are two problems with Bornstein's bold and

unashamed approach. Firstly it fixes the transsexual story as a performance – her third gender is more of an act than a state of being, and therefore not much advanced from a pantomime dame. More acutely, if transsexuals are the only people who can be trusted to write their own stories, then the only transsexual stories anyone will read are those about and by the type of transsexuals who write books.

As sex changes become routine on the NHS, the experience moves beyond the spectacular and into more interesting, more nuanced territory. The way it is for Dru (and for me) hasn't been told in any of the existing stories. Why can't Dru write it? Why can't I fix motorbike engines? I don't know: there are things we can't do, and things we can.

I want to say that changing sex can be amazing but mundane, as marvellous but no more so than a major event in any other life. There can be an absence of glorious renewal, and a sorry lack of Shakespearean disguise and disclosure. I know I'm shooting myself in the foot, but with Dru the story isn't like that. Sorry. It's like this.

*

Dru's first diary dates from the period after she dropped out of Portsmouth Poly. Between this 1979 diary and her last pre-transition thoughts in 2001, Dru's diaries are intermittent, sometimes with gaps of six months or more between entries. Entire years go missing, and half a decade between 1982 and 1987. What they all have in common, until 2001, is complete silence about being a woman trapped in a man's body.

Dru writes most regularly when she's away at sea, because there are fewer distractions and regular hours (*muesli, toast and beer for lunch*), but in the early days she is adventurous, curious, young.

'When I look back at the way I was then,' Dru says, 'I feel so useless, idle and pathetic. I had no sense of direction, but that's how I was.'

Up to a point, Dru. This useless idler, while contributing little to seminars on engineering, went to night school and got an A-grade A level in English. She dropped out of the poly at the end of the year and went back to the farm in Wales, though not to certain defeat. Instead of living in the house she spent the summer in a caravan parked on the hill.

From the diary the dropping out sounds like a good decision, and over the next few years Dru is frequently hitching, and sleeping in fields under banana moons. She hangs out with travellers who claim in past lives in the thirteenth century to have worked as Ottoman librarians, which explains why in 1979 they like going on holiday to Turkey. She is in awe of girls who have discovered the Guru Maharaj Ji, and who now only sleep with Scorpios. She cycles to Ireland, where it rains. She mixes with vegetarians.

One of her bigger adventures involves hitching to Paris in the hope of finding a job, but it's not easy. Men try to pick her up in the parks of Montparnasse, and her only link to home is the essential radio. She listens to the World Service and follows the exploits of Solidarnosc in Poland: *If the Russians invade, I'm going home.*

It reads like a good life for a youngster, full of people and impressions and the gathering of stray bits and pieces. A plaque at Mwnt church near Cardigan:

> Every time I see a church
> I pay a little visit
> And when at last I'm carried in
> The Lord won't say 'Who is it?'

She picks up on the goodness of those who live an alternative life. It's my own observation, though not uniquely mine, that those who reject the standard ambitions of the age are more decent, more moral, more intelligent, though rarely all at once. Dru senses something similar, the counter-cultural proof, in Bob Dylan's phrase, that to live outside the law you must be honest. I've never understood this line in its simple sense that the law is dishonest and therefore to ignore it makes you honest; I always wanted it to mean that if you live life by your own laws, it's only going to work out if you honestly stick by them.

Dru moves back to Portsmouth, where she'll stay until 1989, just before I'm to meet her in Bristol. In Portsmouth she returns to her student house but instead of re-enrolling she signs on the dole and recovers her student lifestyle without the bother of classes. She is always vaguely planning on going to India, or to Iceland on a canning-factory contract, or to pick sprouts near Derby. Instead she goes back to the drama group and finds a girlfriend, a first-year. In the girl's second year the two of them move in together.

Now that I'm a parent, I heave a parent's sigh. This doesn't *necessarily* have to turn out badly.

Dru keeps herself with a four-month stint in the dockyard drawing office, a stretch in the café at the Continental Ferry Terminal, then as cook and counter staff in a wholefood shop. In the summers she cycles off to Kent to harvest apples and hops, where in a good week's picking she can earn close to a hundred pounds. She describes the Poles and various ragbags in the Kent hop fields, including *Dave, a quietly mystical hippie, late of the Glaneirio community near Cardigan, father twice (by two different women), and into the earth-mother thing with a hint of transsexualism.*

The sirens go off, the lights flash. It's a false alarm. There is no further commentary, not even a gap or sudden change of subject suggestive of hidden secret longings. Just that one word, with no special emphasis, and then she's on to an equally interested description of mad slow Eddie from Maidstone prison.

Dru's relationships with women are equally part of the silence. She doesn't write these things down so I have to ask. She first had sex on a trip to London, with an older woman she met in a supermarket. Even with the benefit of thirty years' hindsight neither of us can make this significant. Her first long-term relationship in Portsmouth breaks down, but a parental 'told you so' is premature because Dru and her first girlfriend remain in touch even today. This strikes me as a very girly outcome, in the sense that I can't imagine it happening to me, and I'm not in touch with any of my former girlfriends. If I was a girl, maybe I would be. When Dru told her the news about the transition she said: 'Well that explains a lot.' This remains Dru's favourite reaction of any, and she's told me the story more than once.

The parental instinct changes: should have stayed together, made a bigger effort, not become involved with a divorcee with two children who when they met was living in a car. Then in a squat.

'That was at the beginning,' Dru says, 'then she was in a

Housing Association place. Eventually I moved in there with her.'

Too late. Or perhaps not, because when it comes to relationships parental concern is not a trustworthy guide: the previous girlfriend is always an improvement, partly because she's gone.

'And how long did you last this time?'

'That's a tricky one. We got married.'

*

We arrive at Ian's house in the centre of Presteigne just as he's leaving, a bottle of wine under his arm. It's a Presteigne thing – round the houses, friends in the street, a little something for the neighbours. Ian shrugs. He writes Britain better than anyone, and happens to have stopped in the place he likes best. He waggles his eyebrows, causing an interesting ripple effect across his huge bald head.

'If you can live in the Shire,' he glints, light sticking in the grime on his square-framed glasses, 'why live in Mordor?'

Ian goes out for his Presteigne lunch. He will not be back for five hours. In the meantime, we make ourselves at home, as instructed, and become close friends with Ian's kettle, Ian's shower, Ian's washing machine, Ian's clothes horses and all of Ian's radiators. What a wonderful invention the roof is, and Ian has put on the heating just for us.

I wash every piece of clothing I have with me, which means spending the afternoon in Ian Marchant's silk dressing gown. Later, I wear his trackie-trousers and a pair of his black socks, and sleep in his bed. I briefly transition into the travel writer

Ian Marchant, which is nice, especially in the circumstances, but I wouldn't have the operation.

We take the afternoon off. I read the paper and fill my head with cricket. It is the coldest Test match on record, but I'm warm and safely indoors so frankly I couldn't care less. On the inside pages there's a story headlined '**Sex-change doctor guilty of misconduct**', but there's always something or other like this because the transsexual story is new enough to count as news.

And when it isn't, and needs spicing up, transgender articles can inspire creativity in even the most jaded tabloid hack: '**No Nobby Bobby Keeps Jobby**'.

We've all seen these reports in the papers. Indeed, Dru has been the subject of several of them:

Would you Adam and Steve it?
Transsexual wins £65,000 for taunts by P&O crew

What should they have done with the sex-swap sailor?
Ferrymen flummoxed by flirting

Sex-swap ferry flirt rattled men in engine room

We even had an inventive one all to ourselves in the *Daily Sport*:

Mills & Bone!
Sex-swap ferry worker signs book deal

The media pounce on the transgendered story because, taking

their lead from the cinema, journalists can never quite believe it isn't a performance, and therefore inviting an audience. The press mentality is to expect every cross-dresser to be Priscilla, Queen of the Desert, every transsexual woman to have a show-off sideline in sexy song and dance. Put simply, the press often get it wrong.

While Ian is out, a workman comes to the door of the house. He knocks. Dru opens it.

'Mrs Bowes?'

These moments, each and every one of them, are very precious. Dru politely explains that she is not Mrs Bowes, the owner of the house, but she will certainly leave a message for the tenant. She delicately closes the door, as happy as can be.

When Ian gets back the workman is still doing whatever he's doing outside. He stops hammering and says:

'Do you know where I can find Mrs Bowes?'

'I'm her tenant,' Ian says jovially. He's over six foot tall with a huge bald head and thick black glasses. 'I *am* Mrs Bowes.'

*

Relationships are famously difficult for mariners, and by the time of Dru's marriage in 1985 she's been on the boats for several years.

'You went to sea in 1982,' I remind her. 'I remember you telling me.'

She's not sure. A shake of the head, a wince.

'You don't know the answers to these questions, do you?'

'I could dig the dates out, I suppose.'

It was December 1981. I find it in the diaries. She was

recruited for Western Geophysical by Gareth, a friend from Wales, who in turn had been recruited through a pub in Isleworth where the Western Geo crews used to drink. Dru is not embarking on a career that begins with sensible shoes in a careers office.

As a former crop-picker, wholefood cook and drawing office assistant, Dru is employed at the rank of helper, the lowest rung in the merchant navy, on the North Sea survey ship *Karen Bravo*. This is the kind of adventure she's been looking for, flown out to Esbjerg in Denmark, then the next day in company overalls pumping kerosene on deck as the ship floats slowly down the Kiel Canal. The crew are drinking, whoring ruffians, but Dru soon adapts.

'I talked too much,' she says. She had long hair and a scraggy beard, and they used to call her 'Wurzel', which was better than a lot of other names. Andy, for example.

Life at sea is an enclosed series of routines (*Usual stuff*, reports the diary, *Pumped the bilges, drank tea.*) It's also a traditional escape from an island nation, with the added attraction of intermittent binges on shore. Dru doesn't hang back (*getting really bored with being stoned*) but it's going too far to think she threw herself into a manly seaman's life to avoid self-analysis. It's not uncommon for transsexual women to have an elaborately masculine past. This is in fact a symptom rather than a surprise, or rather it's self-medication, and the psychiatrists call it 'a flight into hypermasculinity'. Hence the existence of paragliding Special Boat Service football-supporting transsexual dads with five children.

For Dru the engine room was never this kind of mistake. She likes engines, she likes ships, she likes a party, and for the next four years she lives two months on the *Karen Bravo* and one month ashore. Survey ships fire pulses of compressed air at the seabed, looking for minerals, and although the ship mainly worked the North Sea there were also trips elsewhere: Ancona, Piraeus, Malta.

'I really must work hard at putting dates to all this.'

I'm not sure they matter at this period. This is life being lived, time passing by. Dru is drinking and smoking and observing. She buys a leather jacket in Tangiers and notes down who from the crew gets thumped in Marseilles bars. Danny the Mate goes for Butch the Cook with a kitchen knife, but all is forgiven by the time they attend the twenty-four hour Bol D'Or bike race, with the ship's Union Jack hanging in the window of the hired minivan.

Her cabin smells of rotting leather, air freshener and fly spray, but there's work, too, and work well done. Dru discovers her practical side and enjoys being valued for her abilities, even if she's sometimes considered odd for eccentricities like reading a book. She is promoted to shift leader, then to acting chief gunner, supervising the high pressure 'guns' and the shifts of seamen needed to operate them.

Her final trip is in 1985. She is sent to Stavanger to join the *Western Discovery* and is expected to give orders to Americans seconded against their wishes from the Gulf of Mexico. Dru is twenty-seven years old. It is a first taste of accredited leadership, a promotion, a chance at a better, brighter future.

'I was out of my depth,' Dru says. 'I resigned.'

It sounds as if she barely made an effort, aware at some level that this was not the brighter future she craved. Another pattern starts to emerge. Sensing that most conventional paths are not for her, Dru never ventures too far down any of them. She also avoids putting herself forward, as if frightened of giving anyone the opportunity to study her too closely.

Back onshore she has a quiet wedding at Portsmouth Registry Office. From her side of the family only a brother attends.

She finds a new job, one she can come home from at night, as relief engine-room assistant on the Sealink Isle of Wight ferry. The hours offshore allow her wife a double life of her own, primarily, possibly, with a regular visitor to the house who is a heroin user and occasional dealer. Dru becomes a user.

Too fast. Slow down.

'How much of my life I've wasted,' Dru says miserably. 'I find that very upsetting.'

Obviously I don't like upsetting Dru, any more than I do anyone else. But I'm curious, and this is the long period of diary silence between 1982 and 1987. How does anyone get into heroin, and drug deals? How did she get that far off the path?

Like this.

Your work is easy and you're married and bored and you fancy an adventure. You take your friend Tony on the back of your 500 cc Laverda motorbike to Holland. You pick up some LSD from Amsterdam, also some dope and a bag of heroin.

The first time Dru sucks up the smoke she's in Leiden, between Amsterdam and The Hague.

'Again in the spirit of adventure?'

'Yes, and curiosity. It made me feel totally brilliant.'

'So. You've left the survey ships, a job you mostly enjoyed. You have a wife who may be sleeping with a drug dealer. You have no qualifications. You have severe gender confusion that is so effectively denied you don't mention it once in any of your diaries. But heroin made you feel brilliant. It was better than acid, then?'

'Very much so. And you get a much worse comedown from cocaine.'

'So at this time you're taking cocaine as well?'

'And amphetamines.'

This had been part of the North Sea ship culture, for adding colour to the nights out in the grey towns of Aberdeen, Den Helder, Bergen, Peterhead. The drugs helped the crews party until daylight – 'Just drinking really.' We British are so dim. We abuse self-knowledge. Given a chance at recreational drugs, we reject the option of freeing the mind in favour of creating a greater capacity for drink.

Dru calls herself a binge user. 'There's a tendency to finish up what you have.' Not injecting, but 'chasing the dragon', inhaling the smoke. Before long she was supplying drugs to the ships on which she worked.

'So you became a dealer?'

Dru objects, and rephrases it more carefully.

'I'd take enough for myself and anticipate other people wanting some as well.'

As would other crew members. It was a co-operative.

'It was so muddled and squalid.'

In brief layoffs from the ferry she got involved in some 'fairly serious dealing of heroin', and some 'serious rip-offs'. She tries to explain.

'Heroin gives you tunnel vision, so that everything is about yourself and heroin. It changes your perspective, but I can only see that looking back.'

The heroin dealing was to supplement their married-two-kids-occasional-jobs lifestyle.

'Not dealing,' Dru insists. 'I was helping out. In that world, at our level, there isn't a clear-cut distinction between users and dealers.'

There is the murky drugs culture with its highs and attendant horribleness, so that coming down it gets always harder to ignore the sickness, the overdoses, the dread threat of a midnight visit from the Mr Bigs of Gosport.

'It was the second-lowest point of my life.'

'What about gender issues?'

I ask because I'm always asking, and they come through, undramatically, as 'a general sadness'. Dru wasn't angry, or jealous of other women. She felt more of an 'unfocused anger' that came out as being 'snidey and sarky' and getting involved in the Labour Party. She delivered leaflets for Kinnock's doomed campaign of 1987.

'I hate so much of what I did it's hard to bring it out into the light.'

I push, and push, on the walk, in the Morris Traveller, in Dru's kitchen, everywhere we go, everything we do, it's when, why, where and does that mean you were always a woman?

At her Portsmouth home Dru was smoking heroin every day, and on the Isle of Wight ferry doing her daily tasks high as a kite, slow as a whale. No one was endangered: her main job as engine-room assistant was to assist the chief engineer with the *Telegraph* crossword.

It was neither a demanding nor a fulfilling life. Dru had no long-term objectives, no sense of purpose, nothing worth recording in a diary for weeks, for months, for years. This was time wasted with other users, like the South African crewmen later killed by dodgy gear in Cairo. People were coming round to the house and injecting, and drugs were not the reinvention Dru was after. They had not transformed her life, or not for the better.

Dru needed to snap out of it. She needed some kind of abrupt renewal, and however it felt at the time, she was about to get lucky. Her wife would provide the catalyst.

'We parted very badly.'

*

That evening in Presteigne I'd hoped to relax, calm down, share some non-Kington time in good company without worrying what anyone else was thinking. It was looking good. We didn't have to go out because Ian cooked us a meal, his friend Rachel brought round a pudding, and the four of us discussed the multiple personalities of Jesus and the more impenetrable mysteries of our respective publishers. All very fine and dandy.

Then Ian fetches a bottle of port that is half full. It dates from 1938, and was liberated from the Newhaven dockside by Ian's father, who once worked on the south coast as a docker. Ian's dad has just found it wherever he keeps his filched bottles of port, and sent it in the post. However, it's not full because the bottle was leaking. That's why his dad decided to send it, before it went to waste. The 1938 port tastes nice. We all agree on that. But it tastes like sherry. I take a closer look at the label. It seems authentic, but I notice, as no one else has, that there's a Sainsbury's sherry cork in the top of the bottle. Ah-ha, I think, no flies on me.

'Ian, is your dad a bit of a joker?'

'He can be.'

I don't mean to go on, but I do. It's supposed to be port but it tastes like sherry. What if Ian's dad is having a laugh? What if he's getting one *over* on us? The 1938 port isn't *real*. Later, the parallels seem so obvious I can barely sleep, even though I'm in a bed in a house with a roof. I'm coiled up with the danger of nothing being as it seems.

We take the bottle to the pub. Ian even takes a glass, though the friendly Presteigne publican points out that glasses they can usually manage. Both barmen taste the port, without any comment from us, both of them think it tastes like sherry. We try some pub sherry, and then some more recent port. No one truly knows, but the need to know diminishes when we then test to see if it tastes like rum. Helps to empty the mind, which is exactly what I need. Appearance, reality, good faith, bad faith, confusion; all soluble in alcohol.

Dru's not bothered. Standing at the bar she tells us there are three ways of drinking rum in the navy: sippers, gulpers and sandy bottoms, which means down in one. The salty sea dog returns. She then steps back, in her sleeveless beige and orange Rohan special-occasion dress, and tells a story that calls for an imitation of a man in a bar with a deep bass voice.

Welsh or English.

Rhinos or Hippos.

Eccles or Chorley.

Port or Sherry.

She is what she is.

VIII

I can't hear it, though
I can see the crow crowing
Through the train window.

I'm having a mid-path crisis. I'd always intended to ask Dru a series of questions about firsts, some of which I've already asked:

When was the first time you dressed as a woman?

When was the first time you had sex?

When was the first time as an adult you went out dressed in public?

At a certain stage in life, men in particular can start doing stupid things. It happens when life starts running out of natural firsts, and new firsts have to be manufactured. My first red sports car. My first mistress. My first mistress under the age of twenty. My first marathon and my first divorce. The only other first times left to us are not of the jaw-dropping, eye-popping, life-affirming kind. First haemorrhoids. First back spasms. First fall in the street. First trouble on the stairs.

That's what you get if you stick to the path, keep going, don't cheat. You get to finish the journey in Prestatyn.

All those years ago when the Dyke defeated us at Hay, I came back on a bus twenty-four hours later and hobbled on until I reached the end. It took me another week. Dru had more sense; she didn't have to prove to herself that courage comes from the inside out, nor check it was there by testing its limits. Did I enjoy that walk? Not as much as Sara Wheeler would have done. I ended up sitting on the beach in Prestatyn among the discarded chip trays. I had my boots and socks off, and that felt good. It felt good to stop. What a Beard.

It's not as though Prestatyn as a destination even comes with any special recommendation. I've seen it, Dru has seen it, Philip Larkin described the poster: 'Come to Sunny Prestatyn/ Laughed the girl on the poster . . ./ Someone had used a knife/Or something to stab right through/The moustached lips of her smile.' Even Jan Morris, who is positive about most places and especially so if they're in Wales, makes an exception for the town of Prestatyn:

> within easy reach of the Merseyside conurbation, Colwyn Bay, Rhyl and Prestatyn form one long proletarian resort between the mountains and the sea, with all the statutory accessories of disco, ice rink, hot-dog stand, indoor surfing centre, trailer-camp suburb and litter.

I know what's waiting if we mindlessly follow the path. The clock. The losing of the marbles. Possibly some acceptable gender-normative behaviour – I could throw Dru in the sea. She'd probably mistake it for horseplay, and never speak to me again.

We spend the early morning on our hands and knees in Ian's front room, poring over maps. There are endless first times out there, if you look closely, nearby places as yet unseen. There are other long-distance paths, like the Glyndwr Way, which I excitedly follow with my finger on the map before realising it doesn't go anywhere. Then there's the Pembrokeshire Coast Path, which passes through the cathedral city of St David's. We like St David's very much, but the city and the path are on the other side of the country. And in the opposite direction to the one we've been travelling.

'We might just as well keep going on Offa's Dyke,' I concede. 'It's easy, it's there, and we're on it.'

Dru sits back on her heels, opens her eyes wide, and stops blinking.

'When you do that I suspect you're not listening.'

'Damn.'

'Last time we went to St David's we cycled. It's not the same. It's miles away.'

The look doesn't change.

'But there isn't a path,' I say, prodding the map.

To get to the Coast Path we'd have to cross the centre of Wales through the Cambrian Mountains. There is no National Trail, and I can only find minor footpaths which may or may not still exist. They won't be waymarked. We'll have to use a compass.

'People have done stranger things, I've heard.'

I decide to get advice from Ian Marchant, because when they're not changing sex this is what friends are for. Ian is a travel writer and has a feel for the stuff worth seeing.

'Prestatyn? Never been.'

We're now eating a cooked breakfast in Presteigne's only

Colombian coffee house. It is run by a real Colombian, because that's the kind of place Presteigne is. 'But probably I wouldn't like it. It sounds a bit like Presteigne and people sometimes get them confused. Big mistake.'

It's hard to stop Ian once he gets started on Presteigne. It's not just that it has the best pub for miles around, and the best Colombian coffee house. Presteigne is a thriving cultural frontier town with a raffish collection of honest outlaws, and Ian rhapsodises the liminality and transgression of the borderlands. I know that, Ian, that's why we're here. But sooner or later you have to jump one way or the other.

'The train,' Ian the train expert suggests. 'Knighton to Llandrindod Wells. It's a special line. Beautiful.'

From there we can walk up into the Cambrians, navigate across the tops, and come back down on the other side in the village of Tregaron, where, according to Ian, there is an elephant buried in the garden of the pub.

'Do it baby!' says Ian Marchant, Britain's foremost travel and rail expert.

So there we have it.

We'll have to leave the Shire, of course, but I'm surprised Ian doesn't know why. The ring. Isildur's Bane. We have to destroy the Great Ring of Power before it destroys us. Christ alive, Ian, everyone knows that.

*

Which is how on our journey by foot – originally among other things a test of stamina, partly to see if Dru still has what it takes – we end up in Ian Marchant's Hyundai Accent on the open roads between Presteigne and Knighton. Then sitting comfortably on a train heading south-west to Llandrindod Wells, in rear-facing seats looking back at where we've come from. What a great and true way of making progress, I think. We're getting where we're going facing where we've gone. Only trains can do this. And boats. And the jump seats in London taxis. But the principle still applies.

When I'm not being a Beard, there's something of the Anglican vicar in me. I want universality, where everything means everything and everything is always good. We're moving on while looking back at where we've been and you know, gender transitioning must be a bit like that.

Like this, too: leaving the Dyke isn't a failure, even if it's not exactly what we had in mind at the start. We had to change direction. It happens. It can happen to anyone.

Dru's first marriage did not end well.

The break-up is a long and involved story, full of the idiocies of men. Dru could never understand it. She had a new contract with British Channel Island Ferries, two weeks on, two weeks off. While she was away at sea, an incidental bloke was shooting up in the kitchen of Dru's Portsmouth home. He set eyes on Dru's motorbike, a 500 cc black Laverda. This is a very elegant machine, if slightly effeminate (Italian). The nobody man wanted the bike to impress a somebody girl. Dru's wife handed over the keys. At a nightclub, this man upset some other men by boasting about the bike, so the men who were upset went outside and set the Laverda on fire.

The manly episode comes to an end. No women were involved. No women were impressed.

When Dru arrives back from the ferry port, her wife claims the bike was stolen then found abandoned and burnt out. To a man (as Dru tells it), the people they know in Portsmouth fail to contradict this story, although gradually the truth comes out: the bike was borrowed, not stolen. But what really hurts is the sense of conspiracy. The organised cover-up revives Dru's sense of being an outsider, and in the confrontation that follows, Dru finds out about her wife and the dealer. Dru attacks the man, but feebly, hitting him then crying, and moves out immediately.

This episode, always starting with the lost bike, the 500 cc Laverda with gold lines on the black tank, is a bone for Dru to chew on, now as then, keeping her awake at night, a proof of her life's rottenness at this time and the rightness of abandoning her marriage. What hurt, what truly wounded Dru, was that she felt she'd always been honest with her wife.

Always, about everything, except waiting until she was out to go through the wardrobe and dress in her showier clothes.

*

Bristol was a means of getting away. Forget the marriage, kick the drugs, become someone else, transform. The pattern repeats: there was *still* a major truth out there waiting to be discovered. So leave home, just like ten years earlier, but this time improve on the details. Go to university (not a polytechnic), and study English Literature. Part of Dru's recurring pattern, though, is that it has to get worse before it gets better.

'There's another disaster coming up before I made the break.'

Though in fact when she tells it the story doesn't sound so disastrous.

Aged twenty-nine, she walks out of her marriage and

moves across Portsmouth into a communal house with a bunch of Physics students. They want to be a rock band. 'They were nice. It was friendly.' She'd bring them cases of duty-free beer from the ship, 'nicey nicey', and life goes on. She raids skips for loudspeakers and a wardrobe, sails her dinghy called the *Belgrano*, and makes many visits to the pub.

By now Dru was less regular with the heroin, maybe once a week, not that she was getting much support or advice from her family. In her new 1987 diary, the first for five years and a sign that things may be looking up, a typical entry describes a routine family gathering: *drink taken, who blames who for what, Dad threatening suicide and being told to shut up.*

Dru had friends in the basement, a young mum, dad and baby who an 'evil buildery type' (Dru's life attracts stock Tory villains) was trying to evict. Houses at that time, like now, were stupidly expensive – the downstairs neighbours asked, Dru agreed, and together the three of them bought a house.

It was madness, of course, because yet again Dru, moving in with a family, was immediately the outsider. *Do yourself a favour.* Dru owned half of the house but the mum, in particular, made her feel like an 'unwelcome guest'. Not that Dru did't make an effort. She had a new girlfriend who insisted on using words like 'herstory' and 'herstorical', and Dru once drove both women to Greenham Common for a sisterhood event at which men weren't welcome. Dru was *throwing* herself into being an outsider. Or she was giving her comrade feminists a lift to earth mother central. It depends.

The co-ownership came to a messy conclusion, Dru eventually getting her money out just before the housing market collapsed. So that's good news. To me, this period and its dramatic event seem drab and perhaps a little tedious. It's a muddle, sure, but no one changed sex or anything. It's another bone for Dru to chew on, grinding away at that sense of being excluded. Other people may have more spectacular problems, but Dru's were happening to her, and in a non-fiction life this kind of unexciting misjudgement can set a person adrift. It would always be cut from the movie.

Dru is not taking the blame, not after twenty years of chewing the bone.

'I've always lived in shared accommodation, or on ships. I'm quite adept at social situations.'

She moved back in with the physicist rock band, who were still playing the same riff by Guns N' Roses. Her girlfriend had a breakdown, and was hospitalised. Ferry work was just work on the ferries. It was definitely time for the clean break, but after so long and with so much prompting it wasn't that clean, and only happened because Dru genuinely wanted to change.

She made up her mind. She'd go to university, start a new life in a new city, be the kind of person who didn't use drugs.

'If you start taking drugs you meet people who take drugs. I'd already met them.'

'Did you hope a degree would solve your problems?'

'It struck me as being a useful way forward.'

There she goes again. She refuses to admit to trumpets sounding from the clouds.

'Why English Literature?'

'It was an academic degree. I wanted to improve my comprehension of what I read.'

'Only later would you realise . . .'

Dru laughs.

'I wanted to know what to do to get the most out of my reading.'

At her mature-student interview, Dru chose to speak about Hardy, Kipling and Evelyn Waugh. She was offered a place.

'Why Bristol?'

'I really liked Bristol.'

She did have a vague notion of afterwards, of After the Clean Break, of Dru Marland BA (Hons), who might conceivably teach in a school. Before – Divorced Drug-Using Ship's Mechanic. After – Qualified Teacher of *Brideshead Revisited*. That's an ambitious personal transformation, but shows that aged thirty-one Dru's interest in radical change remains firmly stamped in the pattern.

I probe and prod. We still haven't met, but will do soon. Before that, Dru has to settle into university life, three years of study for what will eventually be a third-class degree.

She makes friends. In May of the first year, in 1990, she moves into a new flat and in June decides to move out again, *but on reflection* (in her diary) *I'll try sticking it out for a while, try to make it work out.* She still lives in the same house today, and her ability to stick things out and make them work is much in evidence. She reads books and makes essay deadlines with minutes to spare, gets on well with her tutor, drinks with him in the pub after seminars.

There is a strange incident, early in 1990, when Dru is disturbed at home by two plain-clothes policemen. It is not a routine inquiry: Dru is suspected of murder. Or rather, her tutor has phoned the police station after studying an artist's impression of a murder suspect, as posted on the notice-boards of the public buildings of Bristol. Perhaps he saw it in the municipal library, between **Stop Thief!** and a meeting for Local Poets, but the senior Bristol University lecturer with a PhD has examined the poster closely and identified one of his own students as a likely match.

Wrong as he was about the murder, her tutor must have had a distinct feeling, when it came to Dru, that some important aspect of her character remained in hiding. Only it wasn't what he thought it was. Dru waved away the misunderstanding. They're still friends.

Dru is good at making and keeping her friends, and this is where I come in. I'm at large in Bristol doing very little. Dru is in the middle of her studies, and I like her immediately. She is so straightforward.

Of course I wonder now whether I should have sensed anything: the mistake made by Dru's tutor seems prescient, a proof of superior sensitivity. I just accepted what I saw, partly because I first came across Dru as the rival for a girl my friend in Bristol wanted to go out with. The girl was Dru's flatmate but the situation was all very amicable – Dru wasn't possessive and had already slept with her other flatmate and was also interested in the girl who lived downstairs. Not one of these women had a bad word to say about her because (they whispered while she popped out on her bike for baking soda or black-eye beans) she *knew what to do*.

In fact the very first thing I heard about Dru, via a friend of a friend, I think before I met her, was that she was a champion swordsman, an outstanding lover.

'Crikey.'

'Are you? Were you?'

'I *enjoyed* it.'

'That's not uncommon, I gather.'

'All my encounters were initiated by the other woman. Practically.'

Maybe, I speculate, she was a skilful lover because sex represented a kind of wistful narcissism. She was fascinated by women's bodies and could give them all the time in the world.

'Would you say that's right?'

'Could be.'

'Good. Because I've already written it down.'

This is only a couple of years before that first public dressing up on the quayside in Weymouth, but there's still no obvious sign of Dru yearning to express her inner female. She wasn't dropping clues, and in any case my younger self had no idea what to look for, beyond someone I liked spending time with. I'm not sure Dru knew what to look for either. There was a Michael Longley poem that stuck in her head, about Longley's father and the soldiers he led into battle taking off their helmets to cover their balls.

'When we read that in a seminar,' Dru says, 'I thought those soldiers were stupid.'

This is not a guaranteed sign of gender dysphoria. Don't trust it for use at home.

Dru is so honestly uncertain about her feelings at this time that she can't in good faith be accused of a campaign of deception. Neither against the world in general nor me in particular.

I make sure by cross-referencing against her diaries, though I'm not sure what I'm expecting to find: *Met my new friend Richard. Drank too much. Forgot (Again! Doh!!) to mention that I'm a woman.* What Dru writes is what Dru was, or what I took her for at that time. She zips about Bristol in a leather

181

jacket with a badge reading *'psychopathic motorcycling hoodlum'*. She saves bicycles from skips and is forever mending mopeds, motorbikes, cars, most of them belonging to other people. It's in this context that I get my first mention: *Collected Gilera* [another effeminate Italian motorbike] *from Richard. It was in a shocking state. Changed the oil.*

Whatever else she does, Dru always records the names of pubs, in every diary, and the cumulative effect is of a life mapped out from one pub sign to the next, tracing the journey from Newbridge to Bristol and most points in between. She's a regular, at one time or another, at the Cambridge Arms, the Eldon, the Mardyke, the Highbury Vaults, the Adam and Eve, the Royal Oak, the Boat, the Fifth Hants, the Milbury, the Landmark, the Lamb at Glastonbury, Beckett's, the Hat and Feathers, the Lobby, Dick Mack's, Tom Long's Bar, the Moorings and the White Hart.

Dru collects pubs. The Black Bull, the Bridge Tavern, the India Arms, the Railway Hotel, the Cumberland Tavern, the Hop Bine, the Halfway House. I may one day dress as a woman for the end-of-year carnival in Weymouth, she seems to be insisting, but for now I am the bloke in the pub. It is such an obvious role to adopt, especially if you see life as absurd and not to be taken too seriously: 'Bloke goes into a pub, right?'

Look closer into the diaries at this time and there are two fleeting transgender references. In September 1989, the year of the Fresh Start when Dru arrived in Bristol: *Evening; to the University Drama Studio for the Drama Department's Midsummer Night's Dream. Modern dress, highly stylised; flat delivery of lines, intimations of transsexuality, homosexuality; thoroughly boring.*

In the back of the same diary, from a summer earning money on the Channel Island ferry, Dru records three jokes overheard in the engine room. You might know this one – there's two blokes in a pub:

Harry meets George
'Hello Harry.'
'Hello George.'
'It's not George any more, it's Georgina.'
'?'
'I've had a sex change.'
'Oh . . . didn't it hurt when they cut off your . . .?'
'No, wasn't that bad really.'
'What about the silicone implants, then?'
'No problem – what really hurt was when they shrunk my brain and widened my mouth.'

Why this joke from the mess room and not any of the hundreds of others? Why this joke recorded in haste between poems by Matthew Arnold and Ted Hughes, and a 1596 tombstone inscription from Bere Regis ('*Her outside is but painted vanitie*')? Well everyone knows why *now*, but from everything I remember and everything I've read, I don't believe Dru knew even then.

She could fool everyone else because she was fooling herself. The girlfriends, the motorbikes, the cigarettes and roll-ups, the cans and bottles of beer. These are also accessories, convincing male signifiers. Dru at that time was rarely without them, but neither was I. They work a treat. Arriving on the bike with a pillion, pulling a working man's pay from the pocket of a leather jacket, just another bloke in the pub.

Life must have been so much easier then, not like, say, on a train between Knighton and Llandrindod Wells with one of us revealed as a woman. Living as, dressed as, is.

'Alright, gents?'

The guard who also sells tickets is happy for us to leave our rucksacks on the seats. Dru is sitting behind me, and her company has been grabbed by an alcoholic with a battered can of Special Brew who demands to be woken at every station, so as not to miss the stop at Llandrindod, where the good gear is. This could turn nasty at any moment, especially when we're approaching Llandrindod and the assertive wreck of a human being is asleep again. Thank God. Just leave him where he is.

'Wake up,' Drusilla says politely. 'It's your stop.'

Oh Christ. Shouldn't have done that.

'Right,' the man says, standing up abruptly, nearly falling over. He waves the can of Special Brew. 'Thanks for all your help.'

He gets off the train. Thanks for all your help. He means it, too. We get off the train. The drunk staggers away. Loose black dogs fail to worry sheep.

After the train journey we have about ten miles to walk to Rhayader at the foot of the Cambrian Mountains, and the weather looks threatening. We take a quick tour of the town but with this blustery type of rain it's always worth setting out. It might blow over, you never know in Britain, and maybe our weather makes us what we are. Change happens. Adapt. I think that must be so.

We set out, we get out there. However rough the weather we're still walking. We're heading west across Wales to find the path to St David's and St David, Dru tells me, is the

184

patron saint of manual labour. He lived on salted bread and herbs, and stood for long hours in cold water to subdue the temptations of the flesh.

The cathedral city of St David's has been a pilgrimage destination for 1,000 years, and our unofficial guide Jan Morris has even better news. In the twelfth century Pope Calixtus II decreed that two Tyddewi (St David's) pilgrimages were the equal of one to Rome 'in search of the Apostles'. St David's is therefore worth the same as a Santiago de Compostela. This is an excellent exchange rate, especially if you start on foot from Llandrindod Wells.

I'm in charge of the map, and the path is unmarked but we don't get lost. There are new flowers with great names for Dru to call out as we walk – larkspur, eglantine, and the yellow Welsh poppies. There's also bracken unfurling on the hills and grey tube lichen crusting the stiles. Dru's favourite, though, is germander speedwell, which is bright blue and good luck for journeys, also called Eye of the Child Jesus. Knowing all that, I can't help but stop and be impressed: nice blue flower. We see a red kite, the first of many, while a fox trots towards us with a squirrel in its mouth.

We made a decision and went off the path, but when we get to the town of Rhayader where the people are, we end up doing what we always do. We rig up the tent for the last time beside the River Wye, chirpier and brighter here, and then set out to find the least violent pub in town. As a general rule, this means avoiding anywhere with Sky Sports or a blackboard saying 'The Strongest Lager in Rhayader'. We end up at the Crown, and Dru is on auto-destruct, as if a mid-Wales pub is just the place to explore a latent death wish.

'Oh, Brains Dark!' she says deeply. 'I'll have some of that.'

And me, I haven't miraculously made the change and I stick to my timid little tricks. In Kington it was Dru in the chip shop with her back to the street. Here it's a pew-like enclosed booth in the Rhayader death house. Where exactly *is* Rhayader? There's a brochure on the table. 'Right in the heart of undiscovered mid-Wales.' The perfect spot, according to the brochure, for the *Deliverance* sport of off-road quad-biking.

I persuade Dru that she might like a half. Of Brain's Dark, naturally, I'm not completely mean. It goes down quite quickly. I offer to fetch her another.

'A half-pint is quite enough you know.'

I look at her. She looks at me, raises an eyebrow. We fall about laughing. Not too loud!

This is ridiculous. We're no more likely to be aggressed here than anyone else. I look at the girl behind the bar, a bit creepily, trying to work out from her clinging T-shirt whether she has a pierced nipple. She, for one, is not going to beat me up between now and bringing me my steak (rare). She has great tits. I get through my beer quickly, have another one, hope the beer changes everything though probably it won't. I find myself stubbornly unchanged. Or worse, as if to compensate, I find I'm a beer and steak man with an eye for the ladies, a masculine cut-out with clear expectations that in public places Dru should develop a delicate walk, a charming voice, a more womanly aspect. I want her to disappear. When I want her to pass, it's because then she'll fade away, fade out, be silent.

She tells me that in Devon the beer Old Speckled Hen gets ordered at the bar as a pint of Funky Chicken.

'Do you,' I ask, deciding it's about time I confronted this

directly, 'have any tolerance for people who have a . . . "startled" reaction?'

'People are what they are,' Dru says breezily, shaking out a ketchup sachet. 'Hostility is out of order.'

'I didn't mean hostility. I meant . . . doubts.'

'There are levels of accepting,' Dru continues.

'Are they different between men and women?'

'There is civilised and uncivilised,' Dru says. 'Men are more likely to be uncivilised, but the most tedious reaction is a comedy crossing of the legs.'

Damn. Came close to that one right at the start.

The girl behind the bar has put on a sweatshirt, but she's checking us out and I see what she's thinking. Or I have no idea what she's thinking, but by default her thoughts are mine: I project across my fears. When she decides to set her gang of pierced bikers upon us she'll spit it out:

'You're *sleeping* with a tranny.'

Don't be ridiculous.

'You're sleeping with a strange-looking *woman*.'

Oh Christ, right in the heart. See it for what it is. This is what makes me tense: I'm less of a man to be out with this kind of woman. That's what I'm thinking when I want Dru to disappear, condemned to wander the earth unnoticed, the undead. I'm not transphobicphobic. There's no such word. I'm just plain sexist.

And since I'm being a self-pitying baby, I'll confess that with Dru I'm guilty of every checked box of the centrefold syndrome. This is a condition identified by a writer called Gary Brooks as an explanation for breakdowns in male/female intimacy.

Voyeurism – men want to look at women sexually without getting looked at in return. Done that. Do that all the time. Doing it to the bar staff, whenever she isn't looking. Do it without thinking, women's breasts, bums, legs. Enter the data, collate the result, ignite a small pilot flame in the brain, or not. My male gaze, whenever the opportunity arises, clunks on to Dru's breasts. I see her breasts under her tight-fitting tops. When she leans forward to make the tea or thread a pole into the tent I see the usual curves. I've looked, of course I have. What do you think I am? What do you think she is?

Objectification – the female body, as an object, is separated from any notion of character or personality. The woman-gone-wrong look can sometimes carry greater weight than everything I know and like about Dru the person. This is pathetic.

Validation – culturally agreed female sex attributes confirm male sex appeal. If the woman I'm with is not considered good-looking, that questions my status as a man. What kind of man goes camping with a girl who looks like that?

Trophyism – women are the prizes in a competition between men. And frankly, horribly, with Dru this is not a competition I'm winning.

Fear of true intimacy – this is where it all begins. I don't genuinely want to get to know Dru, not really, or only out in the open where no one can see us and where in our intimacy there is no risk.

I tick all the boxes and that, my friend, is truly inadequate. But at the same time it's not so bad. Perhaps this list of deficiencies suggests I'm treating Dru like a bona fide woman, the same person *and* a woman. This is a *breakthrough*.

To celebrate, I buy Dru a half and have another pint for myself. The story doesn't have to end with blood in the streets, because stories are more varied than that. I'm in disguise, I'm engaged in vital undercover activity, I'm not what I seem in the Crown in Rhayader, Radnorshire, Wales. It could have started as one pal taking another pal for a last chance at manly redemption. Yes, that's a story that the people of Rhayader might buy, so let's just plot that one out:

Act 1: [A generic-looking bar; two blokes in a pub.] Dru tells her camping friend Richard she wants to become a woman. Richard giggles. A lout overhears this conversation and after some fancy stagecraft aggression a fight ensues. Richard saves Dru's life. As a reward, she'll do anything, and Richard asks Dru to go camping one last time.

Act 2: [Out in the hills.] Through a series of episodes, Richard fails to persuade Dru to change her mind. Exasperated, distracted, Richard falls off a stile and damages his ankle. He can't walk, and will die from exposure if he isn't moved, but tells Dru she's useless because her hormone treatment means she no longer has the strength to save him. Dru carries him to the nearest pub. He is saved, but doesn't know how to tell Dru that he's been a fool.

Act 3: [The same pub, later that evening.] Richard is waiting with his ankle in plaster and up on a stool. When

Dru finally makes her entrance she is fully made up and transformed. She has let her hair down and is wearing her special-occasion dress and Richard is stunned. 'But Drusilla,' he says, 'I simply hadn't realised . . .'

We sleep together. That's not the climax of the story; that's just what happens every night.

IX

In this strange new land
We name the hills as we pass;
Our feet mark the map.

Morning in Rhayader brings more rain, which calls for some experienced prevarication and a cooked breakfast. It's another mistake, because this is the worst time to get beneath other people's radar. By nine o'clock we're in the High Street, sitting in a coffee-and-cake shop, waiting for our tea and breakfast when an early-bird outing of three old ladies comes in. The bell on the door goes ding-ding-ding. We are the only other people in the room. The white-haired lady at the front of the posse stops by our table:

'Lovely men having breakfast. Lovely.'

Old women are the worst. They're so honest.

Then a couple of workmen in from the rain in fluorescent yellow jackets. They stare at the back of Dru's head, because, sly as you like, I've managed to get her back to the room again. I can't stop her talking though. The men sit side by side, fists ready on the table, and stare as if they're considering how best to open Dru's early-morning egghead – with a knife or a spoon, with a slash or a bash.

Dru sees a caravan pass the window. It's a brand called Leda, or Leda was the name painted on the side of it. I don't see it, Dru does.

'Leda was Zeus.'

'No, Leda was the swan.'

I wish she'd stop talking. 'Those Greeks were always changing. Impossible to know what's what with some people.'

'Who was the child?'

We can't remember who did what to whom or why.

'I used to like Ovid,' Dru adds, 'for obvious reasons.'

I can't stand the looks any more. 'Come on Dru, let's get out of here.'

I seem to say that a lot.

There's a stretch of road that climbs steeply out of the town before we head into the wilds. The sheep are louder here than on the Dyke, and they bleat and scamper on both sides of the kerbless, unfenced road. Looking down, I can see a glint of water ahead, and the sign as we left Rhayader said '*Gateway to the Elan Valley Lakes*'.

'Perhaps that's it,' I say, stopping and pointing. 'Could that be the lake where your family put up the home-made tent?'

'Maybe. The sides look too shallow.' We walk on a bit, and the mist comes down again, and we can't see anything.

'I wonder why I never asked anyone where we used to camp,' Dru wonders. 'Have to have a séance with my dad.'

Dru can hear a curlew, which makes a bubbly kind of sound we have to stop and admire. I wouldn't mind meeting someone, just for a change, but apart from a few Germans we are the only walkers in Wales. This makes it very unlikely, today as on any other day, that we're going to bump into someone I can make *mean* something. A fighter pilot would be convenient, or an opinionated PE teacher. In *Landor's Tower*, Iain Sinclair has a good laugh at a TV programme which had Janet Street-Porter walking Wales end to end: 'Get me Shirley Bassey or I'm out of here.'

By e-mail, Dru had tried to reassure me that this book would be easy: 'I'm a nice, liberal, middle-class person* trapped in a freak's body.' The * was the most accurate part of the sentence – '*Well, okay, not *that* nice, liberal or middle class, but you get the picture.'

Not yet, Dru, but I'm getting there. We're getting there. Up in the mist I keep plugging away.

'If you could change into a bird, would you?'

'No.'

'Ah. Bit of a trick question that one.'

'It was crap.'

Correct. My half-an-idea was that maybe Dru was more interested in change than she was in becoming a woman. It's just that man-to-woman is a metamorphosis currently available on the NHS. The rain keeps me quiet for a bit – it can come from any direction at any time, usually in handfuls. On both sides of the road on the cropped grass there are blackberry brownberry sheep shits.

'If you could turn fluidly into a bird and back again, at will, would you do that?'

'Yes. Wouldn't you?'

'Yes,' I imagine what that could be like. 'Earthworm?'

'No, yes.'

Probably, we agree, just out of curiosity. Of course we would, given the chance. Anyone would.

I check the map and point us off the road into unknown territory. It feels strangely familiar. The act of walking uphill while carrying rucksacks and getting wet is similar to walking and carrying and dripping elsewhere. It's often like this with big decisions – marriage, kids, changing sex. At first nothing much seems to change.

Dru would marry the girl who lived in the flat downstairs. First they had to fall in love, find interests in common, send out solstice cards, lark around in the pagan heartlands with salt and candles and mystical half-onions. They were constantly exploring Britain and having high-tide adventures, camping, picking up stray dogs, boating, swimming, collecting shells and fossils. They were always going somewhere, doing something, and whenever she remembers to write it down Dru in this period lives a non-stop life of *Made haste to . . .* and *Thence to . . .*

They do all sorts of fun things. They swap clothes for the New Year's Eve carnival at Weymouth. It is 1993-4, and Dru is thirty-five years old.

'What took you so long?'

'How was I to know that I wasn't deluded?'

From now on, she knows what she wants. The realisation must have been sudden and complete, because she never mentioned it. The diaries lapse into silence for 1994, and while Weymouth New Year could have been a funny story told by Dru, the bloke in the pub, it wasn't. She never said a word, kept perfectly quiet about the beginning of the long in-between stage, the metaphorical crossing the mountains from one path to another. The silence wouldn't end until 2001, when the marriage broke up and Dru appeared to her friends in earrings.

This period might have been shorter if Dru's wife had been less tolerant, and if neither of them had married for love. Dru's marriage, like her interest in how things work, was not an attempt to compensate, not a conscious stab at traditional male adult life in order to convince herself that this was the life for her. I don't believe that. She got married in 1996 because she wanted to, because she was in love, because she could.

After Weymouth, she could also dress up.

There are marriages that survive cross-dressing husbands, even those that survive the full gender reassignment. Jan Morris is a good example, but as so often she's an exception. A more plausible guide to what to expect is offered by the American writer Helen Boyd, in her book *My Husband Betty*. I want to quote these possibilities in full, because Boyd's list is entirely imaginable in every case bar one:

When a woman finds out or is told her husband is a cross-dresser, she may:

- Want a divorce
- Tell her husband she never wants to hear another word on the subject
- Tell her husband she never wants to hear another word on the subject but that he can continue doing whatever it was he was doing, provided there is no evidence left in her home
- Accept that he is a cross-dresser as long as he under-stands she doesn't want to see him dressed, see photos of him dressed, or participate in any way. She may acknowledge his need to go to meetings, but insist that he remove any trace of make-up by the time he gets home

- Accept that he is a cross-dresser but insist that he can't do it at home for fear that the children will see him dressed
- Accept that he is a cross-dresser but quickly lose interest in having sex with him whether he is dressed *en femme* for sex or not
- Accept that he is a cross-dresser and never want to see him dressed, but go to a meeting or a conference to meet other wives in the same situation
- Accept that he is a cross-dresser and secretly try to figure out how to cure him
- Accept that he is a cross-dresser and start reading everything she can on the subject – more than the husband himself is usually comfortable with
- Accept that he is a cross-dresser and admit she'd like to know more because the idea confuses her
- Fear he's gay
- Fear he wants to be a woman
- Seem to accept his being a cross-dresser, yet pick fights about everything else they've ever disagreed about
- Jump for joy because she's secretly wanted a cross-dressing husband all her life

This last one is a joke. Otherwise, it's reasonable to think that any woman's reaction might be changeable, combining different responses at different times, or developing from one to another. Helen Boyd's husband Betty is a cross-dresser. He does not want to become a woman (at the time the book was published in 2003, although the situation has moved on by the 2007 sequel, *She's Not the Man I Married*) but Boyd describes other relationships in which this next step is nearly always a step too far. Once it's clear that the husband wants to transition, the more negative reactions tend to prevail.

Dru managed to contain this eventuality, or at least to postpone it. After Weymouth she would dress up whenever the opportunity arose, at last giving in to what instinctively she must always have known: there aren't many former cross-dressers – you either do or you don't.

'The world didn't end,' Dru remembers. 'That's what I discovered in Weymouth. I went out in public dressed as a woman and the world didn't come to an end.'

For now, though, the cross-dressing was a home secret, and although it was hidden from her friends it wasn't a secret in her marriage. Dru's wife was understanding, a synonym in this instance, I think, for loving.

At one point they went to Relate, to talk to a marriage guidance counsellor, but Dru did not find this experience helpful. She decided to ask the counsellor a straight question.

'If you could move fluidly through the genders, wouldn't you do it, if you could?'

The Relate counsellor thinks about this. He is a man. As if challenged to his very core, he replies: 'I quite like my penis actually.'

Dru, however, wasn't being honest. I too can think about changing at will between one gender and the other. For the summer, for December, for tomorrow night's party, for this afternoon's meeting. Sometimes you'd do it for fun, and at others for strategic reasons – to make a better impression or get the shorter queue at the toilets. The only reason not to, in either direction, would be a lack of imagination. Or too much imagination: the fear you may never go back, and Dru hadn't yet admitted to this. It must have been increasingly clear to her, and perhaps also her wife, that she didn't want to move fluidly through the genders. She was looking to travel on a one-way ticket, and the counsellor's instinct had been correct: Dru did not quite like her penis actually.

So when and how did she begin to understand this? What's the difference between a cross-dresser and a transsexual?

About two years, as one of the cattier jokes goes.

But only a minority of cross-dressers want to be women, which is reflected in the numbers: if you think you've never met a transsexual you may be right – if you think you've never met a cross-dresser, you're almost certainly wrong.

Cross-dressers enjoy the rituals of apparent transformation, both there and back again, while essentially, in their own bodies, remaining the same. This is transvestite territory, a high-heeled superhero with a phone-box twirl, Eddie Izzard and easy flipping. The classic medical distinction used to be that transvestites are sexually aroused by their dressing up, while the transgendered aren't. By creating categories, the medical professionals could distance gender dysphoria from sexual perversion, meaning a disordered way of seeking erotic gratification. It's now accepted that the situation is rarely so simple.

The rain stops briefly and the cloud lifts, allowing me to check our position. As I thought: in the middle of the Cambrian Mountains. We've come across an old trail marked on the map as Ancient Road, known locally as the Monks Trod. A rocky path can just about be made out between bog and moss on both sides, both yellow springy moss ('sphagnum' says Dru) and green moss in the shape of stars. The monks used to come this way from Strata Florida to trade in Rhayader, but their path has been mangled by the churned tracks of 4x4s. We step over deeply rutted puddles from one block of quartz to another, and between rain-squalls agree that there's a definite light in the west.

'Did dressing up ever end in masturbation?'

(Whoa, but I checked the map – we're a long way off the road.)

'Dru. Tell me. Was wearing women's clothes sexually exciting?'

'I suppose so. It was sexually liberating. That was the real me.'

Recently, the distinction between fetishism and gender dysphoria has been breaking down. One newish theory, much derided by the transsexual community, moves in exactly the opposite direction. A psychologist called Michael Bailey, in his book *The Man Who Would Be Queen*, brought the term 'autogynephilia' to a wider audience. Contradicting earlier assumptions, he suggests an explicitly erotic motivation for transitioning. In brief, Bailey proposes that some men want to get a female body so they can play with the bits.

More new theories may be along any moment now, partly because this is such a recent and therefore unexplored field of research. Transsexual science dates back only to the 1930s, although a history is constantly being reclaimed. Jan Morris was the first to insist that 'myth and history were full if not of precedents, at least of parallels.' Morris reports sex-change behaviour among Phrygians and Scythians and Alexandrians. She wants us to bear in mind the Sarombavy of Madagascar and the Chuckchee Eskimo, Andean sorcerers and Mohave Indian boys, smooth young Tahitians. In later, more academic books, the Native American berdaches are frequently referenced, as are the Indian hijra people. It's clear that gender-crossing wasn't invented yesterday.

In Western medicine, however, the research starts seriously less than a hundred years ago with the work of Magnus Hirschfeld at the Institute for Sexual Science in Berlin. In 1933 an early attempt at a sex change, to the Danish painter Lili Elbe, involved implanting ovaries. Elbe died, but few lessons could be learnt because for Hirschfeld, Germany in the thirties was the wrong place and time to be a homosexual Jew unravelling the complex mysteries of transsexuality. The Nazis destroyed his Institute, but the pre-war discovery of the sex hormones oestrogen and testosterone, in Holland and Germany respectively, allowed for rapid progress once the war had ended.

In this next period, the pioneering figure is Dr Harry Benjamin of New York City. As a reminder of how modern the Western sex-change phenomenon is, Benjamin's first referral, from the sexologist Alfred Kinsey, came only in 1948. Benjamin's great and humane breakthrough, in the succinct words of Pat Califia, was 'to conclude that psycho-analysis was of no use to transsexuals, since they were not in fact mentally disordered.'

They were not deluded. They were real, and as such, Benjamin made another great leap by deciding the best way to 'cure' a transsexual person was to give them what they wanted. He helped navigate an ethical pathway towards gender-reassignment surgery (GRS), and established stand-ards of care that remain today the accepted guidelines worldwide for the process of changing sex.

Since Benjamin, the brain doctors have quarrelled without agreement over the cause, while the body doctors have grown infinitely more accomplished at doing what they do. Their contented patients, some of them, have been free to record the story.

Dru is Dru. Her story is not a close match for Christine Jorgensen, elegant in pearls on the stage of Madison Square Garden. Nor does she have much in common with April Ashley's boop-boop-de-boop: 'I didn't have a clue who Michael Hutchence was. We went upstairs and had champagne and suddenly I was naked.'

The autobiographer closest to Dru is probably Roberta Cowell, who is thought to have had the first ever sex-change operation in Britain, in 1951. The surgeon Harold Gillies practised on a corpse and operated on Cowell twenty-four hours later. The operation was a success, but under threat of being outed by the press Cowell published her own account of her life in 1954.

She's very much Dru's type – a Formula 1 racing driver, a wartime Spitfire pilot and an embodiment of the haunting English spirit of denial: 'The only thing that could really move me was good music, so I was careful not to listen to any.'

Like Dru, while presenting as a man she took scrupulous care to appear a mess, 'revoltingly scruffy. I had a genuine dislike, bordering on hatred, of new clothes.' Initially she was invalided out of the RAF – 'I was not very upset by this, as compared with motor racing, flying was boring', and her attachment to cars was so strong that for years she carried around a tiny bottle of racing fuel, which she could uncork and smell if she ever needed a lift.

Roberta Cowell's memoir exhibits the anxieties of the age. She wants to believe that she has intersex characteristics, and that the operation is simply an acceleration of what would have occurred naturally, given time. She grasps at anecdotal precedents, like a Polish sergeant who 'according to reports' turned into a woman naturally and became a mother in 1936 – 'the baby weighed nine pounds and was quite normal.'

Where Dru is more fortunate than Cowell is that she feels no need to deny the person she once was.

> When I finally knew the full truth about myself, both mental and physical, the tremendous and all-pervading enthusiasm for motor racing vanished completely.

Roberta Cowell protests too much: even within the controlled boundaries of her own book this isn't true. The pages betray her continuing interest in machinery of all kinds, from the working details of faulty fire extinguishers to lead-fouled spark plugs and a casual admiration for 'a three-stage supercharged flat twelve-cylinder engine, with Aspin rotary valves.'

There is something sadly repressed about her new life, as if she feels certain activities are no longer permitted. Some time after the book was published, contradicting her own statements, she did go back to motor racing, and broke several women's records at hill-climbing.

Since then, everything has moved so quickly that I'm now walking in Wales with my transsexual friend as if, almost, this is perfectly normal behaviour. Me and my vigorous, cheery, apple-cheeked female pal on a hike and a ramble in the Cambrians. It could be the thirties, except in the thirties Dru wouldn't have been invented.

'Did you try homosexuality?'

I'm thinking that would make sense, offering a possible

source of relief without identity change or medical treatment. It must have been worth a shot.

'I once went to a Fassbinder film on shore leave in Marseilles. And that was a mistake. I didn't know what it was!'

So that's a no, then.

What Dru did try was to live the life of a cross-dresser. Man by day in public, woman in private whenever possible. She kept it in the family, or made occasional outings to special-interest nightclubs. In the early days after that decisive night in Weymouth, she also went to a meeting of the Beaumont Society. The Beaumont Society, founded in 1966, is there to help – 'The purposes of the Beaumont Society are to form an association of those who cross-dress, are transvestite or who are transsexual and, through this association, to provide a means of help and communication between members, in order to reduce emotional stress, eliminate the guilt and so aid better understanding of them by their families and friends.'

Dru did not get on well with the Beaumont Society. The name sounds like a gentlemen's dining club, and as Dru tells it the hobby that held these boys together could have been cricket, or sheds; it just happened to be dressing in women's clothes. Dru was horrified. The week after her first meeting, in the Trinity Road Library in Bristol's Old Market, she travelled north for her grandfather's funeral. Her short hair was brushed, her shoes polished, she was a man in black glancing along the pew at her brothers and her father and asking 'What kind of person do I want to become?'

She went home and had a purge, destroying the only photo of herself she had from the night in Weymouth. She then bundled up her woman's wardrobe and offloaded the bin bags at Oxfam, where I imagine the ladies were very kind. The poor man. So sad, the death of his sister. Or his mother. They'd go through the skirts and blouses and never quite be able to decide.

'At that time, I didn't want to be a freak. I didn't want to be like the people I saw at the Beaumont Society. I didn't want to be absurd, to look to my brothers and father as those people at the Beaumont Society looked to me.'

Dru took shelter in the familiar routine of two weeks on (the Portsmouth—Channel Island ferry) two weeks off (camping with layabout writers). She was approaching forty, and her intermittent diary entries tell off the days of never enough money, lack of sleep, and mechanical activity. The thread of her life continues to weave through marriage, the pub, fags, *The Archers*, failed MOTs, drink-driving, and seemingly endless cases of duty-free Beck's and Grolsch.

No mention, in the diaries, of post-Weymouth blues. Dru gets a summer's work renovating an isolated farm in Devon. Her wife comes to stay, and while she rescues crane flies from spiders' webs, Dru shoots at wood pigeons with an air rifle. She likes doing these things. There are increasingly frequent references to *strange dreams* and *thoroughly uncomfortable and troubled sleep*, but this hardly comprises evidence of definite repression. In these years, Dru has a fondness for wearing a beret, the best I can do.

It appears the diaries were never the place to look for a combination of Dru and emotional openness. In 1997 her daughter was born. Dru had the usual bundle of extreme feelings, from joy to terror, and I know because I saw her often at this time. In the diary, the emotion gets gruffly downplayed: *Our useful book,* What to Expect When You're Expecting, *has a section addressed to the father-to-be, which advises me, when offered a drink, to say, 'No thank you, WE're expecting.' I have so far failed to employ the phrase.*

Dru was an attentive husband and a doting father. That was my impression then, and I don't think I need to revise it.

This is the period of our spontaneous adventures, and Dru tells me nothing. Maybe we're too busy being men, and men don't talk. She camps, she drinks beer, she rides her motorbike to her dad's house in Scotland and impresses him by re-welding the footrest and fixing his washing machine. She wishes she could spend more time with him. She loves her dad and remembers him saying, at about this time, 'If we were women we'd be able to talk more easily.'

But about what? Would Dru have known how to describe what was happening? Would talking have helped? Her condition wasn't as easily explained as a broken leg, say, so how could she *know*? She couldn't. That's why it took so long to find her way.

'Describe the sense you had that you knew you were a woman.'

'I didn't. I don't know I am, really, for sure.'

Oh my God. Oh my God. Even *Dru* doesn't know if she's real. I look at the map, at the sky, at the grand sweep of the hilltops. The grass of the high Cambrians is a very pale green, as if it's about to fail, despite having been here for thousands of years, since the very end of the pre-Cambrian age. On each clump the sharp tips are white where they've given up the green ghost. The sky is huge, unmapped from start to finish.

Dru has kept on walking, and I have to hurry to catch up.

'I just want to be natural,' she says.

Don't say anything. Don't say anything.

'With lots of feminine signifiers and a better voice.'

'But what does it mean to *feel* feminine?'

'I don't feel very feminine.'

Prestatyn might have changed. It might have become a secretly brilliant place to end up, with charm and regenerated café bars, a hidden hotspot where Fatboy Slim owns a beach hut, in that brief cool space before ruination by the Sunday papers. You can only guess how it is where you didn't end up.

'Stop.'

'Stop what?'

'Let's make some tea.'

The rain backs off, the clouds high enough for us to point out small black lakes. I set up under the lip of the path and brew the tea, throw a PG Tip down a Cambrian mountainside.

'I bet that tea bag didn't expect to end up there,' I say, and sit on my rucksack cover in the soft heather, my unisex mug warm between my palms. Dru is also settled in, hunkered down, out of the wind.

'Not when it left Sri Lanka,' she says. 'Full of hope, its mum and dad saying "Be sure not to come home until you've made some money." '

'Dru, let's not change the subject. There's a kind of contradiction here, isn't there?'

'Is there?'

'You don't know for sure you're a woman but . . .'

I make a feeble gesture: yellow raincoat, Hawkshead top, breasts, one earring, make-up, copper-coloured fringe, cloche hat, capri pants.

'You're a woman but you don't feel feminine.'

'Not all women are feminine.'

'No. But if you're not, it doesn't make your change any easier, does it? Not for you, not for anyone else.'

Dru *knows* all this. She's had years to mull it over and turn it this way and that, like I'm doing now.

'When we used to go camping you gave nothing away. I had no idea. How often were you dressing up?'

'I stopped wearing male underwear two to three years before coming out.'

Oh well, that's something else I missed at the time. I can't ask what kind. That would be prurient, and I refuse to imagine anything lacy or frilly.

'What kind?'

'Black Sloggis.'

'Make any difference?'

'It was a slight nailing of colours.'

I try and revise my memories to incorporate this information. To France on the ferry, watching the matching Hong Kong girls set up the casino, Dru with a pint of lager laughing at the tannoy announcing the ship's band, *Twice as Nice*. In women's pants.

In Bapaume or somewhere like that, Dru discussing war relics with the fisherman who owned the campsite and the next morning calling me outside to see two rusted heavy-ordinance shells left in front of the tent. In women's pants.

Four days to cycle from Cardiff to St David's on heavily laden bicycles, freewheeling slowly into a misty Tregaron like gunfighters. In women's pants.

That time we left Cardiff on the Taff Trail. Every dead-end estate was sponsored by Adidas, and a fat, crew-cut ginger kid ran alongside us shouting 'Hallo you mochyn! Hallo you mochyn!' The cycle path followed the route of a closed-down rail line, burnt-out sofas like waymarks towards the Saturday-night treat of a still-smouldering Vauxhall Cavalier. If only they'd seen Dru's underpants. Then we'd have been for it.

It doesn't change my memories at all. So Dru had big secrets in her life – was wearing women's pants, had trouble in her marriage – but we still had a pretty good time.

Just as we are now, I think.

We get cracking again and before long we cross B Company 9 Para on a wilderness survival exercise, pretending not to notice a man in a pink hat and Drusilla strolling in the opposite direction. They look a little flustered, out of formation, checking their maps. We don't help them because they don't give us a smile, and they're not in a million years going to *ask*.

Some time later, the Monks Trod loses its way. We're in the right place, facing in the right direction, but the path has been swallowed by water.

'This is like a swamp,' I say, up to my ankles. 'It's like a bog.'

'It *is* a bog,' Dru says.

We concentrate especially hard on navigating our way out of it, just in case the Paras come back, and have a eureka moment when we come over the brow of a hill and a road is exactly where it's supposed to be, right under our noses. The rain clouds are breaking up, and the early evening sun dabs a mustard light on the llama farms on the downhill tramp to Ffair Rhos. There's a pub in the tiny village, the Teifi Inn, and we camp in the little garden next to the ducks and beside the shed with the deep freezes in.

As usual, we try to tart ourselves up before presenting at the bar. Dru gets out the trusty dress. I rub my face. None of the men's toilets in our campsites and pubs have had mirrors, and I wouldn't mind seeing how my beard has shaped up since Hay. I've decided to put self-knowledge to its proper use. I'm having doubts about my masculinity. The beard is a reminder and I'm not going to shave it off until I've solved the problem.

'Dru, have you got your compact handy?'

'I have not. And don't call me Andy.'

I ask for an honest opinion of my explorer's beard.

'It's at the in-between stage. Not always a good place to be.'

'Very funny. Your round. I'll have an imperial pint.'

Jacqui the very friendly landlady of the Teifi Inn has some kind of brain virus that makes walking difficult. We therefore stand at the bar so she can tell us the story of her life.

'I just love people, I do.'

She used to be in the merchant navy, as a nurse. Dru holds back. She has also ordered a half-pint of Murphy's. Oh well done, Professor Higgins. I am pleased, and slightly ashamed of myself for encouraging Dru to change.

A pair of locals further along the bar joins in the chat, and Dru is compliant and not part of the conversation but she is being taken for a woman. If she's disappearing, it's because that's her choice, and sometimes, more generously, I want her to pass because that's what she wants for herself. She's my friend. I believe she knows what she's doing, what she wants. Give the poor woman a break.

The locals tell us how much they hate off-roaders. String them up and cut their balls off, those yobs from Bristol and

Birmingham in their customised Range Rovers. Some come from as far as London, and that's a problem before they even arrive. A farmer tells us he charges £400 cash to drag the idiots out by tractor – which tends to stop them coming back. City types. Bastards.

They eye us up carefully. Dru passes the inspection.

'Don't mind walkers, though.'

We escape to a table some distance from the bar. There is no one in this warm and talkative pub who is going to beat us up. There are no transphobics to be scared of, but Gareth and Dai are coming in later, and last time they were here Jacqui was serving until 5 a.m. Don't care, Jacqui, because it's about time *they* faced facts. Any ordinary member of the public should think very carefully indeed before attacking a woman they read as transsexual. Remember the articles from the *Daily Mail*: many of them are former Special Branch policemen and SAS commandos. Dru has a transsexual friend who was in the French Foreign Legion.

Jacqui has made it over with the food and now takes a breather. She asks me where I'm from, then talks about her tankard collection and her decision to sell the pub.

'She assumed we were a couple,' Dru whispers as Jacqui limps slowly back to the bar.

'No, she didn't.'

'She didn't ask me where I was from. Assumed we lived together. How does that make you feel?'

Been there, Dru, done that. And anyway, I ask the questions.

X

Listen – from the mist
The curlew's call comes bubbling;
The bog cotton nods.

After the Cambrian Mountains, there is the Great Bog of Tregaron. The bog is the last but one obstacle between us and the fresh sea breezes of the Pembrokeshire coast. There is only one path through it, and if anyone was to step off it they would sink, very quietly, below the bog asphodels and the broad-leafed pondweed.

There are intractable questions I haven't yet asked, including those about the personal costs of Dru's decision. Haven't wanted to get stuck. But in the Great Bog of Tregaron this is my idea of treading carefully:

'Isn't changing sex, almost by definition, a superficial act?'

It bothers me that appearances are so important. Clothes and the genitals; not the centre, the soul. As April Ashley said, innuendo added for free, if the genitals were that important they'd have a skull around them.

'I want others to share my perception of myself,' Dru says.

'And it's for me, too. I'm actively interested in my own appearance and attach some importance to it.'

'So it's not just attention-seeking?'

'No, I'm not attention-seeking. If I was I'd wear eccentric clothes.'

This one hangs in the still air like a kite on the lookout for scraps of animal, dead or alive.

'Or have a stuffed duck on my head.'

I can't leave the kite hanging. I have the same greedy instincts, and there's an unpleasantness to writing biography. The hunting, the hovering. The kill.

'Some people would say you *do* wear eccentric clothes.'

'I don't care what people think.'

'But you do. You just said you did. You want them to share your perception.'

There is a pause during which we appreciate the silence of the Great Bog. There are occasional solitary trees which Dru can't identify ('those bloody trees!') and the soft flags of bog cotton that tremble as the avid red kites wheel overhead.

'I'm trying to evolve my own style. Get it right.'

Some of the questions that have to be asked will always be hard going, sticky territory that has to be crossed.

Dru's marriage was breaking up at the same time as she was confronting the decision about her identity. From the outside, knowing what I now do, it's difficult to gauge how one influenced the other. Dru appeared in public in the pearl earrings barely a month after her wife had left the flat, taking their daughter with her. At the time, my instinctive reaction was to connect the two events, and a desire for every event to have its cause led to some aggressively rational thinking:

Dru's wife has left her, taking their daughter.

Everyone knows that mothers get to keep the children.

Dru is therefore staking her claim by posing as a rival mother.

Brilliant. Wrong.

I didn't know then about Weymouth, the quiet nights at home playing at sisters, the growing female wardrobe on sale or return from Oxfam. More simply, I thought Dru might be wanting to say: 'Look at me. Look at how screwed up I am (the earrings, the hair dye, wait while I pull on tights and a dress). Don't leave me alone. Don't leave me now.'

That was one way of looking at it: the marriage breaks down, and then Dru breaks down. This is another way: Dru's inner self was gradually and irresistibly emerging.

'It's a one-way trip, once you start,' and for Dru as a woman in public Weymouth was where it started. Despite the setback of the Beaumont Society, her collection of women's clothes gradually reassembled itself, and Dru increasingly longed for safe opportunities to go out and just *be*. What was her wife supposed to make of that?

Perhaps, at the time, I should have paid more attention. I'd pop in for home-made cherry wine and encounter a slightly uncomfortable atmosphere I construed as married life. It was; but married life going wrong.

In the common story of the betrayed wife, the version without added transsexualism, there's a happy family in a viable home and then suddenly, as if from nowhere, there's another woman. Only in this case Drusilla is the other woman. She's been eating at the table, lying in the bath, sleeping in the bed *all the time*. It's a horror story.

This is the Great Bog, this is where Dru could sink, or be sunk.

'And this was so important to you that you were prepared to lose your marriage and your daughter?'

'That was a question I was asking myself six years ago.'

'Don't you think your decision can seem selfish? A very self-absorbed thing to do?'

'Maybe it is.'

From the outside, the dilemma gradually tightens until all that's left is the unyielding unknown that decides most separations and divorces. Think of the children. Is it better for young children (or children of any age, even those who are now adults) to live with repression and stability, or honesty and calamity?

Dru changes the subject.

'Actually,' she says, looking around at the sinking peat and the strange, alone, unidentified trees, 'this is all quite similar to the Lancashire lowlands where I was brought up.'

'Do you always avoid confronting yourself?'

Dru doesn't reply, her mind going round the long way, conceding that we *are* still in the bog, this is where we are, and we're not out of it yet.

'Actually,' she admits, 'this really is *unlike* the Lancashire lowlands. I didn't want it to be one or the other. I wanted to have my cake and eat it, I suppose.'

When Dru talks about her marriage, all the difficulties get scooped together. Not enough money? Lives heading in different directions? Career going nowhere? Every problem becomes the one problem, like consolidating debt on a single credit card. The deficit is just as large, but it seems more manageable – her wife's lack of total acceptance is seen by Dru as the only serious problem in the relationship, when all relationships have more problems than that. Have enough problems *without* that.

Dru's wife is also my friend, and when I started this book I went to see her. She has set up home elsewhere, and has chosen a more recognisable style of life. I had intended to make a list of questions to clarify this stage in Dru's transition, but kept getting stuck. I couldn't get past that first question, the one that always looms at the beginning. Do you believe your ex-husband is a woman? Is Drusilla real? It was an unfair question to ask – the answer would be a book in itself.

Judging from the transsexual memoirs I've read, I don't think insensitivity to the reactions of friends and family is uncommon. In *Crossing* by Deirdre McCloskey, there's an unintentionally horrific scene where Deirdre laments the fact that her student daughter refuses to see her. She drives unannounced to her daughter's shared house. She knows her daughter is in there, but the girl won't answer the door. Deirdre pushes, and the door opens, but now her daughter is hiding in her room. She enters the house, good old Dad in a dress and heels, worrying about her hair, calling out 'Hello! It's me!'

Deirdre seems to think she's still a reassuring person to come creeping around uninvited. It's me. Just me. In that instance, I found it hard to sympathise. Deception hurts, but Deirdre doesn't appreciate this. The fact that a former lifetime of false pretences wasn't much fun for her, or was maintained for the best of intentions, may take some time for her family to digest. The closer the relationship, the greater the deception.

There's a self-righteousness to some of these stories that has no patience with bemusement. Deirdre McCloskey wants 'the courtesy and the safety of a whyless treatment extended to gender-crossers.' She'd rather not allow for curiosity or disappointment. She'd like to dismiss the why you/why us/ why now bewilderment on the part of those closest, who have usually been misled, either by silence or by an understanding that the cross-dressing was under control. This sense of betrayal will not be eased by familiar justifications like 'I've always known.' In that case, why didn't you blinking well *say* something?

'I was the same person,' Dru says defensively. 'I'm the same person this year as last year.'

People do change, or so they say, and not just through surgery. In marriages people grow apart, grow together, but if a conversation starts with 'I've changed', then as a rule you should settle in for some serious trouble.

'We always *feel* like the same person, don't we all feel that?'

'But if you *were* the same person, couldn't you have kept your marriage going?'

Dru could conceivably have lived the rest of her life in shapeless clothes, swigging beer from tins, occasionally pulling on a twinset at the weekend. Even to me that sounds hopelessly Prestatyn, the road to nowhere, but I ask her anyway.

'Was the breakdown of your marriage a catalyst?'

'That came afterwards.'

I have to correct her, and I know I'm being a bastard. I'm in Dru's ear; I just can't let it go. Partly it's because out here I feel less manacled by books, chat sites, support groups, the corrective nagging of the Gender Trust and what I can and can't say. It doesn't take much time on the Internet to realise how politicised this world can be, and by politicised, I mean there are a lot of people out there on a short fuse, alert to every opportunity for an outburst of righteous indignation.

Those people are not in the middle of the Great Bog of Tregaron. Tough cheese. I can still get to Dru, and I want to take advantage. Out here she seems less watchful, more honest, less likely to be looking for truth and redemption in employment tribunals and the Press Complaints Commission.

'She left before you came out.'

Dru doesn't want her wife to be the catalyst. It's a distraction, and she's getting a bit restless. She's looking for wildlife to name ('those bloody bloody trees!'), slowing down and lagging behind. A tiny black-brown shrew, glossy like a mole, comes to the rescue. In distress, it is curling itself up in the grass on Dru's side of the path while squealing and clicking, making the alarm calls of both a rodent and an insect, warning us off in more than one animal language.

'Was the break-up of your marriage a catalyst?'

'I don't know,' Dru says, picking up the pace. 'And nor do you.'

Dru has some scrawled sheets of A4 paper from this time that she was hesitant about letting me see. She was worried about the frenzy, and the negativity, that the 'rant' wouldn't reflect well.

In fact reading those outbursts was the first time I had a sense of the extent of her private anguish. She's writing onboard ship in the middle of the night, reeling out the fears and frustrations of someone anxious and alone in the currents of the English Channel at 0130. The trouble is caused by the euphemism of 'what is intended', and Dru's imagined future as a woman is still no more developed than 'it', as in 'it still seems so far away, where I want to be.' Even at this late stage,

Dru's sex change is a reality not quite revealed to herself, but her distress is harrowing because the anguish is in recognisable form: the pain of not knowing what someone you love is doing, or whether you believe her.

She considers suicide: living as a man by this stage worse than death. And perhaps it is, if you're a woman.

On the path through the Great Bog we stop at a dead vole. Not a day goes by that we don't see something dead: we've seen the corpse of a lamb, a magpie, a badger and many small dead songbirds. The dead vole, however, is worth a moment of anyone's time: it has been eaten and regurgitated by an owl. The tiny crushed skull is visible, as are the bones, and one undigested front paw, intact as if untouched. It looks like a vole skeleton wearing a single, elegant rodent glove.

'When it came to the crunch,' Dru says, 'there was no other place to go. It was the only decision possible at the time.'

She had been impelled by her nature, though often against her wishes and judgement, to move in this direction. Always – since school, the RAF, Portsmouth, the sea, Bristol – it had been a destination out there waiting.

'Whatever happens now happens.'

I'm suddenly reminded of how recent the operation is, only seven months old, that the consequences have barely begun.

'It was like signing the consent form for surgery,' Dru says, 'I knew I could die but I was going to do it anyway. The earlier decision felt the same.'

Dru made the decision and her wife left. Her wife left and Dru made the decision. If the decision was inevitable, the sequence doesn't matter, and having taken the decision Dru at last had a sense of direction.

'How much of my life I've wasted. I find that very upsetting.'

She found herself a new map. There's always a map, and for the transsexual journey there's a website called the TS Road Map. It will get you through from the beginning to the end, from self-diagnosis to the Gender Recognition Certificate. There are many obstacles on the way, but the route is clearly marked, otherwise known as the NHS pathway, and these are the landmark point-to-points:

– To become a candidate for treatment, the patient should approach their GP with a self-diagnosis. The GP will refer the patient to a local psychiatrist.

– The local psychiatrist, perhaps from the Community Mental Health Team, will make an initial assessment. All being well, a second referral will be made to a Gender Identity Clinic, more often than not at Charing Cross Hospital in London.

– At Charing Cross, if the candidate is not deluded, a psychiatrist specialising in gender issues will provide a diagnosis of gender dysphoria and, if appropriate, prescribe a course of hormonal treatment.

– If the candidate wishes to be considered for surgery, she must then live a minimum of two years as a woman, at least one of those years in full-time employment or education. This is known as the Real Life Test, or Real Life Experience.

– Towards the end of the Real Life Experience (RLE), she will have two further psychiatric assessments before being recommended for surgery.

– She will then go on a waiting list (this is the NHS after all), before being given a date for the operation, probably at Charing Cross, but the procedure is also available in Brighton and Leicester.

– After the surgery she can ask for two signed reports

confirming the diagnosis and specifying the procedures that have been carried out. With these she may apply for a Gender Recognition Certificate, the document that authorises the change from **Boy** to **Girl** on a birth certificate.

And that's the end of that.

The NHS pathway broadly follows Harry Benjamin's original Standards of Care, with an extra year added to the RLE. Better safe than sorry. Just knowing that such a pathway exists can bring an order to lives that may have been chaotic for some time, and the freelance alternatives can be terrifying. I've read one pitiful story about self-castration in a hotel room, severing the scrotum, cutting out one testicle, making a start on the second before passing out from loss of blood. This is in the United States where the pathways aren't so clearly marked, but where the bleeding victim was discovered unconscious and rushed to the nearest hospital. In the urgency of thinking the obvious, the ER surgeon made a snap decision and sewed the testicles back in.

The NHS path has to be the better way.

The first time Dru considered the journey in detail she was fresh off the boat, in combat trousers, providing for her family, on another road entirely. It must have made her heart race and her head spin to be contemplating actually setting out. Drink some tea, perhaps some beer. Don't be disheartened by how far there is to travel: take the first step in a journey of a thousand miles.

She gets her ears pierced, buys a pair of earrings at Debenhams, tells her friends, goes to see her GP, studies the Internet, prepares for her interview with the psychiatrist at Charing Cross. It's all good. At Charing Cross they'll ask about her mother, and make sure Dru isn't confusing one thing for another. Would her life have been very different if her mum hadn't died?

'It's the unknowability,' Dru interrupts. 'It's just impossible to know.'

Dru's mother has been insistently absent, an omission through all Dru's teenage years. No one talked about her, and she might just as well never have been. The appearance of Drusilla corrects this omission, fills the gap, brings a female Marland back into undeniable existence. How is Dru to know that replacing her mother hasn't been her motivation all along?

'I'm not daft,' Dru says. 'I did wonder.'

The dresses Dru likes have the same splashed flower design as the one her mum is wearing on the seafront snapshots at Fleetwood, but this is precisely what the pathway is for. If Dru believes that she can recreate her mum, then she's delusional and will not be recommended for surgery. That's what the psychiatrists are there to find out.

Those on the wrong path most commonly have personality disorders, sometimes Munchausen's, occasionally dismorphophobia – a hatred of certain bits of their own body. A doctor friend of mine theorises that this is what Michael Jackson probably has for his nose and face. At the Gender Identity Clinic they're looking out for a hatred of the genitals. Another potential bad or wrong case is someone who's dressed as a woman a dozen times and been to a gay bar and liked it. The psychiatrists also have to make sure that you don't just want to play with the bits.

Dru didn't believe she fitted any of these categories. The Bristol medics agreed, and referred her to Charing Cross, and by November 2001 Dru had a good reason to wear the deep blue almost-ankle-length coat from Long Tall Sally she'd found in a Gloucester Road charity shop. Also her blonde wig. She was off to London by train for an interview with senior consultant psychiatrist Richard Green, and this was her first full day out as herself.

She told me how it felt in an e-mail:

Points arising from London expedition.

You must restrain yourself on Tube station stairways, and take each step one . . . at . . . a . . . time, lest you trip over your long skirt – and anyway, girls just don't leap up stairs.

When walking in St James's Park against the wind, you must wrap your coat about you lest the breeze blow against your skirt and reveal a lump that really shouldn't be there.

You can't go to the pub at lunchtime – on the other hand, a tuna salad and glass of white wine in the Tate Café more than makes up for that.

Some arty people are extremely charming to unconvincing TSs like the Irish girl on the Information desk at the Tate who melted my heart with her smile when I apologised to her for putting her to the trouble of looking up Eric Ravilious and she in turn apologised for being so slow.

If you go into hot cafés while wearing a wig, your make-up melts, and you spend ages fumbling with foundation, lip liner, lippy and powder; and then you stick liplock on and try to do a goldfish impression without anyone noticing, while it dries.

You can ride up the escalator at Paddington to the open-plan pub, and look around at all the fat, flatulent blokes sitting around with their beers, and take the next escalator down and thank God you don't fit in. So then you sit in a poncey café, sipping a Peroni at £2.80 a bottle, while a fat, flatulent bloke just over the way gives you a very mistrustful look.

Don't make eye contact. Don't make eye contact. Well, not very much, anyway.

Dru was very excited, pleased with herself but nervous. She explained to Dr Green that she'd travelled to London for a diagnosis of gender dysphoria and a prescription for female hormones to start with immediate effect. She knew what she wanted, both the gels and the pills, so that she could move to the next stage without further delay.

Richard Green listened closely to what Dru had to say. He encouraged her to tell her story. Then he said no.

*

This is how you escape a bog. Make it to the town of Tregaron and catch a bus. We walk in, can't find anywhere to eat breakfast, but do find the twice-weekly bus waiting by the war memorial, a gift from the gods with 'Lampeter' on the route marker. Lampeter is in the direction of Cardigan, Cardigan is the start of the Pembrokeshire Coast Path, and this is one way to move on – by getting lucky. On the other hand we could always walk. We look at each other, no contest, and jump onboard.

It turns out to be Dru's type of bus: the driver stops for a woodpecker sitting in the road, and waits for it to fly away before continuing. In an absurdly helpful way, he then drives his bus through the village of Llanddewi Brefi. Famously, in *Little Britain*'s fictional TV Llandewi Breffi, there is only one gay in the village, but in real-life Britain, Wales has no funding to refer transgendered patients to the NHS pathway. This means that if you live in Wales and want to change sex you'll have to move. Dru, then, on this buffeting spring morning, is genuinely the only transsexual in the village.

The comedians of *Little Britain* love to dress as women, and men in frocks excite a dependably hair-trigger snicker. How everyone titters at the absurdity of men as women! We know what *they're* like! Put on a dress and have them down, which is maybe not so funny. This is an area where amusement is synonymous with backwardness, like dogfights, and one day *Little Britain* will look as dated as the Black and White Minstrels.

Life across the genders, on the other hand, may soon become as unremarkable as a country bus. Anyone can get on, but not many people choose to do so. There is us in the back seat, and two more down the front, both old ladies.

We get off at Conti's in Lampeter for the breakfast we missed in Tregaron, and I grab a *Times* from the counter and read that this year all the starting *Big Brother* contestants are women. They have a 'Where Are They Now?' side panel of previous winners, and most are working as presenters on non-terrestrial television shows. The transgendered Nadia, who won series five, has not, however, found her place in niche TV. She was recently charged at Highbury Magistrates Court with assault, but cleared when she claimed the man she attacked had insulted her. She is suffering from depression. So not such a funny joke, once the ogling was over.

After breakfast, we buy a pound of Brays fruit drops, and a new Gorilla tripod for Dru (no untoward incidents – we split up) and then we walk to the edge of Lampeter to hitch a ride to Cardigan. For everything to turn out well, Drusilla can't afford to rely on the kindness of strangers, but the kindness of strangers would help.

'You can be hiding behind the hedge while I show my ankles,' Dru suggests.

We're waiting at the '*Normal Speed Limits Apply*' sign on the A475 towards Newcastle Emlyn. It's not an ideal spot, but it's where we are. Hitching self-selects the generous and the weird, but you're certain to meet someone interesting and after a slow ten minutes or so I wonder about making our own luck. We decide to write a sign. I want to write 'Cardigan', on the grounds that it's inclusive. Dru wants to write 'Aberteifi', the Welsh name for Cardigan, because we're in Wales. It's Dru's biography, and she insists on 'Aberteifi'. She also insists on standing like a trooper, legs apart and arms crossed. I move out from behind my rucksack so that drivers can see my shorts, my knobbly knees. I'm a serious walker, me, not a psycho. Trust my appearance.

About twenty-five minutes later we're picked up by a sixty-year-old sheep shearer in a beaten-up Rover saloon. Perhaps he was swayed by 'Aberteifi' because he's definitely Welsh, not Shirley Bassey but he'll do. I sit in the front and we make man-chat about rugby and New Zealand and the price of sheep. I'm good at this. I do not have to choose my pronouns carefully. He's only going as far as Moylgrove but he'll take us into Cardigan because the chat pleases him and the shearing's cancelled due to rain.

Inside the old Rover the speedo is broken, so the shearer has a second-hand satnav screen stuck to the bottom of the windscreen with a black rubber sucker. He uses it for the speed readout because it was cheaper than replacing the speedometer. He doesn't know how to work it, but the first time he left the garage they set the machine to his home address.

'*Turn around when possible,*' the satnav keeps saying, in a reassuring male voice.

He ignores it, and takes another turning.

'*Turn around when possible,*' repeats the voice. Whenever our friend the generous roving shearer goes anywhere in the world which isn't home, this is what his personal satnav will say. He ignores it.

In Cardigan Dru wants to look at shops, but the town is a sad dripping place of stodge bakeries and charity outlets. The High Street moves slowly with poor, fat people. Dru's family used to own a holiday house here, and she remembers the town in better days, pulling me along to her favourite shop. It isn't there any more. There's a shabby new emporium in the place of the interesting hardware store that used to sell mole traps.

Then it dawns on me: 'You never told me about the holiday house. This was supposed to be a new start, a place we'd never been.'

But it seems that for Dru nowhere is entirely new, even though we're now facing in the opposite direction to the one in which we started. For Dru, Cardigan and the west coast is another homecoming, so she takes me down a narrow street to the terraced house where she and her recomposed family came on holiday five years running. Every summer between the ages of twelve and about sixteen or seventeen, eight of them in a two-bedroom house. We stand in front of it. In the cellar the boys stowed the glass-fibre canoes they'd built with their dad, and paddled them in the estuary.

'So the holidays were fun?'

'Up to a point.'

This can be hard work. Dru knows it, and today she's fed up with questions. We have a last cup of tea in a small busy café, where the schoolgirl staff are made to wear black shirts and pink ties. There are no quiet corners here, and Dru gives up on the voice. Rather spitefully, I feel. All the same I think we've made it. We've passed.

I go to the till to pay. While my back is turned, Dru picks up both fifteen-kilo rucksacks, one in each hand, and hefts them between tables and out of the tea shop.

This has been a transition day. We are very tired from all that talking and not walking.

XI

From this high headland
A rainbow on the Teifi
And, now and then, Lleyn.

Next there's the coming out. There's walking the walk. The Charing Cross consultant psychiatrist refused to prescribe hormone treatment, but told Dru to go away, change her name, start living full-time as a woman.

Come back in six months, he said, and maybe I'll change my mind.

'I just went home and stared at the wall for quite a long time.'

Dru's counsellor in Bristol had led her to believe that there wouldn't be a problem. She'd hoped for a significant step forward. Six months! After forty-three years she didn't want to wait that long. She'd been turned back from Charing Cross and feared the decision might be final. The other routes were private and she had limited savings, but in March 2002 she arranged a private consultation with another gender psychiatrist, Dr Russell Reid of the London Institute. Dru punched out her wig, brushed down her coat, put on her face and took the train to Paddington, and from there to Reid's small clinic in Earls Court.

'Dru appears attractively feminine,' wrote Russell Reid in his report, 'with shaped eyebrows, a wig, black trouser suit, women's accessories and female body language. She is articulate and personable.'

The girl done well. In the transgender community Russell Reid is a controversial figure, known primarily for his boldness in using the prescription of hormones as a diagnostic tool. He is not in the business of rejection. Take the female hormones, and you'll soon find out if they're not for you. If the motivation until now has been sexual, then hormones will quickly seem a limp idea. In Dru's case Reid diagnosed 'long-standing gender dysphoria dating to childhood with cross-dressing since adolescence when it was temporarily fetishistic.'

Dru had ignored the Internet advice. She'd worn a trouser suit. She'd been honest and Dr Reid had responded, enacting in good faith Harry Benjamin's enlightened discovery that the best treatment for gender dysphoria was to give the dysphoric what they wanted.

Dru was overjoyed: she had the pills *and* the gels. Yasmin (30 mg ethanol oestradiol with drospirenone), OestroGel (1.5 mg transdermal oestradiol), and 50 mg cyproterone daily. Download the jungle, set the alarms: it is beginning.

After hormones, the message from the medical profession is in all cases clear: live as a woman. Walk the walk. (But what *is* the walk? – elbows in, bounce.) If you feel like it, *do* it.

For God's sake don't just talk about it.

I defy anyone, given this challenge, feeling sick and floppy from the medication, fully informed of the risks of liver failure, impotency, stroke, high blood pressure and heart attack, not to find out fairly quickly whether they mean it or not. On 30 May 2002 Dru formally changed her name by statutory declaration to Drusilla Philippa Marland. No surgery needed for a change of name, nor the chores that inevitably follow: Dru made a start on the paperwork. She obtained new documents in the name of Drusilla for her driving licence, passport and professional qualifications (Basic Sea Survival, Proficiency in Survival Craft, MN Steering certificate, BA Eng Lit, MN Firefighting 1), medical and dental records, tax and National Insurance, personnel and pension records at work, benefits agency, bank and building society, household and motor insurance, rental agreements, credit card, utilities, council tax, electoral roll, library card and union membership.

And once that's sorted, it's into your best frock and outside with you. If this prospect does not fill you with joy, return the hormones unfinished to Dr Reid.

It's like losing your wallet and your clothes at the same time, but much, much worse. After the paperwork, the coming out involves both vast and tiny practical issues such as devising a strategy to finance the treatment, telling everybody who needs to know, negotiating access to children, keeping up to date with the medication, going to work, organising clothes and shoes and hair stuff, self-monitoring behaviour and comportment, cosmetics, the voice, and getting up to speed with the true horror of transphobic crime.

Whatever the TV and tabloids like to suggest, no one is going through this for a laugh.

The next morning we're heading south for the first time. We spent the night above Poppit Sands in a cliff-top field attached to a hillbilly farm. There's a caravan filled above the windows with kitchen rubbish, and free-range children with black feet and clugged noses. There are also cages of fancy rabbits, in much better condition than the kids.

We've changed direction and the weather is calm, bright – this is more than we could have hoped for. At six, or possibly earlier, we look out of the tent and the sky is unexpectedly and memorably blue, almost forgottenly blue, a blue like . . .

'What's it like, Dru?'

We're both on our elbows. Pause to think.

'Sky blue,' she finally decides.

From the tent opening we can see as far as North Wales and the Lleyn Peninsula where we went that time to find B. S. Johnson's God, the mountains hazy in the distance beyond Cardigan Island. We chat about finding water, eating breakfast, who has the plastic bags for the rubbish.

'How many have you got left?'

'Zero,' Dru says.

'That's very clear.'

'We speak the truth.'

We're off to St David's, in search of the Holy Grail. Luckily, it's said to be buried not far from there. Probably. That's the trouble with the Holy Grail – so difficult to actually find. If we'd gone the other way instead, stayed on Offa's Dyke, we might have found it at Castell Dinas Bran, where it's also supposed to be hidden, but in any Celtic place worth the trouble the Holy Grail is there or thereabouts. The real one. Change one path for another and the chance of finding it remains roughly the same. It's like looking for God. The only sure way never to find is never to go out looking.

We put on the tea, and with great precision and pleasure fold the tent's unusually dry and crisp flysheet. Camping is supposed to be simple, and when the weather is like this it is. It becomes fun. Better than that, it's also *good*. We're saving the planet from CO_2 emissions and Malaga, and enjoying the same absence of complication that Apsley Cherry-Garrard remembers from Antarctica: 'there is many a worse and more elaborate life.'

I'm always hoping our walk will shift and fit to the shapes of Dru's past, and sometimes, miraculously, it does. Today it does. The Pembrokeshire Coast Path is unlike the Dyke and the Monks Trod. '*Cliffs Kill*', say the signs, '*Keep to the Path*'. It glints with a sharp ocean-edge beauty, yet on most stretches at some point I think: you could come a cropper here. It is frequently exhilarating.

Partly it's to do with the fences being on the wrong side of the path. The fences are in place to stop the fields and the farm animals from falling into the sea. The path is *between* the safety fence and the drop of many sudden hundreds of feet. The Pembrokeshire Coast Path thereby provides instant proof, should anyone need it, that in this country Health and Safety directives have not run riot: the Coast Path is lethal. It's also a National Trail, so although you might fall off, you won't get lost.

For Dru, the new path is a wonder of fresh discoveries, rich in birds and flowers not to be spotted inland. The ocean is a glittering constant to our right, but beside the path there are sea pinks in abundant clumps, common spotted orchids, sheep's sorrel, sea campion, guelder rose and broomrape. There is spring squill, marjoram. There are, apparently, moon daisies that tremble in the breeze as the stonechats chat. Gulls and fulmars sweep along the cliff faces with rigid wings and at last, after all this time, I find a favourite bird. I love the choughs. They're like crows would be if crows weren't evil and twisted; black and fleeting, pulling their red feet up like a retractable undercarriage and diving the chasms with folded black wings. The choughs also fly in pairs, and I have a soft spot for nature's monogamies.

Later, when I asked Dru to look up Michael Longley's poem about the soldiers, the one that had stuck in her mind at Bristol University, it wasn't quite as she remembered it:

The Choughs

As they ride the air currents at Six Noggins,
Rolling and soaring above the cliff face
And spreading their wing tips out like fingers,
The choughs' red claws recall my father

Telling me how the raw recruits would clutch
Their 'courting tackle' under heavy fire:
Choughs at play are the souls of young soldiers
Lifting their testicles into the sky.

Which is some measure of how this first perfectly sunny day was shaping up. Everything *is* connected. There *are* universal laws. We're on the path and we know where it is we're headed.

As did Dru, after her interview with Dr Russell Reid, after

her statutory declaration of a change of name. Some doctors are prepared to diagnose 'mild' cases of gender dysphoria, but by their definition Dru's case was severe. She wanted the operation. Even at the beginning she was ambivalent about part-time transvestites in female space, her space, on the grounds that unlike her they weren't women. And when challenged (by me, inevitably) she had a clear opinion on what the non-op transgendered needed to give up before sharing women's rights: the testicles. That was Dru's feeling then, and it hasn't changed. If your core identity is female and that's the way you need to be, then the addenda have to go.

In that sense Dru's idea of the pathway had an evident destination – surgery – though there are routes other than the NHS to get there. In the UK, there's going private. The nitty-gritty, the piece of plain white paper slipped into the brochure, shows that the cost is roughly £9,000. The same psychiatric assessments need to be passed (and paid for), although private benefits include less waiting time once surgery is approved, a private room, and the choice of surgeon. The private pathway also conforms to the Harry Benjamin Guidelines, but to his minimum standards, meaning the Real Life Experience can be one year and not the two years required by the NHS.

Then there's Thailand, these days the most popular of the more exotic journeys. I asked Dru to find me the details, which she already had because she'd looked them up at the time. The most prestigious surgeon in Thailand is Dr Suporn, who has a clinic in Chonburi. Although the Harry Benjamin Guidelines are acknowledged, there is a certain flexibility, as the website makes clear – 'It is not Dr Suporn's policy to deny Sex Reassignment Surgery to any patient he believes to be medically and psychologically fit to undergo it.' At the beginning of 2007, the operation at Dr Suporn's clinic costs about £7,000, though Dru tells me the prices have now dropped. Dr Chettawut in Bangkok costs about £6,000, and so on down the scale as far as Dr Pacharapong Patrasinsuntorn who will charge £1,525 for full vaginoplasty, 'including psychiatric assessment if required (at doctor's opinion)'.

To many, the Thai pathway can appear strewn with flowers, a more enticing prospect than the NHS pathway turn left at the lights on Fulham Palace Road. I know this because I was told so by Mr James Bellringer, one of the two consultant surgeons who perform the operation at Charing Cross. He referred to the 'magic of Thailand', and the climatic and psychological attractions of making a clean break in a glamorous holiday location.

Once I started thinking about the operation itself I decided, rather like Dru, that I wanted the guidance of an expert. I went to the man with the knife.

Mr Bellringer is a very pleasant, generous and informative individual whose job stops the conversation at parties.

'Has its advantages, though. No one asks me to take a quick look at them.'

When he opens the door of his house in Wimbledon I'm not sure it's him, because he looks a good fifteen years younger than forty-nine (the same age as Dru). He is red-faced, red-eared like a boy, youthful, enthusiastic. This is a bit misleading; he has an iron gaze, but my immediate impression is of someone direct and uncomplicated who knows he's doing something good with his life.

We get settled in the front room. Mrs Bellringer brings in

the tea. Master Bellringer does his homework (*What does your dad do? He makes vaginas.*) There are a couple of dogs running about.

Mr Bellringer tells me that the Thai surgeons are well thought of, because if their patients weren't satisfied Charing Cross would be correcting the mistakes. That isn't happening, though the Thai doctors perform a slightly different operation, generally thought to achieve good labia minora but to the detriment of the vagina.

'They're a bit secretive,' Mr Bellringer says, sounding disappointed. 'I tried to make contact, to go along and meet them and say hello. We could have shared new ideas, compared techniques.'

It never happened. Instead, there is a biannual international convention but it's not as useful as it might be because in every other country there's money involved, and therefore competition. Mr Bellringer particularly admires the photographs of labioplasties performed by US surgeon Eugene Schrang.

'The pictures he shows are staggeringly good. A nice cosmetic result. Obviously, surgeons are only going to post pictures of their best work, but I wish there was more openness. I wouldn't mind seeing how he does it.'

The level of social acceptance and surgical progress in other countries depends on their religion. Protestant countries are in the lead, while the Catholic countries lag behind. The world leaders are the UK, Holland, Belgium and the United States.

'Are we the best in the world?'

'Of course we are! No. Our results stack up well.'

Mr Bellringer has two claims to fame. He's one half of

Britain's elite high-performance sex-change team. And he does his ward rounds in cycle shorts.

*

Dru would like to find her way on to the NHS pathway that leads to Mr Bellringer or Mr Thomas at Charing Cross, but to start with she has to tackle the acronyms that protect the mystery of most medical procedures: the PCT, the GIC, the SLA, whatever it takes to get on track towards the GRS. Meanwhile, she isn't wasting time. She's coming out. She's *living*.

This includes going to work, because if the NHS route remains closed she'll have to save for the operation. But before the darkness of the engine room, after the bafflement of her friends, there is family.

'I told my dad over the phone.'

'What was his reaction?'

'I don't really remember.'

Yes, I think, that's Dru all over. 'What would your mum have made of it?'

The accepted medical view of gender dysphoria is as an unusual physical condition with a biological and not a psychological cause. In which case (or in the best case) it was Dru's biological destiny to face up to transition, and then if she had the courage to seek out surgery. In other words, Mrs Marland's second son, to be happy and fulfilled, would always have been on track to become her only daughter. If Dru's mum were alive the change would still have happened, and I wonder if putting her through this experience is the life Dru has imagined, with her imaginary mum.

'Maybe I could have talked to her about it,' Dru suggests. 'I don't know. It's unknowable.'

'Going back to your dad,' I say.

'He was bloody shocked.'

After which, Dru believes, her dad had a brief time 'trying hard to understand'. Dru's sense of her father's tolerance may or may not have been wishful thinking, but the family generally struggled to adapt. When her younger brother gets married in a kilt, the family suggestion is that on the day of the wedding Dru wear one too, as a kind of compromise.

It could have been worse. When Kafka's Gregor Samsa wakes up transformed his family do not take the news calmly. The mother faints, the father shapes to punch him and then breaks down in tears. His sister is 'tempted to exaggerate the horror of her brother's circumstances in order that she might do all the more for him', but when self-sacrifice loses its appeal she turns against him: 'I won't utter my brother's name in the presence of this creature, and so all I say is: we must try to get rid of it.'

One example of the ideal family reaction does exist. It has been in the public domain since the outing of Christine Jorgensen in 1952, and was provided by her father when bearded by the New York press pack. 'She's ours and we love her.' Parents since then need only follow Mr Jorgensen's impeccable precedent, whatever people think, whatever people say.

Perhaps after a time Dru's dad would have come round, but in May 2002, shortly after Dru had started on the hormones, he died. The wicked stepmother, trapped now as always in her allotted role, blamed Dru for her father's death. It was a heart attack at the family wedding that Dru did not attend because she wouldn't wear a kilt.

Dru was invited to the funeral, but only if she dressed as a man. So the day they cremated her father was the last day, ever, anywhere, that Dru presented as male.

'What did you wear?'

'I can't remember,' Dru says. 'I could ask my nieces. It wasn't a collar and tie. Maybe it was.'

Again, this time in unremembered clothes, this is the way Dru is. So unsure on the little things, but absolutely, convincingly certain on the big.

'So there was no theatrical symbolic farewell to a former life?'

'Not really. It was a funeral.'

And back in Bristol the last of the trousers and ties into a bin bag for Oxfam, where her sigh of relief was misread by the sympathetic volunteers. They were stunned by the death of the brother, and so tragically soon after.

Dru's dad left her £5,000. In 2002, this was close to the exact amount needed to fund a medical holiday in Bangkok, but Dru was saved from dramatic irony by the more mundane business of the PCT agreeing an SLA to fund the GRS at CX GIC at the end of the RLE. Translated, this means Dru was invited on to the NHS pathway. She could get it on the state.

In practice, the pathway is bristling with dangers. The Real Life Experience of coming out is the period when nature and nurture are most starkly opposed. Dru is a woman (nature) but because she knows more about carburettors than clothes (nurture) she goes out wearing pink and black striped leg warmers. She does not consciously change the way she holds a steering wheel or a beer bottle, but the hormones wreak havoc. Dru experiments with her handwriting, revives an

244

interest in writing poetry. She makes mistakes, and the scrutiny can seem unfair.

I want this to be a positive day, one of flowers (valerian, angelica) and sweet breezes, but I've noticed Dru hasn't asked me many questions on this trip. It's another way in which her femininity is still to emerge, if indeed that's one of the ways in which it ever does. We've been talking about birds versus planes because Dru spotted a merlin on the cliff face, and then digressed to the Rolls-Royce Merlin piston engines used in Spitfires. This is not a conversation to which I have much to add. Dru allows a slightly disappointed silence to develop.

'Don't you get off on military hardware of *any* sort?'

So there's always that, which people are going to notice, like later in the day when in a small cove we sit on a beachside bench beside an elderly lady in a pink polo shirt. Dru does the voice, and in fluent Drusilla asks ever so politely about the nearby missile base.

But at the same time there's this. Up on the tops we come across a dying sheep. It is sprawled right across the path, unmissable, its four legs off the ground and its grimy hooves trembling.

That's inconvenient, I think. Have to step round that.

Dru wants to call the RSPCA. There is no signal on her phone. We move on, she by now fully agitated, as if we'd abandoned a dying swan. It's a sheep, I think, belonging to a farmer who can't even look after his children. Every time we reach the top of an uphill Dru asks me to check my phone. No signal. I'm getting a bit annoyed. A signal appears. I turn off the phone and put it in my pocket. I feel bad. Why should I object to Dru wanting to help a dying sheep? I hand over the phone. She dials a friend in Bristol and gives the details to be passed on. We all feel better.

I don't have the statistical evidence, but I interpret this as feminine behaviour, partly because my own feminism is of the type that believes women are nicer people. Up to a point. I sometimes wonder whether Dru ever bothers about such things.

We see two walkers up ahead, and she only notices when I point it out that when a man and woman go walking for the day, it's the man who carries the daysack. Dru is genuinely surprised, and I can sense her noting this information for the next time she goes walking with a man: don't offer to carry the bag, don't offer to carry the bag.

I find this lack of observation both a little sad and tremendously heartening. Dru doesn't care. She didn't get where she is today because she didn't want to carry the bag on a day out in the hills. She just wanted to *be*, and the purity of her motives equipped her to survive the strange exchanges that punctuate the real life of the Real Life Experience, as recorded in her e-mails of the time:

I have had problems on the domestic front with a new bathroom being installed at the instigation of the landlord. The appropriately named Cox, the builder, has removed the bath and replaced it with a shower which doesn't work properly. He thinks that doing this will solve some imaginary problem with the central heating downstairs. This is because he is a cretin. I try to explain why he is wrong, and he goes a funny colour, puffs up his cheeks, and drills a hole in something. This is a ritual gesture, designed to demonstrate that:

246

- He is a man, and therefore knows what he is doing, and I am either
- A woman, and therefore incapable of holding a worthwhile opinion, or
- A lunatic, which amounts to pretty much the same thing.

I am talking through this with my landlord. And at the end of the chat, as a postscript, I touch on the subject of his persisting in referring to me as 'Andrew' and 'dear boy'. (He is rather old, be it understood) . . .

'You know that I am changing,' I say.

'Oh, yes; it's wonderful what you can do . . .' he replies. 'Will there be any physical changes?'

I look down at my chest. I gesture at my tits. 'These are real, you know.'

He gets all excited and makes little pawing gestures in the air. 'Oh, I think that's marvellous . . .'

. . . the next day, I am up a ladder in his front room, fixing a curtain rail for him. He brings me a glass of whisky.

'It's really rather marvellous, isn't it,' he says again, waving in the general direction of my chest. 'What is it the Indians say? "Ivory minarets, cunningly wrought."'

Everyone is surprised, some are unkind: Dru's old friend from the Air Cadets, the girl who wanted to fly Spitfires and who today is also not a Spitfire pilot, decides Dru 'won't solve anything by flouncing around like a pantomime dame'. There is the spitting incident at the ticket barrier at Temple Meads station. There are various schoolchildren and shop assistants and Body Shop checkout girls who need facing down.

Dru decides she looks like a Greenham Common woman

but with Pre-Raphaelite dreams. She goes back and forth for appointments at Charing Cross, coinciding when possible with the livelier exhibitions at the Imperial War Museum. Along the Fulham Palace Road, on the way to and from the Claybrook Centre, she plays Spot the Tranny. This is not an easy game. I've tried it, and it opens your mind.

'Charing Cross isn't as Stalinist as some people make out,' Dru says, thinking of those Internet dos and don'ts she encountered before she'd even started. 'Be honest with them and they'll be honest with you. There's no reason not to be, because why would any sane person risk getting this decision wrong?'

Part of Dru's honesty was identifying as a lesbian. This is another boggy subject that according to web-lore was best avoided – don't confuse the doctors. Tell them you're a man-loving woman like the women they probably know.

'There was a time when you had to present at the Claybrook Centre as heterosexual,' Dru lets that one hang for a beat, corny comedian that she is, 'otherwise they'd think something was wrong with you.'

At this in-between stage she continues to feel an outsider, even among other outsiders, like when she reads some of her haikus at the Bristol Central Library: 'Typical poetry event. Couple of lesbos, couple of trannies, Angry Young Man and daft old bugger with a large pole (for his Folkie image). God, sometimes I feel like such a cliché.' Nevertheless, she was on the journey, and in the twenty-first century life for the gender dysphoric is not the personal and private struggle it used to be. The condition has at last been recognised, not by tabloid newspapers, but by support groups like the Gender Trust, by endocrinologists and Community Mental Health professionals and consultant surgeons like Mr Bellringer. It can feel like belonging.

The Pembrokeshire Coast Path has as many echoes for Dru as the Dyke. Travelling south, the sun is on the other side of our faces, but apart from that the repeated actions are the same, the tread, the weight is the same. We've stopped by the cliff edge and are looking down at a hazard of rocks through which Dru once canoed with her daughter, three or four years ago, when her daughter was six or seven.

'I'm more timid now,' she says. 'We were alright, though.'

They stayed afloat, between the rocks and the dangerous currents, and they had lifejackets. But looking down, looking back, Dru wouldn't want to paddle through there again.

There are other reminders at different points on the path. The cove where she first went swimming as a woman, at the end of that canoe trip. To Dinas Head as a teenager with her extended family. We walk through a village where her sister-in-law once rented a holiday house, but Dru couldn't go because she was away on the ferries. It seems whichever way we travel, the past is always there.

On a high promontory with a distant view of Fishguard we sit among rocks and get out the bins and watch the magnified Fastcat ferry push out of Goodwick harbour. Then the *Stena Europe* to Rosslare. It reminds Dru of her last years at sea. In spring 2002, at the time of the transition, she was on the catamaran *Condor 10* running between Jersey and St Malo. She'd been on the hormones for a couple of months, and at the end of May had changed her name. On her first shift onboard as Drusilla, at the beginning of June, she made a point not to arrive in anything flash: flatties, denim skirt, comfortable travel clothes. On the car deck the bosun, a young lad, smiled. Dru then went up to the bridge, got a few more smiles, but before I can be disappointed by this sweetness and light Dru confesses the crew were French.

'They were generally much nicer and more civilised than any English crew I've worked with.'

And come October, this was put to the test when Dru transferred to P&O's *Pride of Bilbao* out of Portsmouth. The ongoing crew, as always, gather on the harbour side and wait for the ramp to begin its descent.

'Quite a few looks,' Dru remembers, 'but none of the blokes said anything. Some friendly comments from some of the girls.'

It was fine until Dru had to go into the dragon's den, the ratings' cabins that were to be her onboard home. The men now gawped openly. Two repairmen smirked and dashed into a cabin and burst out laughing.

'It was a bit trying,' Dru says. 'I pretended not to notice; treat it as normal and people will follow suit. That was the theory. Inside I was feeling quite scared, as I often did at P&O, but I would never have dreamt of showing it. Look 'em in the eye and act fearless, or they'll go for you.'

There were some unexpected side effects of working onboard as a woman. Dru's newly pierced ears didn't agree with the ear defenders, and cleaning the dirty end of a Vacuum Toilet System – *crikey*, she notes in her diary, *this clears out the sinuses* – the ammonia fumes turned her elegant silver necklace blue.

So at first it wasn't all bad. The secretary to the HR manager complimented Dru on her appearance, and said she was much better looking than the other P&O transsexuals. Dru tried not to look too pleased, while absorbing the information that she wasn't alone. She suggested a company calendar of P&O TS employees, adding mischievously in an e-mail to me, 'Now THAT should freak out the trolls . . . tasteful, mind. Obviously.'

It looked like it might be possible, in the engine room of a long-distance ferry, to survive as a transsexual.

'Adjective, please,' Dru interrupts.

To survive as a transsexual former drug-user. At the beginning Dru could even josh with some of the engine-room crew that soon every section of the ship would be obliged by law to employ its own transsexual.

'Yeah,' said one of the younger ratings, defending the honour of the section, 'but we had ours first.'

*

By the end of the day we reach Newport Parrog, a pretty village next to a huge sandy beach. Behind the houses juts up Carn Ingli, the Hill of Angels, because the green-grey Welsh hills have followed us right to the edge of the ocean. Dru has been here before, because it features as her *Smash Hits* favourite place, in fact she comes so often she knows the family history of the lady who runs the campsite.

It is a beautiful early evening for sitting outside the tent. Dru polishes her fingernails. I cut mine. We drink cold bottled Heineken from the campsite shop, and eat crisps. Oh, it is a joy to be alive. We watch a young Welsh family erecting a huge tent beside ours, the first time they've unwrapped it, so the dad is hogging the instructions. The toddling kid is in and under and out and over while the baby sleeps in a car seat on the grass. The mum follows orders.

It really is a huge tent, with three separate bedrooms. Dru wonders when the seals and the clowns are getting here.

We walk up the road to Newport village and go into a pub which is also a curry house. England against Brazil is on the telly and I order the pints at the bar, for me Felinfoel Double Dragon, because Dru tells me that's the best. For Dru the same, in a half-pint glass. She coughs, she orders faggots and peas because she doesn't fancy a curry, her voice goes. We drink too much, we watch the football. I watch the football. Dru goes to sleep in her chair.

After fulfilling our gender roles and avoiding random aggression, we walk back to the campsite where the tent next door is not what it seemed. The man was only asked along to put the thing up. He was being used. Once the hard work was finished, he drove off in the car with the toddler and the baby and left the mum on her own. She has now been joined by about twelve friends. They're having a hen party, cackling and chucking it back. I can hear everything they say and I'm hoping for some smutty girl talk but mostly, loudly, they compare how much they usually drink to how much they're drinking now. This seems to be a hilarious and inexhaustible subject and it's still going strong at half past two in the morning.

In the Black Mountains I climbed out of the tent in my long johns and asked the male outdoor pursuits instructors to pipe down. But at Newport Parrog I find I can't ask the hen party to put a timely sock in it. The reason is tragic – I mean properly tragic, because it's a mixture of fear and pity.

Pity because what with the toddlers and babies they probably don't get out that much.

Fear because they're women. I don't know how a dozen

drunk Welsh women will react. I should put my trousers on. I should put my hat on. Maybe I should shave.

Like any other fear, especially night fear, I try to think this one through. What am I actually afraid of? They'll say no, which isn't very scary. They'll laugh at me. Poor thing, and then what? They'll surround me, knock me to the ground, drag me into the tent, pin me to the groundsheet, cut off my penis and testicles and stuff them in my mouth.

That's absurd. I can't be frightened of that. Well I'm not stupid – I *am* afraid of that, but that's not what I think will happen. So no reason to be frightened.

I stay where I am in the tent.

XII

Wind rippling the tent
A nuthatch hops up that tree
Richard snores gently.

R eal Life Experience isn't easy. If it were, it wouldn't be
real life.

'How do they make sure you're doing it?'

'What?'

'The Real Life Test?'

'Well, they don't send round inspectors to make sure
you're going to Tesco in a dress.'

What they do is ask for documentary evidence, like
payslips or gas bills addressed to a woman. Drusilla is a good
name for this. No messing about. In the sex-change story, the
surgery can get more attention than it deserves. The Real Life
Test is where the hardship lies, and for Dru, real life was at
its most real from 2002 until 2004 in the engine room of the
Pride of Bilbao.

People can get used to almost anything. A man and a
woman in a two-man tent, sleeping deeply, becoming attached

to each other and to familiar routines, the smell of meths and a tot of whisky before bed. The longer we live outside, the happier we are to revert to a simpler state of being.

In Newport we wake up to milky, indeterminate skies. I make the tea, or Dru makes the tea. We fold up the tent together, separately, it doesn't matter. We don't have a fixed division of labour, and sometimes I help out more than I'm helped, and sometimes it's the other way round. These things have become natural, like they do with married couples, and there's a deep satisfaction to be had from sharing chores, from seeing what needs to be done and doing it, and knowing that Dru would do the same.

We won't reach St David's today, and probably not tomorrow either, but, certain of the general direction, we'll set out and see how far we get. We'll know when to stop because at the end of every day, when the tiredness sets in, Dru does a kind of furtive go-slow. She takes careful close-up photographs of flowers, and stops to make elaborate searches for nothing through the binoculars. I usually get the message, and then push on a little further, to see if she still has what it takes.

Chris Brasher the Olympic runner was asked why he took part in endurance events like the International Mountain Marathon. It offered him, he said, 'proof that, sophisticated man though you may be, you can still go out with all your worldly needs on your back and survive in the wild places of Britain. That knowledge is great freedom.'

And if you can't survive, that knowledge is a great limitation. It suggests you've been restricted by age, ill health, ignorance, lack of curiosity, fear, or worst of all, general weedy wet blanketness.

There's no physical reason to be constrained by gender. If, however, women were psychologically weedier than men, or vice versa, one gender would be less free than the other. This seems unfair, so I occasionally like to test Dru out. Fewer questions, just the simple physical challenge: can she hack it?

It's another good day to find out, because by mid-morning the rain sets in so decisively that the sense of direction becomes everything: it is too wet to stop and look at flowers, though Dru shouts that nothing can deter a skylark. We can always hear one wittering away somewhere, but if you try looking up to spot it you get rain in your eye.

At first, walking in this relentless rain feels liberating. I'm reminded that it is also possible, at one time and in one place, to think about only one thing. Single-mindedness can be such a relief, putting one foot in front of the other, but then as we yomp along I can't sustain it and soon become an Antarctic explorer, Ernest Hemingway, the Last of the Brays Fruit Drop Kings.

Fantasy is one way of keeping going, and on the Coast Path we begin to forget that we're awfully close to the edge and the deep blue sea. The most astonishing sights become commonplace, smooth cliffs covered in great matted slicks of seagull shit like freeze-framed falls, like blistered and rusted paint. The windblown blackthorns are moulded into curves by gales off the sea, and wherever there's shelter we brush against the purple of dewy, hundred-flower foxgloves.

In the afternoon the rain takes a break, just as we're walking down the steep hill to Fishguard's Lower Town. We start across the wide pedestrian seafront towards Goodwick, where the ferries come in. Not many people about, but a runty little man walks by, turns, gawps, then runs to catch up his mate.

'I fawt it was a girl but it's a boy!'

Sometimes, regretfully, you have to talk to these people in the language they understand, and that language is not Welsh.

'Fuck off.'

There's a harbour-side Tesco and we need to stock up on sweets and pasties. I push Dru into the shop and wait outside on the harbour wall. This time it isn't a phobia of transphobia in the Tesco aisles, nor the thought of the checkout girl checking us out. Nor can I honestly claim I'm hoping for the runt to come back so I can give him an educational kicking.

No, this time I'm reminded of going shopping as a teenager with my mum. I sincerely, passionately didn't want to be seen with her, but that never meant I didn't love her. I love my mum but I didn't choose her, and with Dru that's how it can sometimes feel, including reacquaintance with a supposedly forgotten adolescent terror: don't bring down shame upon me.

This kind of embarrassment is by definition childish, almost certainly hurtful, but not an impossible barrier. I do grow out of it; I did the last time. While I'm on the harbour wall, drinking Coke and kicking my heels against the stonework, I think of the old days when Dru showed me how to cut gaskets, use a chainsaw, or order Jameson chasers in Irish pubs. I thought she was being the alpha male. Now I realise she was mothering me.

Or maybe, enjoying this time to myself, I might just have wanted to wait outside. Not everything is *because*, and it has taken eleven days of walking to work that one out. We couldn't get along if everything was always because, and we are still getting on, out on the Coastal Path.

For the men working in the guts of the *Pride of Bilbao* – and in the engine room they were all men – everything they felt about Dru became *because*. Because who does she think she is? Two years after Dru left the ship, in what she calls 'the most comprehensively deliberated judgement since Paris', an employment tribunal found 'she suffered verbal and physical harassment from the engine room'. She was ignored, threatened, constantly mis-addressed. Dru asked the chief engineer to implement guidelines for decent behaviour, as issued when an officer transitioned on a ship based in Dover.

'But they were an officer,' said the chief engineer, and refused Dru's request.

'There was a visceral, elemental hostility in a couple of people,' Dru says. 'I think the situation raised questions in themselves they didn't want to answer. Things got progressively nastier, but I was not going to surrender.'

She was, however, increasingly living on her nerves, and being told the trouble was her fault for making the men feel uncomfortable. She was tripped in the control room, and this physical assault made her realise that life couldn't be the same. She made a written complaint, but the tribunal judged P&O's internal investigation 'flawed, perfunctory and superficial'. The P&O inquiry was 'so inadequate as to amount to an insult', the P&O human resources manager adjudged to have committed 'a serious managerial misjudgement'. The behaviour of the chief engineer was 'wholly reprehensible', and the 'claim that Ms Marland's own behaviour was inappropriate was unsupported by any evidence.'

Dru was accused of camping it up, flirting, pouting,

working less hard. Whatever she did, her behaviour was inappropriate, because. Because what? Well, just look at the state of her.

Dru must have known that a ferry engine room was one of Britain's wild places, a tough environment in which to survive. For more than twenty years she'd had privileged access to this secret life of men. She knew there were urinals with a plastic ball you can piss into a plastic goal. At any time since 1981, her diaries can record the nights drinking *nine cans of Grolsch, was very drunk when I went to bed. Also nauseous, so went to the bogs and put my fingers down my throat: but couldn't get much to come up.* This is the world of John the Donk and the other sods stealing her lunch from the fridge, of evenings playing Scrabble with sailors who can't spell, and lying awake to the rattle of chains from the car deck overhead.

Instead of men and women, Dru knew engine-room crews were composed of men and officers, an all-white alright-mate culture with posters in the mess announcing 'Saturday is NIGGER NIGHT – blacks only.' She knew all about the endless drudge of manual labour, getting soaked in rancid oil and scraping out shit tanks, and, on a dry ship, not much to raise spirits beyond the pornographic calendar in the engine control room.

On the *Pride of Bilbao*, Miss August 2003 was as nakedly agape as Miss July 2003, and probably very similar to the up and coming Miss September. Someone wrote 'Dru' on the calendar, and then a thick black arrow aimed at the vagina. It was a joke, the men said, think of it as a training manual.

During the next tea break, with the engine-room crew assembled in the control room, Dru took down the calendar and ripped it up. Imagine the courage of that. There were hoots and whistles, curses, threats: she was told she was going to get done.

By the next tea break another calendar was up and open.

I could now disparage the engine room merchant seamen with their bums and bellies, scratching their tattooed arses while smoking tabs and watching *Benji the Hunted* with the sound turned down. It might just as well have been me.

Why should anyone else have to change just because Dru was changing? It was a joke, Dru, get over yourself. 'Banter' among men is as precious as 'horseplay', highly valued, staunchly excused. Both words cover a huge range of possible behaviours, a few sharp words or a knuckle on the skull communicating anything from a display of genuine affection to deliberate and malicious persecution. It's only *banter*, for Christ's sake.

The Gender Trust produces a leaflet with advice on how to transition on the job and stay employed. Tips go from 'You have a clinical condition . . . Let that give you just cause without making you apologetic', but also include 'For the ladies, separates are more practical than dresses in most situations.' The Trust also produce a leaflet for employers – 'To force a pre-operative MtF to use the male toilets despite living as, and looking like, a woman is cruel and discriminatory. Of course, it would be wise to reassure the female employees that the person is, psychologically speaking, a woman, and that as a result of the hormone treatment could not possibly pose a hazard of sexual impropriety. The fact that she still has male genitals is not relevant as they would only be exposed inside a toilet cubicle.'

These guidelines are excellent, but on the *Pride of Bilbao* the chief engineer and captain wanted to deal with the situation in their own way. This meant doing nothing much and hoping any problems would solve themselves.

'I just got on with it,' Dru says, 'and hoped for the best.'

There's a fashion for younger transitioners to dismiss those making the change later in life. Sad old hags, they think, why did the dreary old dears wait so long? What these young women don't understand is just how much more accessible the process has become, both socially and medically. The feisty youngsters also fail to appreciate how thoroughly earlier generations were conditioned in the classic British principle of Mustn't Grumble. Look on the Bright Side. It Might Never Happen.

In the engine-room banter, Dru becomes 'he, she, it, whatever'. The comments sting: 'If he's got balls, he's a gentleman,' and 'When God made man it was Adam and Eve, not Adam and Steve.' Dru would arrive on board in her skirt and earrings, her hair grown long, but whatever she looked like her colleagues refused to believe it. Dru was not a real woman, she was and would always be a man.

'We're all men here,' they said, and once this murmur was accepted as truth it made appropriate behaviour close to impossible. Any of the men who acted as if Dru was real, when the others had agreed she wasn't, had fallen for Dru's deluded little fantasy. That man would look a right fool. Banter becomes horseplay, and Dru is tripped by a motorman as she tries to cross the control room. She's not real, and if she's not real she can't be hurt.

You, my son, are not real. This unbudging disbelief fuels the history of transsexual repression.

April Ashley heard it in a London courtroom. After her operation she'd married, in Gibraltar, a minor aristocrat who was fully aware of her past. The divorce came in 1970 and she lost everything, including her identity, when the judge reached a familiar conclusion. 'I hold that it has been established that the respondent is not, and was not, a woman at the date of the ceremony of marriage, but was, at all times, a male. The marriage is, accordingly, void . . .'

This judgement denied Ashley any chance of a settlement, and British transgendered people lost the right to change their birth certificates, and therefore marry, for the next thirty years. April Ashley the woman was officially not true. She was a charade, a denial of the facts.

In 1979 Janice Raymond published *The Transsexual Empire*, and now essentialist lesbian feminists crowded in with the British judiciary and the heavyset men from the engine room. Basing her argument on the biological difference in the sex chromosomes, Raymond is unequivocal – 'Transsexuals are *not* women. They are *deviant males*.'

In many ways Raymond's book is ridiculous, and many academics who are not essentialist lesbian feminists have laughed at it. She sees transsexualism as a male conspiracy to infiltrate feminism and destroy all genetically born women. Gender surgery is part of a *Doctor Who* plot to replace intransigent independently minded wimmin with transsexual *Playboy* bunnies, a Nazi-style experiment to engineer the 'perfect' woman – an artificial, submissive, super-feminine James Bond girl.

Raymond is such a misogynist. Caroline Cossey was both real and a real James Bond girl, but that doesn't make her submissive. In fact Cossey was instrumental in bringing attention to the April Ashley injustice by contesting her own right to marry at the Strasbourg Court of Human Rights.

Cossey is a very attractive woman, as was Ashley before her, which sends both of them straight to the top of Raymond's hate-list of transsexual Bluebell dancers and nightclub hostesses. It's not their fault they're good-looking, though in fact transsexual women often have an advantage when it comes to working as models. They tend to be taller, have strong features, and great legs because male genetic material is not programmed to seduce cellulite and entrap it to the thighs. This is what leads to that everyday marvel (or patriarchal conspiracy, for Raymond) of the transsexual underwear model. Look at the lingerie, look at the legs. How can you tell?

You can't. No one can, not even men who risk blindness from looking so closely. This is the male gaze, which in the engine room of the *Pride of Bilbao* fell on Dru and accused her of 'acting in an exaggeratedly female way'. The implication is clear. Any feminine behaviour is exaggerated *for a man*. The pursed lips, the raised eyebrows, the walk. They look at Dru on the ramp in her denim skirt, a transformed creature out of a horror story, and they decide the man must still be in there somewhere.

How do I know all this? Because it's nothing I haven't felt myself. There was so much of Drew, over forty years of him, so what happened to Mr Drew Marland, who is no longer with us? The truth is easier to see when the transition happens earlier, before the weight of life gets settled. The truth is there was never Drew and then Drusilla, and I've needed this walk to see and understand that for myself. We've been outside for eleven days, together every minute of every hour except when

I'm outside Tesco kicking my heels. In all that time Drusilla has never flickered, faded, disappeared to reveal a glimpse of poor, lonely Andrew from Lancashire. Never.

Getting tired, Dru has now stopped to explain something geological. Apparently there are three types of rock: igneous, sedimentary and metamorphic . . .

'Aha,' I interrupt, finger in the rainy air.

'Yes, the name gives it away.'

But my heart's not really in it. I know now that there was no great metamorphosis. Gender-reassignment surgery has recently been renamed as gender-confirmation surgery, and the new phrase more accurately describes what happens. The clothes and the lifestyle *are* superficial changes. Dru was a woman from the start.

'Previously, I felt like a freak and people treated me as normal' Dru says. 'Now I feel normal and people treat me like a freak.'

I want to tell the engine-room men, the feminists, the judge, myself: it's like the grammar, dummy. It's unusual but not incomprehensible. Don't waste anxiety on whether Dru is a new friend or an old friend, and where is Drew, and how does that work? Not applicable. She's not a schizo. Nor a psycho. She's been assessed by five different consultant psychiatrists, tested and certificated. There is no haze of crazy around Dru, now as then. She will not stab you in the shower. She is not a creature who on full moons would like to rip out your throat and bite the flesh from your bones.

Nevertheless, she must have been slightly wrong in the head. *I* would never have gone into that engine room, not in Dru's position, not in her clothes. What she did defies most of my deepest senses of self-preservation, but then she was looking after herself, not me. The danger to herself of not making the change must have been extreme, and in this difference between us a gap opens up. I don't understand her – they/we/I will never understand. Women are crazy.

Dru was trapped whatever she did: too feminine and she's constructing a pretence, too masculine and she's not trying hard enough. She's read or she's not read; it doesn't matter because either way she can't win.

On a bad day, transsexual women look so awful they're embarrassing. If only they'd go away.

On a good day, transsexual women look so convincing they're dangerous (they might *trick* us) – if only they'd go away.

Just go away. I mean look at you, you're on *Big Brother* and *Coronation Street* and in City Hall in Cambridge, and those are just the ones we *know* about.

So how many of them actually are there? No one knows the true figure, not even the Gender Trust who admit on their website that 'the rate of occurrence of transsexuality is not accurately known.'

I asked at the source.

'Mr Bellringer, is there any good reason to think they're taking over?'

My favourite sex-change surgeon sipped his tea, considered what I wanted, and replied in numbers. He and Mr Thomas each do about a hundred operations a year. There are roughly fifty operations performed elsewhere in the country and probably, in Mr Bellringer's estimation, about fifty abroad, mostly in Thailand. That's a total of 300 male-to-female gender-confirmation operations carried out on Britons every year.

'What about the total number living among us?'

Between 1966 and 1990, with surgical techniques and social attitudes still in development, Mr Bellringer tells me there were about twenty operations a year performed in the UK. From then until 1999 this increased to about thirty a year, and since 2000 to the 250 a year they're doing now. Add in a generous handful who may have had the operation privately since Roberta Cowell's breakthrough in 1951, and that gives a total of about 3,000 male-to-female transsexual British citizens. There are also those who've gone abroad. In Mr Bellringer's estimation, these would give an accepted figure of between 4,000 and 5,000. The Thai surgeons claim they've done 2,000 in the last five years alone, but Mr Bellringer calls this 'difficult to believe'.

So, about 4,000 to 5,000 post-operative male-to-female transsexual women living in Britain. And about 1,000 female-to-male transsexual men, but that's another story. The country is not being overrun, or to put these figures in perspective, there are about 1,000 more than that living in San Francisco.

As for the future, the numbers are increasing steadily, and show no signs of flattening out. During 2000, when Mr Bellringer started, there were 500 people referred to the NHS pathway. In 2007 there were 1,000, 800 of them male-to-female. Not everyone will make it past the psychiatrists or the reality of Real Life, but Charing Cross is looking to recruit new surgeons.

Personally, I think transphobia is less to do with numbers and more inspired by envy. If everyone could become what they wanted then the world would go to hell in a hand-basket. Except if it happened to me, obviously. In the meantime, not having everything I want remains a basic principle of life, a crabby, small-town belief that is quick to accuse anyone who begs to differ. You're not living in the real world. *Do yourself a favour.*

You could say it of the pre-operative Jan Morris, tuxed-up and young in her white convertible Rolls.

'You don't live in the real world, mate.'

You could say it of the post-operative Dru, with her bacon and egg baps and pints of Beck's.

Reality becomes a shrunken territory, a single, limited version of existence. It's the Real Life Experience in the engine room. It's envy of those who know better.

The shrivelled mind can't cope with Dru's hubris, the cosmological insolence of what she's put herself through. Shifting gender is, after all, a hobby of the gods. Even Thor, the European god of machismo, once changed sex. Physical transformation is a divine, elemental magic, and among earthlings it shouldn't be allowed. Dru has dared to be different, and can't expect congratulations. She should be tied to a rock and have her liver eaten daily by an eagle.

Dru has achieved the universal dream of a second chance, life in someone else's body, and in the engine room of a 7,000-ton ferry at fifty degrees centigrade with no news from home there can't be many ship's engineers who haven't wondered: life in the body of a shoreside harbour master, life in the body of the captain, in the body of Harrison Ford. You're not the only one, Dru. I, too, am dissatisfied and want to be different – a top writer, an elite husband, an astronaut – but I can't just go to my GP and get a referral and jump on the moving pathway.

I envy Dru her certainty. In *Myra Breckinridge* Gore

Vidal's transsexual heroine shrieks 'I know what I want and I know what I am.' Dru has had seven years' enviable clarity of purpose. She found an answer to the questions 'Who Am I? What Am I?' There *was* a big truth out there waiting.

She was prepared to defend it. Forced off the *Pride of Bilbao* by envy and hostility, Dru finally succumbed to the stress of resisting as long as she did. She couldn't face going back onboard, but even when she was lying at home barely able to move from emotional exhaustion, she kept hold of the difference between stress and surrender.

'They inflicted damage to my confidence and to . . . me. I wasn't the me they thought I was. Not a caricature, not a construct.'

Dru kept the fight going, insisting, with the help of an employment tribunal, on correct treatment. She went to work in a Gloucester tricycle factory, and won new battles over toilets and pronouns while preparing herself for the bigger confrontation with P&O, a company with 7,000 employees and a turnover of £1 billion. Dru went into the hearing without a lawyer. She won, was awarded £64,832 compensation, and had her picture in the *Daily Mail*:

Would you Adam and Steve it . . .

*

Walk on. The intermittent sunshine, the sea breeze, the birds and bees and flowers. The rock pipits, the alexanders and wintergreen, and long galleries of caves like halfway space between the shore and the sea.

Dru stops, not for the first time. I stop. She is making a very close study of a big stone at the side of the path.

'This is an interesting rock.'

It must be time to find somewhere to put up the tent.

'Like pumice, only harder.'

I keep us going for another hour or so, beyond the Strumble Head lighthouse, and Dru can take it. It's raining again and a gale blows in from the Irish Sea, but before long we come across the only sheltered, tent-sized flat space for miles in any direction. It is in front of reeds and a boulder, and we have a view over a dip in the cliffs to the ocean, a shallow V in which the dark sea churns slowly. We get the tent up in record time, experienced campaigners.

'We done well,' I say, enjoying the view from inside the shelter of the tent.

'Yes,' Dru replies, passing across the whiskey, 'yes we done.'

After we've eaten the pasties from the Goodwick Tesco, brewed up tea and shared more Powers from the flask, we get into our sleeping bags and watch the sea through the tent opening. Dru is rightly proud of making a stand against P&O, and the tribunal's concluding judgement is further confirmation that transition is not a deluded act of misplaced fantasy. Anyone who stubbornly contends otherwise is rejecting the authority of employment law, entire medical disciplines and everything Dru says. Why would I want to do that? Why would anyone else? Or, as we men say, usually with a view to starting some kind of a fight, *what's your problem?*

Ignorance: it can be cured.

XIII

Rain dashes my face
A splash of sun out at sea
Moves fast as the wind.

Dru is in and out of the tent from first light at about 5 a.m. She can hear wild beasts squealing.

'Fighting?'

'Yickering.'

We're camped on the edge of a cliff, the sea in front of us, and to each side a treeless landscape of stones and wind-stunted grass. The spray of dawn rain on the tent is like untuned radio waves, the pins and needles of noise.

'Go back to sleep, Dru.'

She unfolds herself from her sleeping bag and climbs outside, while I wonder how accurately tent nylon provides a gauge of the strength of rain. There's probably an equation to be written, measuring noise volume against water volume. Campers worldwide would salute this invention. We could call it the Tent Precipitation Index, or TPI for short. The brand name would be Tee-Pee Eye. We'd become rich.

This is a dream, and when I wake up Dru isn't back. I get the water going for tea, and before long she appears from the direction of the lighthouse. She's in a bit of a sulk. She hasn't managed to track the creatures that were making the noise.

'Probably fox cubs,' she says. 'If this was a proper book I'd have seen them.'

We have two days' walking to get to St David's, but already there's a sense of the journey coming to an end. We're lying on our elbows inside the tent, hands round steaming mugs, looking at the greys of mist and sea through the door's maroon arch.

'Dru, has your life been happy?'

'It's been muddled.'

Dru sips her tea, and it's lucky for both of us we have so much good ocean to catch the eye. 'And slightly directionless. I intend to make it different, of course.'

'Why are we going to St David's?'

'Enough people have found it significant for some of that to rub off on us. Maybe.'

The tent is sodden. We do as much packing up as we can inside, scrunch everything into the rucksacks except the tent itself. Dru gets out her mirror, does her make-up. The Amazon jungle reminds her to take her hormone pill. We do not listen to the news. I don't know why, but it's a habit Dru kicked, as if the threat of invasion receded once Britain had its first transsexual mayor.

We then climb out into the rain and dismantle the tent. I'm reminded of men and barbecues; if it's happening outside there's no end to what I'll do to help.

The rain sweeps up over the cliff in bands as wide as the next gust of wind, and this looks like it's going to be another

274

simple day. Follow the coast in the direction of St David's, get as far south as we can, possibly as far as Whitesands Bay. As we set off, I feel nostalgic for the mornings we've left behind, and I tell Dru I've decided that today I will photograph the shoes of every person we meet on the path. Given the weather, this hardly risks overloading the camera's memory.

One hour later, I have a single photograph of four pairs of very wet walking boots belonging to a German family – mum, dad, daughter, boyfriend – who were camping in the field attached to the Pwll Deri youth hostel. In their drenched shoes, the dad is hoping his daughter will speak to him before Milford Haven. The boyfriend is thinking of a girl called Gudrun who likes beaches. The mum is thinking the last boyfriend was better. The daughter wants to know why a stranger is taking a photograph of her feet.

I started with Dru's shoes, the low-cut brown suede KSBs. I'm looking at the photo as I write. It's a reminder that I never could put myself in Dru's shoes, not really, though I did try.

Before setting out on the walk, I decided I should dress up in women's clothes. I wasn't intending to go anywhere or do anything (that's what they all say), just try on a few items in private with no one else around. It seemed a practical addition to my pre-walk reading, an attempt to get closer to the idea of becoming Drusilla. I opened the door of the wardrobe, quite glad that in our flat we don't have closets, and looked at my wife's skirts and dresses hanging on the rail. Too small. I opened drawers, looked at tops, slips, pants. Shut the drawers. Closed the door of the wardrobe. Don't be such a girl, I thought. And also: that's not going to help. Putting on women's clothes was simply not something I had any urge to do. It was absurd.

There's a point at which I can't get into Dru's shoes. The best I can do, as a friend, is to stand alongside and be interested, because empathy only goes so far. To the doors of Ward 4 South in Charing Cross Hospital, for example. I can't begin to imagine what it's like to go into hospital for the removal of my testicles and the erectile tissue of my penis, retaining the skin and scrotum to line a vagina in a hole excavated between my rectum and my prostate. Not only that, but also to be looking forward to it.

I went to visit Dru in hospital on the day she was admitted. After six years of living as a woman, five psychiatrists, one employment tribunal and a year on the waiting list for surgery, in October 2006 Dru finally arrived within sight of the end. It was a Sunday afternoon, and her operation was scheduled for the next day. I got lost.

Found the hospital alright, down the Fulham Palace Road from Hammersmith Tube station, but on a Sunday afternoon the reception hall was deserted. I wandered past many paintings that Dru had once told me were good, and some exotic fish in a huge circular tank. A porter was mopping the seats of some chairs, but he didn't speak English, so I made a guess at the most likely signs and ended up at the Sexual Health Centre. Wrong place, and it was closed.

I did some trial and error, rode some lifts, hesitated about asking anyone in case I got the terminology wrong. Trans-sexual men, women, people, patients. Candidates?

Another lift, round a corner, along a corridor. I find Dru in a four-bed side ward. It is mixed sex, the other patients either waiting for surgery or just coming round. I'd been expecting a dedicated gender department, but across from Dru there's an old lady reading the *Sunday Times*. Next to Dru's bed is an unconscious man with a shaved head and black stubble, and diagonally across a woman called Juliette who might be a man. I don't know. I'm not going to ask. She's wearing surgical stockings, and has an odd stoop to her back. The bones of her spine show through the cotton of her hospital gown but otherwise she's pretty and just back from theatre, so normal signals don't apply. She looks like somebody with whom something has gone wrong. Of course she does. She's in hospital.

Dru is lying on the bed closest to the window but she hasn't undressed. There doesn't seem to be anyone around to tell her what to do. So she waits, in a purple, woolly cardigan, a black dress, and her trusty flat round-toed shoes. On the bedside table, neatly stacked, are Dru's books for the week. *Parallel Lines*, Stevenson's *Kidnapped*, a poetry anthology, and the *Pickwick Papers*. There is also a small bottle of Dr Bach's Rescue Remedy, which Dru has taken a couple of times in the last week to keep panic attacks at bay. That and red wine.

She has a Steiff teddy bear, bought some time ago in the gift shop on the *Pride of Bilbao*.

'He's a lovely bear,' I say, not knowing anyone who finds hospital conversations a breeze.

'He's a she,' Dru tells me. 'Her name is Orsa.'

Right. I remember to fret about pronouns for soft toys. Dru shares the bear with her daughter, who sleeps with it (her – Orsa) whenever she comes to stay.

The man in the next bed is wheeled out because his condition is deteriorating.

Dru is very calm, I think. Or perhaps mildly changeable like weather: mostly calm with a touch of dread. She's come so far and yet still, in one sense, has travelled nowhere. The blood-pressure machine doesn't work.

Dru tells me about the last time she was in hospital, in Portsmouth, after being assaulted by football hooligans. They called themselves the 657 crew, after the time of the London train for all connections to a traditional English bash-up.

'Got to get up early to be a football hooligan,' Dru says, but her mind's elsewhere. I get her to tell the story anyway – the 657 crew asked her the time, she looked at her watch, was headbutted and woke up in hospital. They must have been very proud.

'Men!' I say, shaking my head.

I don't know why we had to talk about something else, but we did. Now that's out of the way, I can ask Dru about the websites I've seen where post-operatives compare the work of the NHS surgeons. Full-colour photographs are uploaded to illustrate cosmetic results, and I want to know if Dru has ever looked at these pictures. She hasn't.

'I've seen enough fannies on calendars at work.'

She has no preference for one surgeon or the other. Not bothered. She thought she was going to get Mr Bellringer, but it turns out it will probably be Mr Thomas. Why would Dru be fussed?

Nurse Louise Ball rescues us. She is very kind and reassuring, as nurses are meant to be. Dru at last gets some instructions, and starts organising herself to get changed and settled.

I offer to fetch something from the shop downstairs. I want to do something. Act, don't think. A paper, *Marie Claire*?

'And some Murray mints,' Dru adds, when I'm at the door.

'Sure?'

'Too good to hurry mints.'

By the time I get back, Dru is in bed. Preparations have started, and the tubes for a catheter have been fixed to the side of the bed. Dru is impressed by the mechanism, and explains how it works, pointing out various valves and bits of plastic as she does so. I instantly forget everything she says.

The old woman opposite has been replaced by an old man, who sits in his pyjamas scratching his balls. In the neighbouring bed there's another new patient, a man who's been beaten up in Kensington. A collection of veiled Muslim women are clustered round the bedside. The doctors close the curtains to examine his genitals – he's been kicked in the groin.

Hospital. What a sickening place to be.

When it's time to go I stand up and say, 'See you later in the week then.'

It seems important to insist on a future, one in which everything must have turned out fine. There's no point asking Dru if she's confident, because I doubt I'm the person who now could help her through. I can't think of any magic question to make her open up, so I kiss her on both cheeks and squeeze her shoulder. Nurse Ball smiles at me on the way out.

Much later, after the operation, after our motorised Sundays in the Morris Traveller, even after the end of the walk, I realise that the secret with Dru is to find the magic question. Like the last time she visited her mum in hospital, when I felt there was more she had to say. I'd left her on her tenth birthday at her mother's bedside, clutching the plastic Airfix plane she had glued together that morning. Yet the moment seemed lighter than the weight it should carry.

'What kind of plane was it?'

By way of answer, Dru sent me this poem, written after her father died. I just had to ask about the plane.

I did not know it then, of course, but it was the last time
                                                    I saw you.
It was just after my birthday, and I brought my model
                                                    aeroplane to show you.
It was a Bristol Britannia.
It wasn't the aeroplane I would have chosen, but I
                                                    suppose father was preoccupied.
I should have preferred to bring you a Spitfire, a purer
                                                    flying machine,
So that you would recognise the fighter ace in me.

You were pale and tired, in the hospital bed,
But you gave me a brave smile
As any fighter ace should,
Preparing for a sortie.

Now I think of those days out on the Moss,
Me sitting behind you on the bicycle
Afraid that my feet might get caught in the wheel,
But mostly happy and safe so close to you
While big brother rode on ahead.

And above the flat Lancashire countryside,
With its sudden smells of ditches and chicken manure
                                                    and cabbage,
A vast world of sky
Made brilliant by the ascending lark.

In the bad old days, those with gender dysphoria were discarded with the homosexuals, lost in the unsorted scrap of mentally ill people who required treatment. Now both groups vigorously stick up for themselves. Homosexuals are not ill and don't require any treatment, thank you very much. Transsexuals, on the other hand, are perfectly sane and they *still* require treatment.

The operation isn't a cure. Mr Bellringer was quite clear about this, telling me that the surgeons offer what his mentor Mike Royle called 'an operation and a chance to be happy'. Unable to put myself in Dru's hospital slippers, too squeamish to pull on a pair of women's underpants, I couldn't help but ask whether the operation was really necessary. Aren't there less drastic ways to make life easier for people with gender dysphoria?

'There could be,' Mr Bellringer said, sitting forward on his sofa. 'The best cure would be a tablet. The patient would take it and then think: "This being a bloke thing is good, innit?"' But it's not going to happen, because gender dysphoria isn't cancer and nobody is actively working on the tablets. This isn't because the condition is insignificant.

Mr Bellringer often answers questions about his job, and sometimes makes appearances on national TV. He's not evangelical about it, he says, but there are misconceptions that need correcting, even inside the medical profession. Mr Bellringer knows that some doctors think gender-confirmation surgery a trivial procedure, and a 'sizeable minority' of nurses would prefer to avoid contact with patients, usually objecting on religious grounds, which is against the law.

'Mostly they're frightened, but often they come round when they see that the patients aren't a bunch of hare-brained lunatics. Then they get to share the immense levels of satisfaction felt by the genders.'

Mr Bellringer refers to his patients as 'genders' like other surgeons have 'hearts' or 'hips'. The satisfaction ratings among his genders outperform every other surgical procedure, including replacement hip surgery where the patient may have suffered extreme discomfort for years on end.

'Sex changes are not frivolous,' Mr Bellringer says. 'The aim is to relieve a major period of significant unhappiness.'

In most cases, it is specifically the operation that achieves this. Jan Morris insists there's something other-worldly involved – 'I had myself long seen in my quest some veiled spiritual purpose, as though I was pursuing a Grail or grasping Oneness' – but I'm stuck on the practicalities, the facts of castration. I'm thinking about a penis and testicles, the full, slightly greasy set, and then a mad lunge forward with a scalpel.

I look at Mr Bellringer, family man, cyclist, dog owner, and ask him how he got into this business.

'Twenty years ago I'd never have dreamt of it. I specialised in other urological procedures, a bit of erectile dysfunction.'

He was then identified as someone who was psychologically capable of doing the work. In other words, he's a no-nonsense operator, a prop forward for the Civil Service rugby club, benching in league fixtures for the first team even at the age of forty-nine. He is not a mad *Doctor Who* professor or a high-tech agent of the patriarchy.

'It's a job,' he says, but I can see he doesn't believe this, and neither do I. It's not true that somebody has to do it. It's only done and done well because there are highly competent surgeons who strongly believe it's the right thing to do.

'There was also the challenge, and this is a big surgical procedure which is mine.'

It's a field in which a surgeon can be creative, ambitious, a little vain, proud of his work in the best possible way.

'What do you do with the testicles, afterwards?'

'We throw them away.'

'No!'

'There's a tissue bank at Hammersmith that's full up. No room left. We've got enough frozen genitals for the next twenty years.'

Even at this late stage Mr Bellringer or his colleague Mr Thomas can turn a patient away. It is very rare, but Mr Bellringer recently sent back one gender who had sex as a man in the week before an appointment for surgery.

For the rest, until the very last moment, there is the terror of being rousted out of bed and sent back down the path. After all that effort, with the end so close, at exactly the moment I and James Bond are praying for precisely such a last-minute reprieve. What feels right for Dru feels for me like the penultimate disaster, the most unnatural of acts, not that acting naturally is always commendable.

As a boy growing up in Swindon, nearly all the 'natural' and possibly male-bonding interludes in my suburban upbringing were provided by Mr LeCoyte at Number 1. These experiences were nearly all disgusting and/or painful. His son Adrian, my friend, broke my arm and shot me in the head with an air rifle. We were boys. It was only natural.

Because Mr LeCoyte was in close contact with the natural world, he kept a shotgun and a fishing rod in the back of his

Peugeot 504 estate. He once found a deer dying on the side of a road, brought it home, and had me and Adrian help gut it as it hung upside down on a rope from a tree in his garden. We were eleven years old and learning the natural relationship of man and his prey, the split and steaming carcass, the stench of the grassy innards.

Another time, while poaching for salmon, we caught some eels. We brought them back alive, in a Tupperware box. Mr LeCoyte put a gaff hook through the lower jaw of the first eel and hung it from a line in his garage. He then made an incision with a sharp knife in the eel's skin just below the head. He got a pair of pliers and pulled the grey skin away from the flesh, far enough to get a good hold with his fingers. He then handed us the pliers, grabbed hold of the eel skin with both hands, and stripped the skin off the flesh of the squirming, living eel.

This is essentially the same technique as is used in the second step of a vaginoplasty.

*

The rain eases for a moment and we find a cove where a fat brown seal is lying on a rock close to where we can make tea and share the final Ginsters pasty. It starts raining again, which means walking again, no stopping, and we risk getting truly miserable, tramping one of the finest routes in Britain without seeing it.

We're rescued by an enchanted tea shop. It's uncanny, but at about teatime it appears out of nowhere in the brick storehouse of an old slate-quarry port. Shop downstairs; tea shop upstairs. I have scones and cream. Then I have scones and cream again. Dru has a slice of bara brith, and criticises the paintings of fish on the walls. We may stay here forever.

We don't, because as on every other day it turns out that Dru *can* hack it, even though I keep giving her the option to stop.

'Now I just want to get there,' she says, when on several occasions I wouldn't have minded stopping. Dru insists on keeping going, and I never really doubted she could make the walk, any more than when I left Charing Cross on the Sunday evening I thought she'd flinch from the operation.

Women are tough. I've seen childbirth. Now I also know a woman who had the courage to have her testicles removed and her penis skinned. Whatever the limits of my will, I'll reach them well before Dru does, because right from the start she knew how bad it could be.

The pain of the operation is a recurring feature of the autobiographical journeys. April Ashley tells of the days immediately afterwards, when 'she was soggy all the time. My middle was grotesquely swollen and bound inches deep with bandages into which blood continuously spilt and congealed.' Renée Richards, who had her operation in 1975, describes 'an overwhelming awareness of pain. My torso was afflicted with several different kinds. Sharp, shooting pains of searing intensity came from my now non-existent penis and testicles. It was as if someone were repeatedly poking a firebrand into my groin. Mixed with this was a tearing sensation; it was as though someone were ripping at my organs with a pair of pliers. Underneath these sharp aspects was a dull, sickish ache such as you might have if someone had beaten you with a baseball bat in the area of your lower back. Beneath the ache was a pervasive sense of pressure, as if something inside me were enlarging, pushing outward.'

Surgical techniques have improved, but these were the hazards marked on the map by those who'd been here before. Dru was not discouraged, even when Mr Bellringer went through the risks with her one last time. The urethra, the bladder and the rectum can be damaged. A fistula (passage) can open between the rectum and the vagina, allowing for leakage of faeces from one to the other. A colostomy bag is sometimes needed.

Reached the limits of the will yet? There's a risk of infection and internal bleeding, the neoclitoris may die, the urethra may heal shut, the skin taken from the penis and scrotum may lack a sufficient blood supply and shrink, perish, and in the worst cases fall out of the space between the rectum and prostate.

The limit of Dru's will? Can't even *see* it from here. I can't imagine her courage.

*

On the Wednesday, I'm back at Charing Cross.

Dru is . . . radiant.

There is no other word. She is elated and rosy-cheeked, bright-eyed and interested in everything going on in Ward 4 South. She's been moved into a women's ward, a mixture of three ancient, East End crones and four post-operative trans-sexuals. There is a wartime spirit at work, the elderly Londoners and the gender-confirmed women getting on famously and bailing each other out. Fruit and magazines are being shared. Dru has donated *Parallel Lines* to the small ward library, and when no visitors come the women shuffle up and down making visits amongst themselves.

It's almost bonfire night and in the far window, directly opposite Dru's bed, we can see fireworks. There is the flash and fall, and then some time later, the bang. Dru lists the various tubes that have already been removed, and utterly fails to describe how much she enjoyed the morphine.

Looking around, I'm glad to see that a dislike of sport is not a key indicator for gender dysphoria. A policewoman is wearing her Barcelona shirt while being visited by her football team. Another of the new women looks like Neil from *The Young Ones*. She has a shambling nightgown and a receding hairline and reeks of defiance and stubborn indifference, of not living happily ever after. She has no visitors and is taking a *Woman and Home* across the ward to lend to one of the Blitz survivors.

'Thank you most kindly. What did you say your name was?'

'Alison.'

The old lady looks for her glasses and sucks on her false teeth, opens the magazine and licks her finger. She is tremendously unconcerned.

'Alison. That's a funny name for a bloke.'

All week, Mr Bellringer has been conducting the post-operative ward rounds. His reputation goes before him, and on Dru's first day after theatre he greets her cheerily:

'You've heard about the cycling shorts, I suppose?'

Sheet up to her nose, Dru nods. Bellringer knows they look strange, but then what else is he supposed to wear? He likes cycling. He cycles to work.

'I'm Lance Armstrong with a few more pounds.'

In his tight Lycra cycle shorts, on the first day after the operation, he and Lisa the gender nurse peel back what Dru describes as 'a large and bloody nappy'. They make admiring noises.

'No, really,' Dru says. 'They did.'

Next the drains come out, and finally the packing that stops the new vagina from collapsing. It makes Dru laugh, because the packing is a tape that appears, and goes on and on appearing, like a red ribbon from a magician's hat.

On the last day, Mr Bellringer gives his considered expert opinion – 'all well and with good depth.' Dru is delighted, and as she gingerly gathers her belongings she's reminded of seafaring days: gear stowed, ready to pay off, waiting for the gangway to be lowered. All she has to do is prove she can pee twice on her own and then she can leave.

Many women suffer from complications, but Dru is not one of these women. She is lucky, and this must feel reassuring, as if it was meant to be. She is also emotional. 'It's quite a highly charged time, coming to terms with a new geography that looks a bit like a road accident.'

With a mirror, when the swelling finally goes down, she gets to inspect what's there. 'I realised I just didn't know my way around, let alone the names for what I could see.' She doesn't know where anything is, and only finds out back in Bristol when she borrows a copy of *The V Book*. She learns about the vagina, the vulva, the vestibule. I find this endearing, and not so alarming. Dru didn't take the journey because she preferred the design ('*So much more elegant. Put me down for one of those.*') It's like her failure to notice that men carry daypacks, or not giving much thought to her name. Her driving energy was more essential, more elemental:

because it was an expression of her true self, it didn't change who she was.

She remains the kind of person who sticks it out, as I do. We plug on for more than twenty miles carrying our sodden fifteen-kilo rucksacks, determined to make the beach at Whitesands. On the final miserable slog there are nearly always flashes of white in our peripheral vision, the waves booming in caves and shattering on rocks below. The path becomes a series of streams, then a constant river, except in the rare places where the path is flat and the brown rain settles. Welsh rain is like snow. When it's heavy it sticks.

Somewhere close the Grail is buried. In at least one of the stories it's up one or another of these hills, their tops hidden in mist. Close up we can see pale rocks and green moss, and hear the white noise of hard rain on our rain-hoods.

Maybe it could have been better another way, with another destination. I think of Prestatyn. This is another of the unknowable questions, or it would be if I wasn't so literal-minded. After we get back I look up the weather in Prestatyn on exactly this day, when we walked through rain from morning into night. As I suspected: rain over Prestatyn. Possibly worse.

With Whitesands Bay in sight as a pale blur in the downhill distance, I check that Dru's okay. We've had an epic day's walk and it would be good to know there aren't any ows in unmentionable places. She says she's fine, looking forward to getting there, putting the tent up. Having a swig of Powers.

'Does all your equipment,' I'm searching for the right words, since this is a subject that's been on my mind. I want to get my meaning across without sounding smutty. 'Does all your equipment work as efficiently as you'd like?'

'Yes,' Dru says without hesitation, and I'm amazed at how definite she is. No 'up to a point.' No 'to a certain extent.' It must feel wonderful to know that everything turned out well, a complicit wink from a benign destiny.

'Except the shoes,' Dru adds, 'they've been letting the water in.'

XIV

Motley old weather;
I rove the sky and light on
The hoped-for rainbow.

The beach at Whitesands Bay is within easy walking reach of the city of St David's. The next morning Dru has already been out and about, but she gave up when it started raining again and is now back in the tent and asleep. I poke my head outside.

Mist stubbornly obscures the hill that, in some of the myths, covers the Holy Grail. This is not how the end was supposed to be, but I think yes, we have no rose-tinted dawns, yes we have no sunbeams. I pull on damp socks, lace my heavy, drenched shoes, and, beneath the gloomy clouds, go for a maudlin walk along the gunmetal beach, thinking about a girl from twenty years ago and wondering if she's still the same. If I am. It's quite enjoyable. I do it twice.

Back at the tent Dru is awake and looking glum.

'I was *so* sure the sun would be out.'

Me too. Last night we were wet and used up, but confident

from forecasts and a principled optimism that the morning would bring new hope and sky-blue skies.

'I thought we'd earned a perfect arrival,' Dru moans. 'But at five there was rain in the air and a howling gale. All I could think was oh no, I'll never be dry and warm ever again.'

She wraps the top of her sleeping bag around her shoulders. This is unlike her.

'Of course you will,' I say, because that's what people say.

We pack up slowly, preparing ourselves for St David's and civilisation. The rain holds off and Dru practises the voice, but her body also has a memory and sometimes it refuses to forget. If her voice squeaks, and single words slip out sharp and scratched, she automatically clears her throat.

'Laa!' Good. Cough.

'Oh God.' Low. Bad.

'We can get some coffee,' I suggest, meaning that should perk us up. 'We can sit at a table that isn't a rock, in a place which has four walls and a roof and where if we pay good money someone may bring us cake.' This is meant to be encouraging. 'We could make a start on some of the recommended portions of fruit and vegetables we've missed over the last two weeks. Fourteen times five a day.'

'Let's say seventy,' Dru says. 'I could murder a salad.'

For yesterday's epic walk we survived on the following provisions between two:

4 toffee waffles
1 Ginsters Cornish pasty
2 Scotch eggs
2 cheese and ham rolls
1 flapjack

2.5 Mars Bars

2 scones cream and jam

1 slice bara brith fruitcake

4 litres tea

2 litres water

2 dl Powers whiskey

That was a day without a sit-down meal. If we'd found somewhere to stop and eat, we could have had all that and chips too.

In the days when two pilgrimages to St David's were worth one to Rome, if you made it to Rome you could ask for almost anything. As we fold the sopping tent, probably for the last time, I ask Dru what she's going to ask for, what intercession she feels she needs.

'What do you mean?'

'Well that's what happens at the end of a pilgrimage. You get to the shrine or whatever and you pray, you ask for something. What are you going to ask for?'

We're out on the road and walking towards St David's before Dru answers.

'It's a bit muddled,' she says.

She's wearing her special-occasion dress, because the end and St David's cathedral counts as a special occasion. It would look better without the yellow coat and the rucksack, though for the last leg she's packed away her walking shoes and is wearing her red-laced flatties.

'Can you unmuddle it?'

'Possibly. But not in my head at the moment.'

Thanks, Dru. She's going to refuse me any epiphanies, right to the very end. Her life hasn't been simple and she isn't going to pretend it is just because I make a point of asking. The cloud cover remains grey and low and the weather refuses to brighten. Come on, sun, for narrative reasons. But the sun does not come on.

There's a direct road from Whitesands inland to St David's, but the city itself is off our map and we get lost after distrusting the straightness of the road. We flag down a car and ask. What the hell. Then we're back in the right direction, claret-stalked nettles at every gatepost, skylarks in the air.

'I want the strength to get on with things,' Dru says.

'*Things?*'

'Yes. Things.'

'Would these be things other than the sex-change thing?'

'They would.'

This changing-sex business wolfs up the time. The pathway takes years, and the process itself has been getting in the way of the person Dru wants to be, someone characterised by competence, enterprise, and adventurousness. These are the qualities I've always admired in Dru, though I know her competence is both infinite and limited. I wouldn't trust her to make any repair that would last a lifetime, but I'd trust her absolutely to be able to repair her repair when it broke.

Her resourcefulness is surely going to help with whatever happens next, because if changing sex had ever been Dru's sole objective in life, she would now have nothing left to live for. In that sense, the standard jolly Hollywood transsexual story – 'we are among the few people in the world who have overcome obstacles and fulfilled their lifelong dreams' – can never end happily. After the operation, there's nowhere else to go.

'Do you actually *want* a new objective?'

'It seems kind of alien to me,' Dru admits. 'Apart from happiness.'

Everyone wants that. This is the prayer everyone makes, and the value of prayer isn't dependent on the existence of a god (though a god would possibly help). More pragmatically, prayer encourages abstract notions into words, helping us clearly to see what it is we're missing.

'Some material well-being, to make life easier. A secure and good place to live.'

Dru's hopes for the future invariably involve her daughter, family added to home, what we instinctively recognise as the core of every life, the centre. It feels disappointing yet true that Dru can't answer, bright-eyed and popsterish, 'Yes! I'm happier all the time! Now and for ever! Amen!' There's something irresistibly sincere about her doubts, and about the fact that she hasn't changed in any meaningful way. Apart from the cock and the balls, obviously, which are not that meaningful. The feminists are right – gender isn't so important.

'I want people to treat me as the same person *and* as a woman.'

'Is that your prayer?'

'I'm not doing bullet points for God.'

'But you feel the same?'

'The same.'

'But happier?'

'Yes.'

As the same person and as a woman. It's unusual but not incomprehensible, and after a fortnight together I think I see how it's done: the objection that a man can never become a woman is to look at this completely the wrong way round.

Dru is a woman. She was then exposed to vigorous and unrelenting male conditioning.

If more girls, without knowing what they were supposed to like or dislike, were exposed to RAF glider flights and motorcycle mechanics and naval engineering they would find the fun in each activity and acquit themselves well, just as Dru did. Nobody should worry for the femininity of these girls, or for their sense of themselves as women. You can even encase a young girl in a boy's body and give her male genitals and the woman inside survives. Place every obstacle in that girl's path and she will do everything a boy can do, yet the girl will still insist, sooner or later, on becoming known.

The transgender experience demonstrates that girlness and boyness are fantastically resilient. *And* it proves the strength of cultural conditioning. Dru doesn't identify with the maleness of the pasty and the pint and the full cooked breakfast. Her upbringing allowed her to enjoy these things (as a misread boy), and now as a woman she appreciates the pintness and the pastiness and the fried breakfastness, pleasures pure in themselves. As do many other women the world over.

Dru has always been Dru, and her basic interests now are the same as they always were. It is not 1955, and unlike poor Roberta Cowell she is not obliged to give up engines for more 'feminine' interests – 'Cooking was unexpectedly exciting.' Dru always liked cooking, but she also likes camping and outdoor pursuits and fixing stuff. She'll allow men to help her lift her canoe on to the roof rack of the Morris Traveller, but only if they're passing and they offer. If no man comes along, she'll do it herself.

Dru is a girl who likes boy things who was mistakenly born in a boy's body. Her pain was therefore less immediately evident. She's keen on machines and comforting nourishment but is neither emotionally articulate nor especially interested in other people. Dru is not the only woman on earth like this, but no wonder it took a little while to straighten things out.

That's it. That's my conclusion. Dru is a girl who likes boy things who was born into a boy's body. Her earlier life is not darkened by a desperate shadow, and she has the integrity of not being or feeling like two people split cleanly by a hello-goodbye medical procedure. There was never a hidden Drusilla aching to overcome a miserable Drew, and Dru's personality has not miraculously blossomed as Drusilla. She is different but the same, the same but a woman, and her femininity is no more or less a mystery than anyone else's. Women are infinitely varied, so varied that some women start out as men, just as at Charing Cross there are also men who start out as women.

We know that femaleness is neither defined by sexual orientation, nor the ability to carry a child, nor a liking for salads and cats. The uterus does not compete directly with the brain for an adequate blood supply, and chromosomes do not determine an ability to knit or squeal at the sight of a spider. But there is something essential and indivisible about what we mean by 'female', by 'male', and whatever it is, Dru's experience shows that it will insist on its right to be recognised.

She's still learning, becoming her own woman in her own time, adapting not just to the change of external gender but going from anonymous-looking person to striking-looking person. Broad and strong-faced, she will improve at this, developing strategies as effectively as the rough and bluff members of the Raglan History Society, openly checking out restaurants with strangers and insisting on the right size of glass for sherry.

No one wants to be invisible, Dru included, and in the streets of Bristol people look at her all the time, not because she once lived as a man but because she drives a 1971 Morris Traveller. People will carry on looking, and not always kindly, as long as her behaviour remains fluid, moving back and forth between fixed perceptions of gender – the frocks and the mascara but also the Beck's, the bacon sarnies, the open-air farting and, probably, small-tent camping with a man who is not her brother or a partner. How much she gives up on the one hand and takes up on the other is up to her, but she shouldn't *have* to let go of anything, any more than any other woman.

This is where the real world intervenes. I asked Dru for an example of something she'd had to give up, and she mentioned a truck-stop café near Cirencester.

'Last time I was in there I felt uncomfortable,' she said. 'And that's the end of that.'

In the meantime I admire her for holding on, enjoying life out on the hills, sometimes with a deep voice, and when she feels like it with Ginsters pasties and a fine disregard for vitamins. Because you know what? It's not all bad being a boy. It's not *always* worse than death.

She has no sense of belonging to a third gender, a powerful space beyond the limiting boundaries of maleness and femaleness, but seeing as I had an available expert, I did ask Mr Bellringer what he made of Bornstein's idea.

'There has been a bit of interest in this neutral gender,' he said, but then he reminded me of the male-to-female brains cut open in Holland and found to contain biologically recognisable female patterns. 'I personally don't think there is a neutral gender.'

For Dru there are men and there are women, and to me it seems there are few people better placed to have an opinion. She's been through it, and that's what she thinks.

'Do you have any regrets?'

'No.'

Dru is not among the 1.7 per cent of people who go through surgery and then wish they hadn't. Compared to most other clinical procedures this is a tiny failure rate ('I can count those who want a reversal in ones,' Mr Bellringer told me), though the few who do have regrets can always attract attention. Five former transgender patients recently gave evidence at a GMC inquiry into the professional conduct of Dr Russell Reid, the gender psychiatrist who first prescribed hormones to Dru. Reid was reprimanded for 'lack of caution'. That was the newspaper story I read at Ian's house in Presteigne – **'Sex-change doctor guilty of misconduct'**, but Dru, like the majority of Reid's patients, is a staunch supporter.

'Everyone should take responsibility for their own actions,' she says. 'No one *forced* them to go and see Reid.'

'So no regrets of any kind?'

'Lots.'

'I mean about this.'

'I will never be shapely and beautiful.'

'Meaning?'

'Sexually active.'

It would have been better for Dru to make the change younger, as with any biological glitch – if your child has a birth defect, you seek help as soon as you can. This doesn't mean that Dru would never have seen the inside of a ship's engine room. She can't be 'cured' of being the person she is, but right from the start she'd have belonged to the engine room as Ms Drusilla Marland, MN. She is an extraordinary woman.

'Do you miss your brothers?'

'No.'

'Even though you may never see them again?'

'It's in my past.'

Dru was the only child to take the alternative route. Her brothers are army and engineers, and Dru is now only in contact with the youngest. She broke off with the others after her dad's funeral.

'It was always me who was calling.'

Isn't it always? Dru sees her two nieces, in their mid-twenties, and her girl cousins, because it's the girls who stay in touch.

We walk into St David's past a church hall with smashed windows and a chipboarded door. Our first sight of the ancient city centre is the square bell-tower in the mist, and we have to make an effort not to be sucked down the hill towards the cathedral. We exchange morning mornings with an elderly gent in a kilt and a turquoise velvet shirt. He is on a cycling holiday, and this kind of random eccentricity is partly why we liked St David's the last time round. Also for the powerboat trip that bumps across Ramsey Sound beside the offshore rocks called The Bitches – the boat has an all-woman crew.

In a coffee shop we lounge on sofas upstairs. Dru criticises the artwork for a change. I prop myself next to a narrow window and watch the street and the wonderful girls of St

David's go by. We get more coffee, and Dru leans forward over the low table, about to write on a piece of paper I ripped from my notebook. She scratches her head with the end of the pen, almost writes again. She wants to jot down her requests for St David, to be ready when we get to the cathedral. So far the paper is blank.

I take this opportunity, like every other opportunity, to look her over. I try to see what other eyes might see, rather than the Dru I know, and I'm reminded of a joke on the US gender scene about the three phases of male-to-female transition. Step 1: Hey, that guy looks a little weird. Step 2: Hey, that person looks *really* weird. Step 3: Whoa, that chick is ugly!

There is also a Step 4 – no one bats an eye. And Dru, I think, can shift between all four of these. This is why she gets so antsy when she hasn't had time to get ready, when we've spent too long outdoors.

She wants to be at Step 4 all the time, and the women in the Internet support groups call it Stealth. Deep Stealth (as the girls capitalise it) is when nobody knows and nobody is told, but I don't find this terminology very helpful. It suggests hiding, creeping about, getting away with it, when there is no invisible man to hide.

Dru still hasn't written anything down.

'Is deep stealth your objective?'

'I want to be as stealth as possible, but not to hide anything from people I'm close to. I want to be viable.'

That seems a better word, where viability includes the achievement of not having disintegrated, not having cracked up.

The problem with deep stealth is that effort and anxiety are no guarantee of happiness. A perfect cover is like Hollywood's version of the Witness Protection Scheme. A pleasant fantasy (Act 1), with a mown lawn and roses on a trellis, but in the film version and perhaps in life, too, the past always catches up (Act 2). And then (Act 3) it's betrayal and violence and tragedy.

Faces don't lie – Dru is a woman for whom something has gone wrong. Which was that she lived the first forty-three years of her life as a man. This past that is readable in her face will never entirely fade. This is her story, and for anyone who takes the trouble to look closely enough, the story in this book is the one her face will tell.

I want to say I'm sorry. It must be horrible and tiresome having people look all the time, having *me* look all the time. Christ, *I* wouldn't like that, to be looked over so closely by someone like me. Which is why I don't often do it. I will shave off my beard as soon as we get back. I won't think twice.

*

It's hard to predict how for Dru, in the long run, it's going to turn out. Many transgender women choose not to respond to follow-up medical questionnaires, and decline invitations to transgender gatherings. They don't want to be defined all their lives by this one aspect of themselves, and Jan Morris (who else?) pioneered an attitude of utter disdain for post-operative curiosity. Academics writing for an interview could receive a one-sentence reply – 'When I hear the word *gender* I reach for my pistol.'

This is the ideal ending, when any of Mr Bellringer's or Mr Thomas's patients can stop thinking and hearing the word gender. Can stop explaining themselves to themselves; at that point the illness is finished.

I've had glimpses of this already. I like it when Dru relaxes, and on good days refers to Charing Cross as Tranny Central. I like it when she calls this book *Travels with a Tranny*. But I can also understand, in what is still a new and fragile world, that she doesn't want to concede any unnecessary ground. It's important not to offer the enemy any openings, at the risk of forgetting, sometimes, that not everyone is the enemy.

In the short term, our walk will soon be over, and with it the temporary relief that living outside can bring. The simplicity of camping and walking appeals to an instinct we all have and increasingly know to be true – stop *worrying*. But the benefits gradually fade, and Dru has to go back to the flat, the flatmate, the routines of mornings in Waitrose, lunch at Lello's Pure Pasta in Bristol Market, the pale green interior of the Morris Traveller. She can look forward to visits from her daughter, the adventures that arise from a native sense of adventure, and the female virtues of relatedness and support as offered by the TS crew who live in the computer, gangs of middle-aged gals with colourful pasts.

She'll also be looking for a job, applying for interviews as Dru and not as a privileged shaman of the third gender. Recently she's been illustrating books for a Bristol publisher. 'Today, local history,' she once told me, 'tomorrow . . . more local history.'

She does some cleaning, getting other people's houses shipshape for the Captain's Inspection, but sometimes she forgets she needs money. In her last job she cleaned fifteen hours in exchange for a Mirror dinghy. She has applied, unsuccessfully, for work as assistant curator at the Bristol

Industrial Museum, as a paramedic, as an assistant at both the Central and Branch libraries, as a temp for Bristol City Council, as part-time assistant at the Bristol Museum and for what she called the 'dog-drowning job' as Bristol Docks duty officer.

This is the everyday life Dru will return to, but Dru doesn't really do everyday, or not in the sense that every day should be the same. In our twenty-four hours in Bristol for packing the rucksacks, her everyday included popping round the corner and fixing her publisher's bicycle brakes. She then recommended her neighbour solve the problem of a cracked wall with waterproof concrete and a drain, and returned a call to the not very bright friend who bought the Sierra with advice on how to change a clutch cable.

What is she supposed to do? Pretend that she doesn't know these things?

Even Jan Morris eventually concedes that in the early years she exaggerated the demands of femininity. *Pleasures of a Tangled Life* is her second, less well-known book of memoirs. She calls it the 'obverse' of *Conundrum*, a companion book about the happy side of her life.

> There was a time when, new to life as a woman, I tried to forget that I had ever lived as a man, but it had grown on me over the years that this was not only intellectually dishonest, but actually rather dull of me.

Dru, too, would rather not be dull, and because an empty day is a wasted day, when we should have been packing the radio and the matches we spent the afternoon in Bristol harbour, sailing the Mirror dinghy. I remember Dru struggling to get into her lifejacket, 'I didn't have boobs the last time I wore this.'

Such is the life of the one person that Dru is, that is legally Ms Drusilla Philippa Marland. She can be a crusty reactionary, a snob opposed to 4x4s and screechy mums and anyone under the age of thirty. But she's also a communist non-nuclear liberal, a Greenham Common sympathiser and former strike-action National Union of Seamen engine-room representative ('**Islands ferry set to sail**' reports the *Dorset Evening Echo* of 7 May 1988, 'Marland denied there had been a climbdown').

I do sometimes worry that Dru might lose her way, I mean really lose her way. That she'll drop into a life of special-interest groups and Oxfam scavenging and the occasional indignant letter to the *Daily Mail*. Or end up a bag lady on a permanent shuttle between Lidl and the Gloucester Road charity shops, too old to jump into skips, her day made or broken by whether there's bottled beer in the house come five past six.

But then I worry about everybody I love, and in the second-worst scenario they usually end up at Lidl. I can also see brighter futures, with Dru an eccentric lady bimbling round Bristol in her Morris, getting mistaken by people of a certain age for the district nurse. The lucky children in her street will know her as the mystery woman with many bangles who when asked politely (but not before) will mend a puncture before Mum gets home. And solve any problems with a bully.

*

We leave our rucksacks at Tourist Information and stroll

unburdened down the hill towards the cathedral, this our second visit so the equivalent of arriving at the Church of St Peter in the Vatican. I feel the sun trying to come out and dispel the mist. It really is. That's not something I can help.

The cathedral close, the cathedral gates, the cathedral porch. Just before I push open the heavy wooden door I remember to snatch the pink Tilley hat off my head and say, 'Hats off!'

I enter the cathedral, the pink hat scrunched in my hands, and the vast stone floor of the nave looks more uphill than I remember it. The floor hasn't been level for centuries, and last time we were here I thought it was like a ship in mid-ocean, the foredeck with the altar rising to the crest of a wave. The swell has grown slightly stronger.

Dru hasn't followed me in. I look around. No sign of her anywhere. I go back outside and there she is sitting on a bench with her nose in the air. Oh Christ, what have I said *now*?

'I was going by the Pauline rules,' Dru says.

'I'm sure you were right to do so.'

'"But every woman praying with her head not covered disgraceth her head." You should know that.'

'I'll do my best to remember it.'

We cut the gender stereotypes and go inside. Dru is the only woman wearing a hat, but looking about at the slightly older women – and the cathedral does not draw a young crowd – the splashed-flower design on dresses of all colours and lengths is very popular. It never goes out of style.

Both Dru and I light a candle to dead people we wish were alive. We watch the flames and the reflection of the flames in the melting wax, Dru with her hat on in church, specks of mascara black on her bronzed cheekbones. Then we walk uphill, even here uphill, to the ossuary of St David, the saint himself. It rests in a small chapel towards the back of the cathedral, a kind of thoroughfare behind the high altar, and the reliquary containing the bones is on a stone shelf set into the ancient wall. This is called the pilgrim's recess, and the clasped oak casket is protected by an iron frame like a portcullis. To get a good look at it we stand on a hard slab of grey slate commemorating the service of Edward Vaughan, bishop, 1509-1522.

Above and to the side of St David's bones there is a prayer on a piece of laminated A4 paper, a reminder for pilgrims who may have forgotten or mislaid their thoughts on the journey. It is a statement of thanks and good intentions, looking back and looking forward.

Dru drops to her knees. In the candlelight she faces the relics of St David, a little embarrassing and completely real. Then she closes her eyes and moves her lips as she tells out her prayers, whatever they may be.

Acknowledgements

For many of the facts and figures in this book, as well as memorable perspectives on the transsexual experience, I'm particularly indebted to the work of Jonathan Ames, Amy Bloom, Kate Bornstein, Helen Boyd, Jennifer Finney Boylan, Pat Califia, and Jan Morris. A full list of books I found either helpful or interesting can be found at www.richardbeard.info.

I'd like to thank the surgeon Mr James Bellringer for his time and patience, and for so generously answering my many questions. Also Ian Marchant for his hospitality in Presteigne, and Adrian LeCoyte for asking his dad if I could tell about the deer and the eels.

Zoe Waldie, as ever, has been a valued source of support and encouragement, while Stuart Williams at Harvill Secker has been wise, precise and positive – the full house of editorial virtues.

And thanks yet again to Laurence, this time and all the other times, for thinking it no bad thing I should spend days on end in a tent with Dru.